D0S92575

CROSS-CULTURAL CONSUMPTION

It is increasingly common for goods produced in one culture to be consumed in another. When goods are exported, they can act as a means of communication, social distinction or cultural domination. However, there is no guarantee that the meanings and uses invested in goods by their producers will be recognized, much less respected, by the consumer from another culture.

Cross-Cultural Consumption is a fascinating guide to the cultural and ethical implications of the globalization of the consumer society. Chapters address topics ranging from the 'fashioning' of the colonial subject in South Africa and the rise of the hypermarket in Argentina, to the commodification of Guatemalan handicrafts and the internationalization of the British palate.

Through their examination of diverse representations of 'otherness' and identity, and such issues as cultural imperialism and appropriation, Howes and his contributors show how the accelerated global flow of goods and images challenges the very idea of the 'cultural border' and creates new spaces for cultural invention.

David Howes is Associate Professor and Chair of the Department of Sociology and Anthropology at Concordia University, Montreal. He is editor of *Law and Popular Culture* and *The Varieties of Sensory Experience* and co-author, with Constance Classen and Anthony Synnott, of *Aroma*.

CROSS-CULTURAL CONSUMPTION

Global markets, local realities

Edited by David Howes

London and New York

First published 1996
by Routledge
11 New Fetter Lane, London EC4P 4EE
Simultaneously published in the USA and Canada
by Routledge
29 West 35th Street, New York, NY 10001

Typeset in Garamond by Routledge
Printed and bound in Great Britain by Redwood Books,
Trowbridge, Wiltshire

British Library Cataloguing in Publication Data
A catalogue record for this book is available from the British
Library

Library of Congress Cataloguing in Publication Data
Howes, David, 1957–
Cross-cultural consumption: global markets, local realities /
edited by David Howes
p. cm.
Includes bibliographical references and index.
1. Consumption (Economics)—Social aspects. 2. Culture
diffusion—Economic aspects.
3. Diffusion of innovations—Social aspects.
I. Title.
HC79.C6H673 1996
339.4'7—dc20
96–7701
CIP

ISBN 0–415–13888–4 (hbk)
ISBN 0–415–13889–2 (pbk)

CONTENTS

CONTENTS

FIGURES

CONTRIBUTORS

Marian Bredin is a Post-Doctoral Fellow in the Communication Studies Department at Concordia University, Montreal. Her research focuses on aboriginal media in Canada. She is the author of articles in *Resources for Feminist Research* and the *Canadian Journal of Communication*.

Constance Classen is the author of *Inca Cosmology and the Human Body*, *Worlds of Sense: Exploring the Senses in History and Across Cultures*, and co-author with David Howes and Anthony Synnott of *Aroma: The Cultural History of Smell*. Her current research centres on the relationship between sensory codes and gender ideologies in pre-modern Europe.

Jean Comaroff is Professor of Anthropology at the University of Chicago. She is the co-editor of *Modernity and its Malcontents: Ritual and Power in Africa*, author of *Body of Power, Spirit of Resistance: The Culture and History of a South African People*, and co-author with John Comaroff of *Ethnography and the Historical Imagination* as well as the two-volume study *Of Revelation and Revolution*.

Mary M. Crain's recent writings include the article 'Poetics and politics in the Ecuadorean Andes' in *American Ethnologist*, and the chapter 'The Remaking of an Andalusian Pilgrimage Tradition' in the collection *Culture, Power, Place*. Her research focuses on the anthropology of gender, politics and cosmology. She is a Visiting Professor in the Departments of Social Anthropology and Latin American History at the Universidad de Barcelona.

Carol Hendrickson is Professor of Anthropology at Marlboro College, Marlboro, Vermont. She is the author of *Weaving Identities: Construction of Dress and Self in a Highland Guatemala Town*. Her other publications include the essay 'Twin Gods and Quiché Rulers' in *Word and Image in Mayan Culture*, and 'Images of the Indian in Guatemala' in *Nation-States and Indians in Latin America*.

David Howes is the editor of *Law and Popular Culture* and *The Varieties of Sensory Experience*, co-author with Constance Classen and Anthony Synnott of *Aroma: The Cultural History of Smell*, and the author of numerous articles in law and anthropology as well as cultural studies journals. He is Associate Professor and Chair of the Department of Sociology and Anthropology at Concordia University, Montreal.

Allison James is a Lecturer in Social Anthropology at the University of Hull. She is the author of various articles on the anthropology of food. Her other research interests lie in children and childhood, and in this connection she has published *Childhood Identities: Self and Social Relationships in the Experience of the Child* and co-authored *Growing Up and Growing Old* with Jenny Hockey.

Christine Jourdan edits the journal *Culture*. She has published articles in linguistics and anthropology in *Annual Review of Anthropology* and *Journal de la Société des Océanistes*, among other periodicals. Her research focuses on pidgin and creole languages and processes of urbanization in Melanesia. She is an Associate Professor of Anthropology at Concordia University, Montreal.

Jean-Marc Philibert is an Associate Professor of Anthropology at the University of Western Ontario and past-President of the Canadian Anthropology Society. He is the co-editor of *Customs in Conflict,* and author of numerous essays on economic anthropology, including 'Consuming culture: a study of simple commodity consumption' in *The Social Economy of Consumption*.

Brad Weiss is an Assistant Professor of Anthropology at the College of William and Mary, Williamsburg, Virginia. His research centres on consumption, commoditization and everyday practice in Tanzania. He is the author of the article 'Plastic teeth extraction' in *American Ethnologist*, and the book *The Making and Unmaking of the Haya Lived World*.

ACKNOWLEDGEMENTS

The idea for this book originated in the context of a lecture series on 'Culture and Consumption', which I organized in the 1991–2 academic year. The inaugural lecture of that series, by Jean Comaroff, is also the lead chapter of this book. It was first published in French in a special issue of the journal *Anthropologie et Sociétés* (which I also had the pleasure of editing), together with the essays by Carol Hendrickson, Allison James and Brad Weiss. I am grateful to the managing editors of *Anthropologie et Sociétés*, Mikhaël Elbaz and Yvan Simonis, for permission to reprint these four essays in revised and translated form here.

There are many people I want to thank for the many engaging discussions we have had regarding cross-cultural consumption and related subjects over the years, all of which contributed materially to the ideas expressed in this book: Joan Acland, Vered Amit-Talai, Eric Arnould, Gregory Baum, Gilles Bibeau, Valda Blundell, George Classen, Sally Cole, Ellen Corin, Pieter de Vries, Homa Hoodfar, Gordon Howes, Annamma Joy, Nicholas Kasirer, Roger Keesing, John Leavitt, Ken Little, Grant McCracken, Kristin Norget, Gavin Smith, Joseph Smucker, Anthony Synnott, Chris Trott, Gail Guthrie Valaskakis and my fellow contributors. I am also indebted to my editors at Routledge, Mari Shullaw, Anne Gee and Joanne Mattingly, for their advice and encouragement. My deepest thanks go to Constance Classen, who has helped me become a far more discerning consumer than I ever dreamed, and whose love is the most precious good I know.

INTRODUCTION
Commodities and cultural borders
David Howes

Indian takeaways now outnumber fish and chip shops across the British Isles, and Chinese food and pizza have become standard fare. What has happened to British taste? Who are you if that's what you eat?

Brand names and trademark symbols such as Marlboro, Nike and Rolex are now known around the world. These marks transcend language and make it possible to display one's status or signal one's desires by simply pointing to the appropriate symbol. Can communication get any more transparent?

West African villagers recoiled in horror when an American multinational introduced a new line of baby food with pictures of smiling babies on the labels. Accustomed to seeing the contents of packaged food depicted on product labels, the villagers assumed that the jars contained, not food made *for* babies, but food made *of* babies. Are Americans cannibals, they wondered?

The Hopi Indians of Arizona were dismayed to see caricatures of their gods or *kachinas* in the pages of a popular comic book, where they were portrayed as 'bad guys' and dominated by an 'All-American' superhero. Surely there are laws against such 'cultural theft'? the Hopi ask, offended by the blasphemy. But what law? Is there a right to cultural integrity?

This book is about cross-cultural consumption, or what happens to commodities when they cross cultural borders. In the following pages, I shall describe how the study of this phenomenon promises to transform our understanding of culture and consumption, and sketch some of the more pressing analytical and ethical issues raised by the globalization of the consumer society.

WORLDS OF GOODS

It is now widely recognized that cultures and goods stand in a relation of complex interdependence. As Grant McCracken states in *Culture and Consumption*: 'One of the most important ways in which cultural categories are substantiated is through the material objects of a culture . . . [objects are] created according to the blueprint of culture and to this extent they make the categories of this blueprint material' (1988: 74).

1

McCracken's position agrees with that of Mary Douglas, who holds that goods are needed for 'making visible and stable the categories of culture' (Douglas and Isherwood 1979: 59). As the material part of culture, goods afford sets of markers which both structure perception and facilitate social interaction. For example, we often infer what people are like based on the clothes they wear, the make of car they drive, or the way they furnish their home. In other words, we judge them on the basis of the 'assemblages' they construct from the total cultural repertoire or 'system of objects' (to borrow Jean Baudrillard's phrase). As Douglas observes, 'goods in their assemblage present a set of meanings, more or less coherent, more or less intentional. They are read by those who know the code and scan them for information' (1979: 5).

The idea that goods 'substantiate' the order of culture has inspired an extensive body of research in the sociology and anthropology of consumption, as well as in the recently reinvented field of material culture studies.[1] However, the conclusions of this research are thrown into confusion by the type of situation with which we are concerned in this book – that is, in situations of *cross*-cultural consumption. For when goods cross borders, then the culture they 'substantiate' is no longer the culture in which they circulate.

Moreover, given the accelerated pace and increased scope of world trade, it is now more normal for goods to cross borders than ever before. With goods passing in and out of cultures all the time, the interpretive power of notions like 'blueprint' (McCracken), 'code' (Douglas) or 'system of objects' (Baudrillard) seems compromised. What system? Whose blueprint? Which code? What happens – when the culture of production and the culture of consumption are not the same?

The relationship between goods and culture needs to be rethought, taking the constant displacement of things in the increasingly global marketplace into account. In particular, we need to know more about the social relations of consumption – or in other words, the logic by which goods are *received* (acquired, understood and employed) in different societies.[2]

In the past, anthropologists writing about small-scale societies, like those of Amazonia or Melanesia, were inclined to tidy the presence of Western goods away, or ignore them 'for the sake of analysis' (Hugh-Jones 1992: 43; Lederman 1986). Conversely, anthropologists who witnessed their subjects begin to produce artefacts or put on rituals for the tourist trade were often quick to lament or even denounce such developments (Crick 1989). The latter reaction was motivated by the assumption that the commodification of tradition automatically spelled the end of cultural authenticity and meaningful social relations.

In this book, instead of absenting 'foreign' objects, the focus of the contributors is on their presence, and instead of treating cultures as meaningful wholes existing in pristine isolation, the emphasis is on their interface. As a result of this orientation, the essays presented here enable one to attain both a deeper awareness of the extent of capitalist penetration in the twilight of the twentieth century, and a fuller appreciation of the resiliency of non-Western (and Western) cultures in the face of globalization.

THE GLOBAL HOMOGENIZATION PARADIGM

Contemporary thinking about the cultural effects of the migration of goods within the world market system has tended to be dominated by the paradigm of *global homogenization*. According to this paradigm, cultural differences are increasingly being eroded through the world-wide replacement of local products with mass-produced goods which usually originate in the West. This process of colonization (or re-colonization) of the non-Western world through the institution of new regimes of consumption is sometimes referred to as 'Coca-colonization' (Hannerz 1992: 217).[3]

Let us briefly examine how the diffusion of a product like Coca-Cola can be seen to contribute to the homogenization of cultures. It is said that the replication of uniformity is the main reason for Coke's success. Coca-Cola is made from the same formula and marketed according to the same strategy – 'one sight, one sound, one sell' – throughout the world. A key component of the Coca-Cola 'sell' has, in fact, been its much touted capacity to transcend barriers:

> Ever since the 1920s, when the ad campaign 'the pause that refreshes' debuted, Coke [has] been positioned as the universal cola, a single, unchanging soft drink that suited the taste of everyone – young or old, female or male, white or black, American or foreign, rich or poor. It was 'your good friend', 'a democratic luxury', ready to satisfy whenever you needed a lift.
>
> (Rutherford 1994: 44)

This universalist aspect of the Coca-Cola image was highlighted in the popular 1970s' television commercial which showed a group of teenagers of diverse ethnic origins on a hilltop singing 'I'd like to buy the world a Coke and keep it company'. The implication: open a Coke and enjoy *instant communitas*!

While Coca-Cola is promoted as a universal or transcultural product, it is at the same time closely identified with the culture and ideals of the United States. Coke is intimately bound up with the so-called American Dream – or what is to say the same thing, the ideal of living in a 'consumer democracy' (Ewen 1988: 32). For example, some American soldiers in World War II, conscious of the lack of Coca-Cola overseas, thought of themselves as fighting not just for God and Country, but also 'for the right to buy Coca-Cola again' (Pendergrast 1993: 210–11).

In a related vein, it is commonly supposed that the recent collapse of the communist regimes of Eastern Europe was precipitated by the irrepressible demands of the youth of those countries for Coke, blue jeans and all the other 'good things' of American consumer democracy. The consumption of Coca-Cola is thus apparently allied with the internalization of American political ideology and economic values. Coke offers a taste of 'freedom'. This notion is nicely captured in the pop art image of the Statue of Liberty holding out a Coke (instead of the more traditional symbol of freedom, the torch) to those who enter New York Harbour.

The film *The Gods Must Be Crazy* provides another illustration of the association between Coca-Cola, political change and consumerism. In this film, a Coke bottle tossed out of an airplane window falls in the middle of the Kalahari Desert, and is discovered by a !Kung man, who takes it home to his camp. The bottle becomes a catalyst for the complete transformation of !Kung society: it is responsible for introducing the idea of private property, shattering the 'primitive communism' which had prevailed; it awakens a craving for other commodities, provoking a radical break with the traditional strategy of 'want not, need not'.[4] Thus, Coke is attributed an almost magical power to re-make societies in the image of its country of origin. It is one of the most 'fetishized' commodities the world has known (Marx 1967; Taussig 1993).

It was observed earlier that the replication of uniformity is the main reason for Coke's success. It cannot be ignored, however, that Coke changed in 1985, when the formula was altered. Such was the outcry over this 'adulteration', that Coca-Cola Inc. felt compelled to re-introduce its original brand, now called 'Coca-Cola Classic' as distinct from Coca-Cola. Although this re-insertion was ostensibly in response to customer demand, many suspect the 'response' was preplanned. The result of this smoothly managed crisis was a significant increase in Coca-Cola's market share: there are now two classes of Coke drinkers (Coke Classic and Coke) where formerly there was one. Thus, Coke owes its current market dominance not only to the replication of uniformity, but also to a strategy of 'the generation of difference', or 'Coca-*classic*ization', as it were.

Coca-classicization is a form of customized mass-production/consumption.[5] It involves the exploitation of differentiation (within definite bounds) as opposed to standardization. It has emerged as a major marketing strategy of the late twentieth century. But what is the significance of the differences it introduces? Some would say that the differences are virtual, rather than actual, that substantively speaking there are no differences. While this position is often overstated, it is not without some substance (cf. Waldman 1992; Barber 1995: 116). Whatever the case may be, in what follows Coca-classicization will be treated as subsumable under Coca-colonization, as a variation within the latter paradigm, and hence a putatively homogenizing (rather than hetero-genizing) factor in the global scheme of things.

MUTABILITY OF THE COMMODITY FORM

The fact that the same mass-produced and marketed goods – Coca-Cola, blue jeans, Hollywood movies – are not only increasingly available in countries all over the world, but sometimes appear to serve as a catalyst for cultural and political change in those countries, is a powerful argument in favour of the paradigm of global homogenization. There can be no question that items like Coca-Cola have displaced local products – coconut milk, fruit juice, even water in many regions (Barnet and Cavanagh 1994: 246; J. James 1993: 177). Yet the assumption that such goods, on entering a culture, will inevitably retain and communicate the values they are accorded by their culture of origin must be questioned. When one takes a closer look at the meanings and uses given to specific imported goods within specific 'local contexts' or 'realities', one often finds that the goods have been transformed, at least in part, in accordance with the values of the receiving culture.

Rena Lederman provides some illuminating observations on this process from her experience among the Mendi of the Southern Highlands of Papua New Guinea.

> The Mendi we know do not see [consumer] objects in the same way as we see them: their purposes supplied *for* us . . . In our objects, they perceive multiple possibilities for satisfying needs the manufacturers never imagined . . . They use safety pins as earrings in place of blades of grass and combs made out of umbrella spokes instead of bamboo . . . women we know reuse the plastic fibres of rice bags, rolling them into twine with which to make traditional netbags.
>
> (1986: 8)

In addition to acquiring new uses, imported objects often become imbued with alternative meanings upon incorporation into a new cultural setting or 'local reality'. For example, in *Entangled Objects*, Nicholas Thomas describes how, in the nineteenth century, the construction of narratives around European trade goods (firearms, tools, liquor) played an important role in the process of their assimilation by the cultures of the South Pacific. The narratives indigenized the objects, reconstituting them in accordance with local cultural schemas.

THE CREOLIZATION PARADIGM

The process of recontextualization whereby foreign goods are assigned meanings and uses by the culture of reception may be termed 'hybridization' (García Canclini 1992) – or to align our discussion with current usage, *creolization*.[6] For purposes of exposition, this process may also be seen as a paradigm. The creolization paradigm contrasts with the Coca-colonization paradigm as follows: firstly, whereas Coca-colonization refers to the flow of goods and values from the West to the rest of the world, creolization is concerned with the in-flow of goods, their reception and domestication (whatever their provenance, whatever their destination). Secondly, whereas Coca-colonization is centred on the presumed intentionality of the producer, creolization also takes in the creativity of the consumer.[7] What the concept of creolization highlights, in other words, is that goods always have to be contextualized (given meaning, inserted into particular social relationships) to be utilized, and there is no guarantee that the intention of the producer will be recognized, much less respected, by the consumer from another culture.

No imported object, Coca-Cola included, is completely immune from creolization. Indeed, one finds that Coke is often attributed meanings and uses within particular cultures that are very different from those imagined by its manufacturer. These include that it can smooth wrinkles (Russia), that it can revive a person from the dead (Haiti), and that it can turn copper into silver (Barbados) (Pendergrast 1993: 245–7). Coke is also indigenized through being mixed with other drinks, such as rum in the Carribean to make *Cuba Libre*, or *aguardiente* (an alcoholic beverage) in Bolivia to produce *Ponche Negro*. Finally, it seems that Coke is perceived as a 'native product' in many different places – that is, you will often find people who believe the drink originated in their country, not in the United States (1993: 218).

As this cursory treatment of Coca-Cola illustrates, and the chapters in this book will show both in force and in depth, recognizing creolization as an integral dimension of cross-cultural consumption can significantly enhance one's understanding of the migration of goods both within the world market system and at the local level. The creolization paradigm sensitizes one to all the ruptures and deflections, rejections and subversions that can take place at each point in the economic cycle of production–exchange–consumption. Items 'Made in USA' become 'Re-made in Japan' (in the sense of 'Japanized') if that happens to be their destination (cf. Tobin 1992), or 'Re-made in South Africa', 'Re-made in Argentina', and so on – as alternative meanings are added and novel uses are found for them with each new border they traverse. Viewed from a creolization perspective, the economic cycle begins to look more like an etching by the Dutch graphic artist M. C. Escher, with its endless detours and transformations, than it does the linear process leading from production to consumption familiar to us from economics textbook discussions.

It is important to emphasize that creolization is not simply the opposite of global homogenization, or what we have been calling 'Coca-colonization'. The opposite of the latter would be 'fragmentation', or the universalist tendency Benjamin Barber calls 'jihad' in his controversial book *Jihad vs. McWorld*.[8] Creolization is an intermediate construct, rather than a universal tendency (or ideal type); it is always the product of a conjuncture, an intersection, hence not amenable to abstraction. Indeed, one of the most consistent themes of the analyses in the chapters which follow is the particularity of the *articulation* between the local and the global in each and every situation of cross-cultural consumption. Neither homogenization nor fragmentation (nor any dialectical synthesis of the two), but the multiplicity of possible local–global articulations is, therefore, one of the main messages of this volume.

The idea of articulation, with its syncretistic as opposed to synthetic connotations,[9] like the notion of creolization, differs from many of the other formulas which have been advanced to characterize the current state of the 'world system' (Wallerstein 1974, 1984, 1991), such as 'the spread of modernity' (Tomlinson 1991: 173), 'the globalization of fragmentation' (Firat 1995: 115), 'the process by which the world becomes a single place' (King 1991: 12).[10] All of these formulas project an encompassing unity on to the external world without being reflexive enough about the particular position from which the author speaks, and without addressing the prior question of whether it is even possible (and not simply an illusion of modernity) to hold the world in a single view.[11] The problem here is that globalization or world system theory continues to be spun from a centrist standpoint, which is also somehow 'above it all', even while its proponents question the division of the world into First, Second and Third, into centre and periphery, etc. (cf. Buell 1994; Appadurai 1990). As such, the theory has very little resonance with the experience of peoples on the margins – namely, those on the receiving end (but also sometimes the initiators) of global trends.

One type of individual for whom globalization theory would and does have special resonance, however, is, of course, the executive of the transnational corporation. Indeed, it is often difficult to distinguish the discourse of the world system theorist from that of the transnational capitalist. Whether it is the Marxist critic Armand Mattelart describing 'differentiation within global-ization' (1994: 216) or the President of Sony discussing his company's strategy of 'global localization' (Barnet and Cavanagh 1994: 65), whether it is the sociologist Anthony King cogitating upon the world becoming 'a single place' (1991: 12) or the advertising executive pushing the phrase 'On planet Reebok there are no boundaries' as a slogan for the Reebok athletic shoe company (Barber 1995: 24), the advanced theorist and the late capitalist speak a remarkably similar language.

The world as seen through the windows of the corporate boardroom situated on the twentieth floor of some glass office tower may well look like 'a single place', and alterity just another market opportunity. But as we know from anthropology, there is rather more going on 'out there'. Indeed, anthropology has a vital role to play in the reconstruction of globalization theory and transnational marketing alike, because of the unique insights which result from the special position which the anthropologist, as 'marginal native', takes up – a position on the border (looking both ways) rather than in the boardroom (looking out and down).

The anthropological perspective is bi- or multi-lateral as opposed to global (in the business sense), and marginal instead of central. As such, it has the potential to disclose aspects of the globalization process that are *invisible* from the boardroom – not to mention inaudible, for the business executive does not have the access that the anthropologist does to all the arguments that go on over the meaning and use to be assigned to 'exotic' goods locally (cf. Weismantel 1989; Wilk 1994), or the debates over the definition of the very borders that distinguish one culture from another (cf. Clifford 1988; Arnould 1989; Hoodfar in press). Moreover, while the executive may know all there is to know about 'product positioning' in the marketplace, it is the positioning of products in the home and other post-purchase contexts – their sensual presence in relation to other objects – that is the ultimate arbiter of their meaning and value.[12] Here again, it is the anthropologist who is in the best position to study these 'local arrangements', and thus to grasp the motivation behind the 'assemblages' people construct (Douglas and Isherwood 1979).[13]

CROSS-CULTURAL CONSUMPTION

This book is divided into three parts. Part I, 'The Mirror of Consumption', examines how goods exported from 'the West' (i.e. Western Europe, the United States, Canada, Australia) are received-transformed in other regions of the globe. Part II, 'Consuming the "Other"', explores what becomes of goods which are imported to the West. In Part III, 'Consumption and Identity', the focus is on the strategies of resistance and accommodation different aboriginal peoples have devised in an effort to contain the commodification of their 'way of life' and continue to live it. The Epilogue expands on certain points of discussion from earlier chapters and delves into some of the more pressing ethical issues raised by the globalization of the consumer society – issues such as cultural dumping, transnational advertising, and environmental degradation.

The genesis of this book can be traced to a lecture given at Concordia University in 1991 by Jean Comaroff entitled 'The Empire's Old Clothes', at which many of the contributors were present. While the theoretical impetus may be traced to that talk, the practical impetus for the chapters which follow came from the need experienced by each of the contributors to sort out the articulation of the global and the local in their chosen area of study. The chapters are therefore rich in ethnographic detail and at the same time reflect, as well as anticipate, vital new directions in anthropological thought.

Before introducing the individual chapters, I would point out that while *Cross-Cultural Consumption* is addressed to the general reader, it is also designed for use by students of disciplines and subjects ranging from economic or symbolic anthropology and the sociology of consumption, to marketing and development studies, material culture studies and social theory. In fulfilment of its pedagogical objectives, this book contains two chapters (Chapters 2 and 6) which may serve as points of departure for student essay assignments, as well as an epilogue, which raises a broad range of ethical issues for in-class debate.[14]

THE MIRROR OF CONSUMPTION

The recognition that culture is constructed through consumption, not just production, is not confined to sociology and anthropology. Historians have increasingly come around to this view as well. The result is that numerous history scholars are now involved in a complete 'historical reperiodization of consumer culture', reconceptualizing its causes, and revaluating its moral and political consequences (Agnew 1994: 26; Brewer and Porter 1994). For instance, it is now thought that the Industrial Revolution presupposed – and may even have been preceded by – a 'Consumer Revolution'; hence, the birth of the consumer society is no longer presumed to be explicable in terms of technological innovation and changes in the forces of production alone. Conceptualizing the relationship between mode of production and mode of consumption has thus become far more complex (and interesting) of late (cf. Fine and Leopold 1993). To date, however, there has been little serious attention paid to the construction or reconstruction of culture through consumption outside of 'Western history', such as in Africa during the colonial period, or in the recent history of Latin America or Oceania. The chapters of Part I seek to redress this situation.

The lead chapter of Part I, by Jean Comaroff, explores the role of clothing in the making of colonial subjects and 'ethnic' communities in Southern Africa. Comaroff asks why the nineteenth-century British missions to Southern Africa devoted so much attention to clothing African nakedness, and why this effort was seen as integral to the revolution the missionaries hoped to foment in African hearts and minds. She points out that clothing was considered to represent the 'fabric of civilization' by the British missionaries, and as such, was seen as a major means of fashioning new social identities for the Africans. Comaroff goes on to describe how the second-hand clothes from Britain did indeed foster the Europeanization of Africans, but also touched off a complex politics of dress, playing into the making of new ethnic and class divisions, as well as encouraging syncretisms with indigenous styles.

One example of such syncretism given by Comaroff is that of a South African chief who ordered a European-style suit to be made for him out of leopard skin. Some colonialists thought that this was because he wished 'to make himself a white man'. Given that leopard skin was the traditional symbol of chiefly office, however, there was clearly more going on here. The chief was not simply emulating European fashion; rather, through cross-cultural dressing (i.e. through combining the potent indigenous symbolism of the leopard skin with the powerful foreign symbol of European dress) he was seeking to double his authority in his community, to construct a power that was greater even than the sum of its parts.

Indigenous uses of Western commodities are often disparaged for the apparent failure on the part of the natives to 'get things right'. However, as the case of the leopard skin suit illustrates, the failure may lie with the observer who sees only mimesis, and does not grasp how Western goods and values are being reworked in the context of local practice.

In the second chapter, Constance Classen also takes an historical approach to the study of consumption. Her analysis is in the form of a family tale. She relates how three generations of her family, living in a provincial capital of Northwestern Argentina, have experienced the influx of foreign commodities from the turn of the century to the 1990s. Her narrative is sensitive to the

sudden materialization of products, substitutions and often jarring juxtapositions – all of which have lent a surreal atmosphere to consumption in the
Argentine Northwest. There is the surreality of fur-suited Santa Clauses
appearing in the middle of summer, a clothing boutique that is called El
Sportsman Drugstore, and a 'hypermarket' that uses the Statue of Liberty as its
logo.

Classen's chapter reads like a surrealist story in places, but there is nothing
foreign about this genre. As she points out, the folklore of the region often
presents a surreal juxtaposition of the extraordinary with the everyday. The
narrative she has constructed to describe the reception of imported consumer
goods in the Argentine Northwest is thus continuous with the narrative means
the people of the region have traditionally used to interpret the incursions of
the extraordinary into everyday life. As such, her account provides a vital
counterpoint to the prevailing 'biography of things' approach to the study of
consumption (Kopytoff 1986; Ferguson 1988).

The third chapter, by Jean-Marc Philibert and Christine Jourdan, takes us to
the South Pacific. The authors are interested in how the peoples of Vanuatu and
the Solomon Islands continue to participate in the traditional Melanesian mode
of production, which is fundamentally agrarian, and to subscribe to the social
norms and 'world view' or classificatory system associated with it, while
engaging in occasional wage labour and embracing modes of consumption that
are ostensibly modern and Western. This duality has led to an intriguing
mingling of consumer and agrarian ideas and values, according to Jourdan and
Philibert.

Jourdan describes how, in the Solomons, manufactured objects of foreign
provenance are classified along with natural objects like trees as things which
are replaceable, because they replenish themselves 'naturally' – that is, without
any apparent expenditure of human effort. Being replaceable, such objects are
also disposable and, therefore, tend to be 'abused' rather than maintained in
good repair. One consequently finds a regime of conspicuous consumption-
bordering-on-destruction in the Solomons, where broken-down commodities
(VCRs, refrigerators) lie strewn about peoples' yards.

So, too, in Vanuatu would the consumer society appear to have arrived, but
Philibert's careful analysis of the consumption patterns of the affluent reveals
that there is little evidence as yet of the atomization or privatization that a
'properly' Western regime of consumption would entail. In fact, it is new-
found poverty that constitutes the gravest threat to the reproduction of the
particular form of social life at Erakor (the village studied by Philibert), because
poverty prevents individuals from participating in the collective rituals that
customarily mark the attainment of new social statuses.

CONSUMING THE 'OTHER'

The chapters of Part II are concerned with analysing what becomes of goods imported to the West. Most of the recent research on this subject has focused on artefacts which end up in museums or private collections (e.g. Clifford 1988). Studies of the domestication of exotic products (e.g. Mintz 1985), of their role in everyday life as opposed to the privileged space of the collection, are rare.

Part of the interest of the following chapters lies in their depiction of the West as no less caught up in processes of hybridization or creolization than anywhere else. This disclosure gives new meaning to the concept of 'Westernization'.[15] The chapters also bring out the vagaries of commodification, by showing how 'the great transformation' (Polanyi 1944) involved in the coming to be of the world market economy remains unfinished and jagged in some cases (e.g. in its encounter with the local reality of coffee production in Tanzania), yet more invasive and totalizing than ever in others (e.g. the marketing of handmade items from Guatemala in the United States).

Addressing the link between food and cultural identity, the lead chapter of Part II, by Allison James, explores some of the changes which have occurred in British patterns of food consumption since the 1950s. James notes, for example, that Indian food now outsells fish'n'chips, and that British Rail has been known to offer a 'Dishes of the World' series which features a range of international cuisine. The result of all these divergences in available tastes is that the British subject has a veritable smorgasbord of culinary signposts to choose from for the purposes of constructing an identity. The question arises, therefore, of whether the increasing globalization of foodstuffs – either through the importation of exotic foods (as above), or through the expansion of fast-food franchises like McDonald's – should be interpreted to mean that food has lost its potency as a determinate marker of identity.

According to James' analysis, this apparent globalization of the British palate has, in fact, been offset by the discovery and revaluation of 'authentic' British fare, which in turn supports an insular sense of identity (cf. Chambers 1990). British taste has also been modified by the appearance of hybrid (domestic/foreign) dishes, as attested by the growing preference for curried chips. James concludes her discussion by asking whether these developments in British cuisine reflect an abandonment of national, regional and class identities – traditionally refracted in and through the food domain – or, conversely, their rephrasing.

Brad Weiss, in 'Coffee Breaks and Coffee Connections', describes how the Haya of Tanzania use locally grown coffee as a masticatory, and how this product fits within the fabric of Haya social and ceremonial life. The Haya also produce large quantities of coffee for export to Europe, but profess to be mystified about what Europeans do with it all: 'We Haya grow this coffee, we harvest it, and then we sell it to you in Europe. But what do you Europeans do with it?' According to Weiss, this uncertainty on the part of the Haya about the ultimate purpose of the fruits of their labour points to a significant disjuncture in the world market system, and raises important questions about the values and rationality of the 'global economy'.

In the second part of his chapter, Weiss follows the trail of Haya coffee, both historically and geographically, from its production in Tanzania to its consumption in Europe. He finds both significant conjunctions, and even more significant disjunctions, in the way this commodity has entered into the definition of class relations, work relations (e.g. the 'coffee break'), and domestic relations in the two settings. By straddling the two worlds, Weiss' analysis provides many valuable insights into the making and remaking of a commodity.

Chapter 6, by Carol Hendrickson, explores how various handmade items from the Third World are presented in the pages of US mail-order catalogues. Hendrickson is particularly interested in artefacts sold under the label 'Guatemala' or 'Maya'. Her analysis of the imagery used to promote these products reveals the powerful marketing value of 'cultural difference' in the West (cf. Giroux 1994: 15), and some of the distortions of local realities which can result from this stress. For example, the industrialized cities where many of the Guatemalan artefacts come from are represented as pre-industrial villages in the catalogues. This is so as to agree with the American purchaser's preconceptions about 'Mayan life' as well as to foster associations with both 'tradition' and 'uniqueness'.

Other selling techniques the mail-order catalogues use to move merchandise include presenting the artefacts in intimate and familiar terms – suspenders as 'handwoven for you', for example – and/or linking their purchase to support for the struggles of indigenous peoples. These heartwarming representations pose a serious challenge to conventional theoretical perceptions of capitalism as a system devoid of conscience, and market relations as intrinsically impersonal (cf. Zelizer 1989: 342–7), for they suggest that capitalism has a conscience and that market-mediated relations can be cosy. On the other hand, it could be that all these representations attest is that commodification will indeed stop at nothing.[16]

CONSUMPTION AND IDENTITY

The third part of the book explores how various aboriginal communities of North and South America have responded to the globalization of the consumer society and, in particular, to the commodification of their *own* way of life as a result of international tourism, mass media representations and other such forces. According to some commentators, the 'marketization of culture', or commodification of tradition, has become essential to cultural survival (Firat 1995: 116–21). It brings international recognition and creates employment opportunities for youth, thus saving many cultures from becoming 'museum items'.[17] The question remains, however, of how those who find themselves subjected to this process respond. And if they object, what strategies can they employ to protect their cultural identities from being commodified?

The first chapter in this part, 'Negotiating Identities in Quito's Cultural Borderlands' by Mary Crain, examines the situation faced by native women from the town of Quimsa in the Ecuadorean Andes who are employed as domestic servants in an international tourist hotel in the nation's capital, Quito. As is typical of 'ethnic tourism' ventures of this kind, 'native traditions' are disassembled and rearranged in order to recreate a marketable semblance of 'authenticity'. In the case cited, this involves the women being required to dress in a gaudy version of their traditional clothing for the purpose of attracting tourists.

However, Crain asserts that the native women are not mere passive subjects. Rather, by means of a calculated reconstruction of their gender and ethnic identities, they have actively reshaped the role assigned to them by their employer, and attempted to use it to their own advantage. In other words, they have proceeded to 'occupy' and exploit the very stereotypes which were intended to dominate them.

The Quimsa women's strategy for dealing with commodification may be described as one of 'accommodation': they have chosen to live with their negotiated identity, while at the same time exploiting it. An alternative strategy would be for the members of a community to seek to restrict the representation/appropriation of their way of life – that is, to remove their culture from the market and render it *extra commercium hominum*. This 'oppositional' strategy is practised by various aboriginal groups of the United States and Canada, including the Hopi of Arizona, as I discuss in the next chapter, 'Cultural Appropriation and Resistance in the American Southwest'.

The Hopi have come to feel beleaguered by the endless stream of representations of their culture. This feeling came to a head in 1992 when Marvel Comics came out with an issue in which various Hopi sacred beings were caricaturized. Having already experimented with diverse forms of political action (protest, lobbying), interest at Hopi shifted to finding out what forms of cultural protection might be offered by the law. According to the analysis of Anglo-American legal doctrine undertaken in this chapter, most of the available recourses (invasion of privacy, copyright, etc.) would not suit Hopi purposes, but one that might is the action for breach of publicity rights. This is the same action many North American film and sports celebrities use to control the marketing of their personalities. There is risk involved in pursuing this strategy, however, since treating one's culture as property may eventually lead to its removal from the dynamics of everyday life. Such are the stakes, however, that there may be no other option: it is either mobilize the law, or *koyaanisqatsi* (global chaos).

Another strategy which a people may use to counteract the forces of misrepresentation is to *themselves* employ modern media of communication to represent their culture and world. This is the possibility explored by Marian

Bredin in Chapter 9, 'Transforming Images'. Bredin presents the results of her study of the reception and transformation of diverse communications technologies by the First Nations peoples of northern Canada, focusing specifically on the operations of the Wawatay Native Communications Society, which services some 45 widely dispersed Cree and Ojibway communities in northern Ontario.

As Bredin notes, electronic media are typically seen as homogenizing forces, hence the widespread discourse on 'electronic colonialism', 'media imperialism', and the like. The power of such media to disseminate the values and practices of the dominant society should not be underestimated. However, in the aboriginal communities of the Canadian North, it appears that the introduction of radio and television has had the effect of stimulating demand, not just for mass-market programmes such as *Happy Days* and *Dallas*, but for local programming in local languages. In responding to this demand, native communications societies, like Wawatay, have had both to adapt traditional communicative practices to the new technologies, and adapt modern media to the transmission of traditional messages. The result is oral traditions going electronic.

At one point, Bredin remarks on how Wawatay media 'both facilitate and necessitate border crossings'. Here she is referring to the way Wawatay reporters take up a position on the boundaries of their culture and operate as cultural translators between the world at large and their community. The Wawatay case illustrates a point made by Frederick Buell in his discussion of the transformation of cultural boundaries from barriers into junctures, and the construction of post-colonial subject positions, within the 'new global system':

> in the construction of these positions, old boundaries have *not* been effaced but reassembled in fluid, strategic, situational ways. In fact, the new positions from which one can speak have increasingly evoked, not erased, the borders they have transformed: but they have done so *not* to divide, to exclude, but to interface and construct.
>
> (1994: 341)

A similar set of considerations may be seen to lie behind Mary Crain's use of the term 'cultural borderlands' to refer to the space in which identities are constructed in Ecuador.

The last chapter of this book, the Epilogue, is written by Constance Classen and myself. The Epilogue interweaves the various perspectives presented in Parts I, II and III. Its aim is to map the global dynamics of consumption, as goods cross and recross cultural borders, and highlight the social and ethical conflicts which can arise as a result of this process. In its concern with the ethics of consumption, this chapter provides a counterpoint to those approaches which treat consumption as a purely 'symbolic' phenomenon (e.g. Sahlins 1976; McCracken 1988). Each section of the Epilogue concludes with a series of questions which are meant to stimulate reflection on what Néstor García

Canclini (1995) has identified as the principal ethical contradiction of our times – the contradiction between being a consumer and being a citizen. It is hoped that these questions may help clarify aspects of our future as citizens of a global consumer society.

NOTES

1 In the sociology and anthropology of consumption one thinks of the work of Baudrillard (1968, 1970, 1975, 1981), Sahlins (1976), Douglas and Isherwood (1979), Bourdieu (1984), Appadurai (1986), Ewen (1988), McCracken (1988), Leiss, Kline and Jhaly (1988), Rutz and Orlove (1989), Tomlinson (1990), Featherstone (1990a), Shields (1992), Lee (1993), and Bocock (1993), as well as the pioneering work of Simmel (1904) and Veblen (1912). In material culture studies, there is the groundbreaking work of Miller (1987), and that of Riggins (1994). Another important stream is constituted by the writings of Benjamin (1989), Adorno and Horkheimer (1973) and de Certeau (1984), whose works have profoundly influenced cultural studies approaches to consumption (cf. Buck-Morss 1989; Chambers 1986; Willis 1990; Laermans 1993; Nava 1992).

2 Some anthropologists who have noted this lacuna – and made important contributions to our understanding of the local logics by which foreign goods are received – include Philibert (1982, 1989), Gell (1986), Arnould (1989) and Wilk (1994) (cf. especially Arnould and Wilk 1984), as well as those whose work will be discussed later in this introduction.

3 Another common name for this phenomenon is 'cultural imperialism' (Adam 1980; Tomlinson 1991).

4 To prevent further social disruption, the main protagonist of the film sets out to return the Coke bottle to its source, and encounters the spectacle of South African consumer society, which is gently mocked by the film (cf. Volkman 1988). For a good critique of what has been called the 'Coke bottle in the Kalahari syndrome' see Solway and Lee (1990).

5 The regime of Coca-classicization, or customized mass-production/consumption, is sometimes referred to as 'post-Fordism' in the literature. As Larry Grossberg explains: 'If Fordism controlled consumption to create demand for standardized mass-produced products, post-Fordism makes production conform to the continually changing demands of consumption', for example, through the use of hyper-adaptable machinery and labour practices (1992: 340–1). The profitability of Coca-classicization depends on economies of scope rather than scale. On this subject generally see Lee (1993) and Mattelart (1994: 215–17).

6 The use of the term 'creolization' in this book follows Hannerz (1992) and Jourdan (1994a), but also owes something to Ivor Miller (1994). Cognate terms include 'domestication' (Tobin 1992) and 'localization' as used in Friedman (1990) and Appadurai (1990).

7 As Daniel Miller notes, 'a system of categorization is an inherent attribute' of every artefact, and 'some notion of intention is also usually attributed to their creation' (1987: 112). Philibert calls this indwelling intentionality of the commodity its 'structure of recognition' (1989: 61). It is to this that I refer when I use the phrase 'intention of the producer'.

8 According to Barber (1995: 205), the characteristics of 'jihad' include 'parochialism, antimodernism, exclusiveness and hostility to "others" ', or basically any form of fundamentalist opposition to modernity.

15

9   On the difference between the syncretic and the synthetic, or the 'diathetical' and the 'dialectical', see my discussion in '*We Are the World* and its Counterparts' (Howes 1990a); see also Sherry (1987) and Arnould (1989).

10   The formula advanced by Roland Robertson, according to which we moderns are witnesses to 'a massive, twofold process involving *the interpenetration of the universalization of particularism and the particularization of universalism*' (1992: 73) appears to solve the problem of reflexivity, but remains inadequate with respect to conveying the sort of cobbling process that the word 'articulation' suggests. 'Interpenetration' is simply too smooth a term, when one considers how jagged and syncretic the real world of globalization is in all its 'boundary-violating strangeness' (cf. Buell 1994: 4–5, 27, 341) and injustice (cf. Barnet and Cavanagh 1994: 138, 427).

11   On the difficulties with the visualist or 'world picture' paradigm implicit in world system theory see Mitchell (1991), Little (1991) and Classen (1993).

12   On positional meaning and the significance of the sensual characteristics of things see Turner (1967), Howes (1990b), and Howes and Classen (1991).

13   Of course, the business community is not blind to the possible advantages which the 'local knowledge' anthropology has to offer might confer on their enterprises. Indeed, there has been a marked opening of business schools and corporations to anthropology in recent years: one now finds 'ethnography' being taught to students of marketing, and 'culture' being recognized and exploited as a basis of market segmentation (cf. Piirto 1991: 135–8; Rossman 1994; Solomon 1994; Giroux 1994: 15–20). The present book may be considered an opening in the opposite direction: it offers an anthropology of marketing, which both complements and critiques marketing anthropology (see the Epilogue).

14   To elaborate on how this book may be used for teaching purposes, Chapter 6 by Carol Hendrickson provides a model of how to do a content analysis of print advertisements for imported goods. Students could be invited to collect examples of similar sorts of advertisements, and then to identify the themes that run through them, and discuss their implications, in light of Hendrickson's analysis. Chapter 2 by Constance Classen provides a model which could be used by students to develop a series of interview questions concerning how patterns of consumption change over time. These questions could then be addressed to older members of the student's family, or other persons with experience of the social and cultural transformations precipitated by changes in consumer goods over a period of years. Students might also wish to draw from their own experience as consumers.

15   The implication is that 'Westernization' (or 'modernization') is not solely a process which goes on 'out there', in the developing parts of the world; it is at the same time the process by which the West constructs itself as 'Western' through representing other parts of the world – and the people and goods which come from them – as 'exotic' or 'primitive' or 'other' (cf. Said 1978, 1993).

16   This suggestion is supported by recent work on the commodification of the body (Haug 1986; Joy and Venkatesh 1994), smell (Classen, Howes and Synnott 1994) and touch (Hornik 1992; Chambers 1986: 12). Capitalizing on the sentiments, including our feelings of solidarity, puts the finishing touch to the civilizing process under late consumer capitalism (Giroux 1994; Rojek 1985, 1995).

17   The Ainu of Japan, as described by Friedman (1994: 109–12), present a classic example of what could be called the marketization strategy (after Firat 1995). The Ainu are not recognized as having autonomous ethnic status by the Japanese state, so they have resorted to tourist production and display in an effort to gain recognition as a separate ethnic group. Official recognition has yet to happen, but the Ainu have achieved widespread popular success.

Part I

THE MIRROR OF CONSUMPTION

1

THE EMPIRE'S OLD CLOTHES
Fashioning the colonial subject
Jean Comaroff

It might be argued that modern European empires were as much fashioned as forged – that as social fields, they arose as much from the circulation of stylized objects as from brute force or bureaucratic fiat. The banality of imperialism – of the mundanities that made it ineffably real – has seldom been given its due by colonial historians, although most would probably agree that cultural revolutions must root themselves in rather humble gound. Even the most formal of economic structures may be shown to arise from ordinary transactions. Marx understood this well; after all, he vested his mature account of capitalism in the unobtrusive career of the commodity, that 'very queer thing' (Marx 1967, 1: 71) whose seemingly trivial production, exchange, and consumption built the contours of a whole social world.

This insight turns out to be highly relevant to an understanding of European colonization in nineteenth-century South Africa, especially the project of those 'humane imperialists' who hoped to found God's Kingdom in the savage wilderness. The civilizing mission merged bourgeois Protestantism with imperialism – both fuelled by expanding industrial capital. But the record of such evangelism speaks less of a theological crusade than of an effort to reform the ordinary, a pursuit in which common objects were as central as the Holy Book. Particularly striking was the place of dress in this enterprise: clothes were at once commodities and accoutrements of a civilized self. They were to prove a privileged means for constructing new forms of value, personhood, and history on the colonial frontier.

In what follows, I relate these sartorial adventures to the more general British effort to incorporate African communities into a global economy of goods and signs. These stylized transactions were not mere representations of more 'real' historical forces; they themselves began to generate a new cultural economy. Indeed, both parties to the colonial encounter invested a great deal in the objects that passed between them; for these goods were 'social hiero-glyphics' (Marx 1967, 1: 74), encoding in compact form the structure of a novel world in the making.

My immediate case, in this paper, is that of the Nonconformist mission to the Tswana peoples of Southern Africa, a project that relied heavily on recasting local modes of consumption. Consumption, here, must be understood in its nineteenth-century European context, one that idealized the power of the market to convert difference into a single system of value – a 'commonwealth'. With its characteristic Protestant ardour, the civilizing mission professed the faith that commodities could conjure new desires, bodily disciplines, and exertions; indeed, new forms of society *tout court*. And nowhere was this faith more visible than in the realm of self-presentation – especially in modes of dress.

My argument will trace one strand of a more encompassing colonial encounter.[1] I shall explore the Nonconformist campaign to cover African 'nakedness' – in particular, to make the Southern Tswana susceptible to the aesthetics of European fashion. This project was driven by a clear sense that civilization was promoted by encouraging discerning consumption. The aim was to draw would-be converts into the system of surplus production by evoking a competitive urge to create new identities with coded things. The case centres on a feature quite common in European colonialism: its early moments frequently focused not only on making non-Western peoples want Western goods, but on teaching them to use them in particular sorts of ways (cf. Sahlins 1988). Indeed, imperialists and their merchant associates often sought to prevail by transplanting highly specific regimes of consumption; their conscious concerns, in the first instance, dwelt less on the brute extraction of labour or raw materials than on trade that seemed capable of forging new self-sustaining orders of desire, transaction, and value. The sense that culture is constructed through consumption, then, is clearly no mere figment of the 'post-modern' or 'post-industrial' imagination, as some have assumed (Baudrillard 1975; cf. Appadurai 1993). It is as old as capitalism itself.

Attempts to explain the rise of colonialism – and the rest of modern industrial society – in terms of the logic of expanding European *production* alone tend to miss this point. Yet we have long realized that imperialism was a more complex cultural process, both in motivation and consequence. The effort to redress Africa, for instance, was driven as much by the urge to civilize as to garner profits – at least in crude material terms. Already by the early nineteenth century, commodity consumption was indissolubly linked to the production of civilization. Thus, when British mission propagandists advertised the commercial opportunities available in Africa, they did so to glean support for what they saw as a more profound moral enterprise. But while they drew alike from the gospels of Jesus and Adam Smith, the evangelists would learn that commerce and civility did not always go hand in glove. Though the Christians shared a faith in commodities characteristic of their culture, they were also aware of the contradictions of competitive consumption, especially for those of Puritan heritage. In time, they would try vainly to rein in the material forces they had mediated, especially as these fell prey to the more cynical designs of colonial capital.

In outline, I argue that attempts to reform Tswana consumption had unintended outcomes – that they played powerfully into the making and marking of new social classes, rupturing existing communities of signs and hastening the conversion of local systems of value to a global currency. But these efforts also set off playful processes of experimentation and synthesis. For novel goods spurred the African imagination, although from the first, many refused to 'buy in' to European cultural dictates, epitomized by the mission's strict codes of dress. Old élites were especially resistant to such sartorial discipline, seeing it as a foreign assault on their subjects. But, as the century wore on, few Tswana would escape the constraints of the colonial economy, and their room for creative manoeuvre was severely reduced. Forced to be more dependent on the market, the majority would adopt a dress that – more than any other medium – made visible their marginal place in the new imperium. Experimental syntheses were replaced by a more enduring style; its female form (a 'folk' costume to the European eye) contrasting with the work garb that became the uniform of male migrants here and elsewhere in South Africa. Women's dress seemed to 'ethnicize' what had become a peasantariat, a unit in the national reserve army of 'tribal' labour. Their dress would be made almost entirely from store-bought materials. Yet these commodities would be used to craft a novel conservatism, an existence beyond the exigencies of innovation and endless metropolitan mimicry that defined black petite bourgeois culture.

'Ethnic' dress, in fact, seemed part of a local effort to stabilize a radically compromised identity. Yet it was also a mark of displacement from the centres of social and cultural production. Fashion seems especially appropriate for this task in the modern world, for it epitomizes the power of the commodity to encompass the self: not only does fashion's insistence on 'pure contemporaneity' render those who do not wear it 'out of date' and parochial (Faurschou 1990: 235); it also confirms the fact that, in a commodity culture, identity is something owned *apart* from one's self, something that must continuously be 'put on' and displayed (Bowlby 1985: 27–8; cf. Williamson 1992: 106). This turns out to be a crucial aspect of the remaking of African space and time, African selves and societies under colonialism.

THE HEATHEN BODY

From the start, in Southern Tswana communities, the most tangible signs of the European presence were worn on the backs of the people themselves. Clothing is a 'social skin' (Turner n.d.) that makes and marks social beings everywhere. But the early evangelists came from a world in which garments were central to the rising industrial economy, and distinctions of dress crucial to the work of 'self-fashioning' (Greenblatt 1980; Veblen 1912). Mission activities suggest that, at least in this Christian culture,[2] clothedness was next to godliness: it was easier for a camel to pass through the eye of a needle than for the ill-clad to enter the Kingdom of Heaven.

At the core of the Protestant mission lay a tension between inner and outer verities, the life of the spirit and of the sensuous world. Dress epitomized this conflict. It was a fitting means for showing self-improvement, but it was also the stuff of the flesh. Unless it could be seen to effect reform that was more than skin deep, it remained an exterior overlay or vain deception. The concern with dress revealed what was often a vain effort to fuse the cultivation of the body with the conversion of the spirit. At the same time, the evidence suggests that many Southern Tswana acknowledged the ritual resonance of dress – albeit from a perspective of their own, one that gave voice to a distinct understanding of the colonial encounter. As they read them, the European gestures with clothes were unambiguosly embodied and pragmatic.

These gestures began with, and were at first frankly preoccupied by, the covering of African 'nakedness'. Nakedness, of course, is in the eye of the beholder. In mission practice, it implied neither savage innocence, nor even mere degeneracy. It spoke also of darkness, disorder, and pollution. Pioneer evangelist Robert Moffat expresses a widely shared sense of the rampant heathen body – that it threatened the whole fragile cultural order built on the Christian frontier:

> As many men and women as pleased might come into our hut, leaving us not room even to turn ourselves, and making every thing they touched the colour of their greasy red attire . . . . They would keep the housewife a perfect prisoner in a suffocating atmosphere, almost intolerable; and when they departed, they left ten times more than their number behind [i.e. lice] – company still more offensive.
>
> (1842: 287)

There is no effort, here, to disguise the distaste for African intruders who breached the bounds of domestic propriety. Moffat's prose is not without precedent. The notion of the 'greasy native' had gained currency in the texts of late eighteenth-century travellers and anatomists (Comaroff and Comaroff 1991: 104), probably reflecting the use of animal fat and butter as cosmetics in much of South and East Africa, where a gleaming skin radiated beauty and projected status (J. Comaroff 1985: 110).[3] But for the Europeans, the epithet also carried more prurient associations. It suggested a lascivious stickiness, a body that refused to separate itself from the world, leaving (as an unnamed writer put it) red, 'greasy marks upon everything' (Religious Tract Society n.d.: 85). Nothing could have been further from the cool, contained, inward-turning person of the mission ideal; a self both 'discreet' and 'discrete'.

The bogey of such bestial bodies was well rooted in the English imperial imagination. First the Irish, then Native Americans had been seen as dirty primitives in animal hides (Muldoon 1975). In each case, the trope was tuned to the tenor of its times. Hence, in early nineteenth-century Africa, the 'lubricated wild man of the desert' contrasted with the 'clean, comfortable and well-dressed believer' as did 'filthy' animal fat and skin with the 'cotton and woollen manufactures of Manchester and Leeds' (Hughes 1841: 523). The early evangelists assumed that the benefits of 'decent dress' would be self-evident to the Africans: while Moffat (1842: 348) found it understandable that Tswana might at first oppose Christian doctrine, he thought it 'natural' that they would adopt Western attire 'for their own comfort and convenience'. But appeals to practical reason are always also moral injunctions: Rybczynski (1986) has shown that the concept of 'comfort', seemingly so transparently physical, is itself an historical construct denoting a set of material and moral assumptions born of bourgeois domestic order.

Of course, the Nonconformists were also heirs to a moralistic language that had long waxed eloquent on the issue of shame and modesty. The frequent eruption of corporeal images in staid mission prose confirms their

Figure 1 'The abandoned mother: a scene in the life of Robert Moffat'
Source: reproduced from Adam & Company, *The Life and Explorations of Dr Livingstone* (1874), frontispiece

23

preoccupation with the erotic. It also lends credence to the claim that, in order to extract power from the repressed body, modern Protestantism had constantly to evoke it (Foucault 1978: 115 ff.). One early evangelist told the Tlhaping that the Word would melt their flinty savage hearts, bringing forth penitent tears and 'wash[ing] away all the red paint from their bodies' (Comaroff and Comaroff 1991: 214). Redness and rudeness were made one, for the daubed body invoked a brace of nineteenth-century associations, from the 'rouge' of female depravity to 'Red' Indian warpaint. The Tswana had to be made aware of their brazen nakedness, their sinful passion. If they were to become vessels of the Spirit, their corporeality had to be reconstructed: confined, turned inward, and invested with self-consciousness and shame.

Western dress was at once a sign and an instrument of this transformation. To European and African alike, it would become the most distinctive mark of association with the mission (Etherington 1978: 116), a fact graphically conveyed to the British public in pictures sent from the field. In the oft-illustrated incident of Moffat ministering to an 'abandoned mother' (Comaroff and Comaroff 1991:110-11), for example, the evangelist's black assistant, a male convert, stands attentively behind his mentor, faithfully replicating his dress (Figure 1). The heathen, by contrast, lies in tatters in the bush, her breasts flagrantly bare. Absent altogether from the heroic scene is the mission wife, primary agent of the early campaign to clothe Africa.

AFRICAN ADORNMENT

The Western trope of 'nakedness' – which implies a particular idea of bodily being, nature and culture – would have made little sense to Tswana prior to the arrival of the missions. In South Africa, what the nineteenth-century missionaries took to be indecent exposure was clearly neither a state of undress nor impropriety in indigenous eyes (although local notions of unclothedness existed; uncovered genitals and undressed hair were considered uncouth in Tswana adults). African dress and grooming *were* scanty by European standards, but they conveyed – as such things do everywhere – complex distinctions of gender, age, and social identity. In their seeming nakedness, the Africans were fully clothed.

What was most unsettling to the evangelists was the place of apparel in the whole Tswana social order. As I have said, in the European world, discerning consumption was the major index of social worth. In fact, consumption was increasingly set off from production as a gendered and markedly female sphere of practice. Women's domestic demesne centred on the display of adornments that would signal the status of their male providers, men whose own attire, as befitted their endeavours, was relatively sober and unelaborated (Turner n.d.). Moreover, while men of the bourgeoisie controlled the manufacture and marketing of clothes, the labour which produced textiles and garments was largely that of poor women and (in the early years) children, members of the lower orders who were conspicuously excluded from the stylish self-production that engrossed their more privileged sisters.

OTHER KINDS OF CLOTHES

Above all else, it struck the evangelists as unnatural that, while Tswana women built houses, sowed, and reaped, 'men ma[d]e the dresses for themselves and the females' (LMS 1824). Refashioning this division of labour was integral to reforming 'primitive' production in all its dimensions; and this, in turn, required the creation of a distinct – feminine – domestic world centred on reproduction and consumption. In this regard, the churchmen were disturbed by the fact that, although it was marginally distinguished by rank, female attire was largely undifferentiated. In direct contrast to bourgeois fashion, it was mainly men's clothes that signalled social standing here (cf. Kay 1834, 1: 201). In fact, European observers pronounced male dress to be quite varied – even dandyish (LMS 1824, 1828).

Such distinctions apart, however, Tswana costume seemed to be unremittingly rude and rudimentary. For the most part, those of the same sex and age dressed alike (Schapera 1953: 25). Nonetheless, it soon struck the Europeans that, albeit in a register of their own, indigenous clothes also spoke volubly of status. By contrast to infants (who wore little besides medicated ornaments), adults of both sexes wore long skin cloaks (*dikobó*; singular *kobó*) that were significant 'sign[s]' of wealth' (LMS 1824).[4] Cloaks were first donned at the conclusion of male and female initiation, denoting the onset of sexual and jural maturity (J. Comaroff 1985: 105 ff.); interestingly, during lapses from full participation in social life – such as after bereavement – people put on their *dikobó* inside out. Royal males wore especially fine karosses, often incorporating the pelts of wild beasts, although that of the leopard was reserved for reigning chiefs (Philip 1828, 2: 126). The skin cape was to prove extremely durable in this economy of signs, surviving amidst a riot of market innovations to give a distinctive stamp to Tswana 'folk' style, where it lived on, in the form of the store-bought blanket, as a crucial element of 'tribal' costume.

Early accounts suggest that Tswana were especially creative in fashioning new ornaments which seemed to radiate personal identity. They favoured shining surfaces (recall the glossy cosmetics) and a gleaming visibility that would contrast markedly with the dullness of mission modes, which countered 'flashiness' with a stress on personal restraint and inward reflection. There is plentiful evidence of novel adornments made with the sparkling buttons and glass beads that found their way into the interior, for by the early nineteenth century, the latter had become a widespread currency linking local and monetized economies.

But bright beads were not all equally desirable; Campbell (in LMS 1824) noted that, by the 1820s, Tswana 'greatly prefer[ed] the dark blue colour'. This is intriguing for, as we shall see, dark blue was to be the shade favoured for the dress of converts by the mission. If Campbell was correct, the European's chosen hue had a fortuitous precedent, having already been associated with prestige of foreign origin. Blue beads were globules of exchange value, imaginatively congealed into local designs. Clear blue appears to have had no other place in indigenous artistic schemes: patterns on housefronts, pottery, and ritual artefacts tended to play on the three-way contrast of black, red, and white (J. Comaroff 1985: 114). It is tempting to suggest that blue – so clearly the colour of the mission and its materials (as well, in Tswana poetics, of the pale, piercing eyes of whites) – was the pigment of exogenous powers and substances. The Christians would certainly wield the blues in their effort to counter 'heathenism', for when it came to heathens, they saw red.

CIVILITY, CLOTH AND CONSUMPTION

Above all, the evangelists would try to force Tswana bodies into the strait-jacket of Protestant personhood. The Nonconformists acted on the implicit assumption that, in order to reform the heathens, it was necessary to scramble their entire code of body management; thus 'decent' Western dress was demanded from all who would associate with the church. Tswana soon appreciated the role of clothes in this campaign. When Chief Montshiwa of the Tshidi Rolong perceived that the Christian influence in his realm had begun to extend even to his own kin, he ordered his daughter publicly 'to doff her European clothing, . . . to return to heathen attire' (Mackenzie 1871: 231). His royal counterparts elsewhere also fastened on to such discernible signs of allegiance, and many struggles ensued over the right to determine individual dress. From the first, Southern Tswana tended to treat objects of Western adornment as signs of exotic force; those introduced by the mission were soon identified as *sekgoa*, 'white things' (Burchell 1824, 2: 559). But some items of European clothing had preceded the mission into the interior,[5] where people often seem to have regarded them as vehicles of alien power (1824, 2: 432). An early report from Kuruman tells how the Tlhaping chief addressed his warriors prior to battle in a 'white linen garment', his heir wearing an 'officer's coat' (Moffat 1825: 29). In a published account of this incident, Moffat (1842: 348) revealed that the garment was actually a chemise of unknown origin. Such attire seemed to lend potency to indigenous enterprise, in part because its qualities resonated with local signs and values. White, the usual colour of the baptismal gown (itself, to the untrained eye, much like a chemise) was also the colour of the transformative substances placed on the human body during indigenous rites of passage (J. Comaroff 1985: 98). Similarly, the military uniforms carried inland from the Colony by Khoi soldiers might have had cogent connotations associated with this forceful frontier population. But the interest which they evoked seems also to have been fed by what appears to have been a long-standing Tswana concern with the dress of combat (J. Comaroff 1985: 112; Comaroff and Comaroff 1991: 164).

European costume, in short, opened up a host of imaginative possibilities for Southern Tswana. It offered an enhanced language in which to play with new social identities, a language in which the mission itself would become a pole of reference. In the early days, before the Christians presented a palpable threat to chiefly authority, royals monopolized the Western garments that travelled into the interior. These were worn in experimental fashion, often in ceremonial audiences with visiting whites (Philip 1828, 2: 126-7). Already at this point, several aspects of the synthetic style that would be much in evidence later on in the century seem to have taken shape – among them, the combination of European garments with skin cloaks. This was a form of mixing which the evangelists abhored, yet would never manage to eradicate.

But the missions would expend great effort and cost to ensure that, in Moffat's telling phrase (1842: 505), the Africans would 'be[come] clothed and in their right mind' (cf. Luke 8.35). As Western dress became more closely associated with expanding evangelical control, the early phase of playful experimentation came to an end. By the 1830s, once a regular mission presence had been established, most senior royals had discarded the dress of *sekgoa*, identifying with an ever more assertively marked *setswana* (Tswana ways). Some were said to 'ridicule . . . and even abuse' those kin who 'laid aside' the dress of their 'forbears' (Smith 1939, 1: 337).

I have noted that the campaign to clothe black South Africa was inseparable from other axes of the civilizing mission, especially the effort to reform agricultural production. Thus in order to dress Tswana – or rather, to teach them to dress themselves – women had to be persuaded to trade the hoe for the needle, the outdoor for the indoor life (Gaitskell 1988). In this endeavour, the Nonconformists relied largely on the 'domesticating' genius of the 'gentler sex' – on their own wives and daughters (cf. Hunt 1990), most of whom started sewing schools almost at once (Moffat 1842: 505); these also served as a focus for the exertions of female philanthropists in Britain, who sent pincushions and needles with which to stitch the seams of an expanding imperial fabric. Recall that, in pre-colonial times, clothing was made of leather; an extension of animal husbandry, it was produced by men. It is not surprising, then, that sewing schools had limited appeal at first. In the early years, moreover, there was no regular supply of materials. But by the late 1830s, once merchants had been attracted to the stations, those Tswana women most closely identified with the church had begun to take in sewing for payment (1842: 17). This was one of several areas in which the evangelists encouraged commercial relations well ahead of a formal colonial labour market.

But even if the missionaries had succeeded immediately in persuading Tswana to clothe themselves, local manufacture would have fallen short of the task. Thus the Christians appealed to the generosity of the great British public. The growth of the fashion industry encouraged obsolescence, and by this time had already provided a steady supply of used garments (or recycled commodities) for the poor and unclad at home and abroad. When, in 1843, the Moffats returned to Cape Town from a visit to the United Kingdom, they sailed with fifty tons of 'old clothes' for the Kuruman station (Northcott 1961: 172). The famous David Livingstone, sometime missionary among the Tswana, was scathing about the 'good people' of England who had given their cast-off ballgowns and starched collars to those 'who had no shirts' (1961: 173). But a letter from Mrs Moffat to a woman well-wisher in London shows that she had thought carefully about the adaptation of Western dress to African conditions:

> The materials may be coarse, and strong, the stronger the better. Dark blue Prints, or Ginghams . . . or in fact, any kind of dark Cottons, which will wash well – Nothing light-coloured should be worn outside . . . All the heathen population besmear themselves with red ochre and grease, and as the Christians must necessarily come in contact, with their friends among the heathen, they soon look miserable enough, if clothed in light-coloured things . . . *I* like them best as Gowns were made 20 or 30 years ago . . . For little Girls, Frocks made exactly as you would for the Children of the poor of this country, will be the best.
>
> ([1841]1967: 17-18)

Clothing women and children was her priority. And while any European clothes, even diaphanous ballgowns, were better than none, more sombre, serviceable garb was ideal. Dark blue garments, especially, resisted the stains of a red-handed heathenism that threatened to 'rub off' on the convert. Indigo-dyed prints, now being mass-produced with raw materials drawn from other imperial outposts, conformed well with the long-standing European association of dark hues with humility, piety and virtue. Ochre and grease aside, Mrs Moffat suggested, African converts were like the virtuous British poor, whose inability to produce their own wealth was marked by their exclusion from the fashion system, and by the dismal durability of their dress. Great efforts would also be made to stir a desire for self-improvement in these neophyte Christians.

The fact that Mary Moffat wrote about such matters to a woman was itself predictable. Not only the acquisition and maintenance, but also the dispatch of clothing in the form of charity had become a key element of a feminized domestic economy (Davidoff and Hall 1987). But such recycling carried its own dangers: it could inhibit ambition in the poor. Care had to be taken not to evoke indigence. Here the Protestants put their faith in the sheer charm of commodities. Comfortable and attractive garments, they hoped, would awaken the desire for property and self-enhancement, for a life of righteous getting and spending.

And so, through the effort of mission wives and their European sisters, the germ of the fashion system arrived on the African veld. It bore with it the particular features of the culture of industrial capitalism: an enduring impetus toward competitive accumulation, symbolic innovation, and social distinction (Bell 1949). But its export to this frontier also underscored the deep-seated contradictions in the material expression of the Protestant ethic. Ascetic angst focused most acutely on female frailty. For, in as much as the fashion system made women its primary vehicles, it strengthened the association of femininity with things of the flesh. Willoughby was far from alone in grumbling that many Tswana women were soon in thrall to ridiculous hats and expensive garments.[6] Also, while the Nonconformists might have striven to produce an élite driven by virtuous wants, they had also to justify the lot of the less fortunate majority. They had, in other words, to sanctify poverty and the postponement of physical pleasure in the interests of eternal grace. Their most humble adherents remained the deserving recipients of charity, dressed in the strong dark blue cottons whose colour and texture were to become synonymous with the mission rank-and-file. This would be the nucleus of rural 'folk', whose style and predicament would come to typify Tswana peasant-proletarians in modern South Africa.

As the century wore on, the evangelists would devote their energies increasingly to the cultivation of a black petite bourgeoisie. But in the early years, they encouraged 'improvement and self-reliance' as an ideal for all; hence their attempts to bring traders and, with them, the goods needed to make Christians. Revd Archbell began to pursue merchants for his Wesleyan station among the Seleka Rolong in 1833; and by 1835, Moffat had persuaded David Hume, a factor catering to the 'demand for British commodities', to establish himself at Kuruman. The mission played a large role in stimulating that demand, not just for ready-made garments, cotton prints, and sewing goods, but for all the elements of the European sartorial economy. The Nonconform-ists, for instance, stressed the fact that, unlike 'filthy skins', clothes had to be washed and repaired, binding wives and daughters to an unrelenting regime of 'cleanliness' – epitomized, to this day, by the starched and laundered uniforms of the black women's Prayer Unions. It was a form of discipline that the evangelists monitored closely, ensuring brisk sales of soap and other cleansing agents (cf. Burke 1990).

From 1830 onwards mission reports speak with pleasure of 'decent rain-ments' worn by their loyal members. They also note that trade was healthy, and that there was a growing desire among Southern Tswana to purchase European apparel (Moffat 1842: 219; Read 1850: 446). Not only was the campaign to clothe the heathen masses under way, but a distinct and sedately styled Anglophile élite was increasingly visible in the interior.

SELF-FASHIONING ON THE FRONTIER: THE MAN IN THE TIGER SUIT

The growing supply of Western apparel in the interior towards the mid-century also had another effect on the Tswana, one less palatable to the mission. It incited what the Christians saw as an absurd, even promiscuous syncretism:

A man might be seen in a jacket with but one sleeve, because the other was not finished, or he lacked material to complete it. Another in a leathern or duffel jacket, with the sleeves of different colours, or of fine printed cotton. Gowns were seen like Joseph's coat of many colours, and dresses of such fantastic shapes, as were calculated to excite a smile in the gravest of us.

(Moffat 1842: 506)

Such descriptions give a glimpse of the Tswana *bricoleur* tailoring a brilliant patchwork on the cultural frontier. To the evangelist, they offered a disconcerting distortion of the worthy self-fashionings he had tried to set in motion. Such 'eccentric' garb caused the Christians much anxiety. As Douglas (1966) might have predicted, it came to be associated with dirt and contagion. State health authorities by the turn of the century were asserting that 'Natives who partially adopted our style of dress' were most susceptible to serious disease (Packard 1989: 690). If the selective appropriation of Western attire flouted British codes of costume and decency, it also called into question the authoritative norms of Nonconformism. This was particularly evident in the counterpoint between the colourful, home-made creations of most people and the 'uniforms' introduced by the mission to mark the compliance of those in its schools and associations. (The latter attire, being both novel, yet closed to stylish innovation, anticipated subsequent 'folk' dress in several respects.) But the creative couture contrived by so many Southern Tswana suggests a riposte to the symbolic imperialism of the mission at large. It speaks of a desire to harness the power of *sekgoa*, yet evade white authority and discipline. The *bricoleur* contrasted, on the one hand, with those who ostensibly rejected everything European and, on the other, with those who identified faithfully with church aesthetics and values. Style, here, was clearly implicated in the making of radically new distinctions. And as the colonial economy expanded into the interior, the means for such fashioning was increasingly available through channels beyond the control of the mission.

Indeed, as the century progressed, the growing articulation of the Southern Tswana with the regional political economy was tangible in their everyday material culture. For a start, the volume of goods pumped into rural communities rose markedly. A visitor to Mafikeng in 1875 (Holub 1881, 2: 14) reported that, apart from a small élite, the population persisted in its patchwork of indigenous and European styles. But the make-up of the mixture had subtly altered. Mafikeng was by then a Christian Tshidi-Rolong village that had no white mission presence. Still, store-bought commodities comprised a growing proportion of its cultural *mélange*. British aesthetics were being used in ever more complex ways; both in the honour and in the breach they marked widening social and economic differences.

The deployment of Western style was particularly evident in the changing garb of 'traditional' rulers and royals. As noted above, they had responded to

30

the earlier missionary challenge by reverting, assertively, to *setswana* costume – and by insisting that their Christian subjects do likewise. By the late nineteenth century, however, with the colonial state ever more palpably upon them, few but the most far-flung of Tswana sovereigns harboured illusions about the habits of power. Some, in fact, sought to outsmart the evangelists at their own game; Mackenzie (1883: 35) records the fascinating case of Chief Sechele who, in 1860, had a singular suit tailored from 'tiger' (i.e. leopard) skin – all 'in European fashion'. According to the missionary, many of the Kwena ruler's subjects thought he wished 'to make himself a white man'. But the matter was surely more complex. In crafting the skin, itself a symbol of chiefly office, the chief seems to have been making yet another effort to mediate the two exclusive systems of authority at war in his world, striving perhaps to fashion a power greater than the sum of its parts! Other rulers, most notably the Tshidi and Ngwaketse chiefs (Holub 1881, 1: 291), took another tack, now choosing to dress themselves in highly fashionable garb, clothes whose opulence set them off from their more humble Christian subjects – missionaries included! These early examples of royal dandyism involved only male dress; but the nascent local bourgeoisie had already begun, like its European counterpart, to signal status on the bodies of its women, whose clothing became ever more nuanced and elaborate (cf. Willoughby n.d.: 25, 48).

MIGRANTS, MERCHANTS AND THE COSTUME OF THE COUNTRYSIDE

In the closing decades of the century, it was labour migration that had the greatest impact on Southern Tswana dress. Whites in the interior had insisted, from the beginning, that 'natives' with whom they sustained contact should adopt minimal standards of 'decency' – covering at least their 'private' parts. Men who interacted regularly with whites soon took to wearing trousers, and those who, in later years, journeyed to the new industrial centres had little option but to conform to the basic rules of respectability pertaining to public places. By then, however, the Christians had already established a widespread 'need' for European garments, if not necessarily for European styles. Schapera (1947: 122) is not alone in suggesting that the desire for such commodities as clothes was powerful in initially drawing migrants to urban areas.

But desire is seldom, in itself, a sufficient explanation for large-scale social processes. The migration of Southern Tswana to the cities occurred in the wake of regional political and ecological forces which impoverished large sections of local populations. Nor was the consumption of European fashions a specifically urban affair. Willoughby indicates that, by the late nineteenth century, Tswana living near rural mission stations had learnt very well how to craft themselves with commodities; some spent 'as much on clothes in a year as would keep my wife well-clad for Ten Years'.[7] None the less, it is clear that those who did migrate to the industrial centres were immediately confronted by an array of

31

'Kaffir Stores' that pressed upon them a range of 'native goods' designed especially for the neophyte black proletarian.[8]

Advertisements attest that clothes were by far the most significant commodities sold by urban 'Kaffir storekeepers'.[9] The sheer volume of this trade at the time suggests that migrants were devoting a high proportion of their earnings to self-fashioning. And the standardization and range of goods indicate that some customers, at least, were putting on the dress of industrial capitalism, with its distinctions between labour and leisure, and manual and non-manual toil. Contemporary advertisements also invoked class distinctions: texts aimed at literate Africans, for instance, suggested that discerning taste conferred social distinction. The moral economy of mission and marketplace overlapped ever more neatly.

RURAL TRANSFORMATIONS

In rural areas, too, important transformations were unfolding. The closing decades of the century were marked by the proliferation of a striking array of local fashions. Style had become integral to the internal stratification of local Tswana communities as they were drawn more tightly into the regional political economy. Among the evidence is a published collection of photographs, *Native Life on the Transvaal Border*, produced *circa* 1899 by the Revd Willoughby of the London Missionary Society (LMS), which gives an intriguing insight into the development of local material culture, especially in respect of dress and domestic design.

Figure 2 'Milly, one of [Chief] Khama's daughters, and Sekgome, Khama's only son'
Source: reproduced from Willoughby, *Native Life on the Transvaal Border*

These pictures suggest that the contrasts discernible a couple of decades before had undergone transformation. Wealthy royals remained the most expensively and stylishly clad (Figure 2), but they were now less distinguishable from the Christian élite, which also dressed itself in elaborate (if sober) versions of current English fashion. This convergence stemmed, in part, from the fact that colonial rule had established new Eurocentric hegemonies; the expansion of the bureaucratic state had continued to erode the bases of chiefly power and had enhanced the status of those schooled by the mission. What is more, nominal membership of the church now extended to most Tswana, including senior royals. Here, as elsewhere, class distinctions were literally being tailor-made. Style did not just reflect new Southern Tswana alliances; it was part of their fabrication.

The crowd scenes in the pictorial archive offer little evidence of 'heathen dress' among adults, although it clearly remained common among youths and unmarried girls (Figure 3). Having acquired the status of the primitive and childlike, such clothing might still have been worn by adults in areas not yet penetrated by the white gaze. But most Tswana chiefs had become aware of the stigmatizing implications of 'backwardness', and were themselves urging their subjects to dress in European style. In such a climate, the evangelists testified proudly that 'traditional costume' was all but extinct (Willoughby n.d.: 84).[10]

Figure 3 'Rising generation'
Source: reproduced from Willoughby, *Native Life on the Transvaal Border*

FEMINIZING THE 'FOLK' ON THE ETHNIC PERIPHERY

However, history has a habit of leaping across such rigid breaks. In this respect, perhaps the most telling feature of Willoughby's pictures is found in the middle ground between the élite and those in childish 'heathen' attire – the appearance of ordinary people, especially women. By now, almost all Southern Tswana had been drawn into a world dominated by commodity manufacture. Yet unlike their élites, who strove to effect Eurocentric models, the rank-and-file developed a distinctive style, one that shaped industrial materials to a heightened sense of *setswana*. Neither straightforwardly Western nor 'authentically' indigenous, this style combined elements of both to signify a novel sense of anachronism: that of membership in a marginalized 'ethnic' culture. Like the dress of other peripheral peoples in South Africa (cf. Mayer 1961: 25–6), or in Europe, it drew on global commodities to mark the fact that its wearers were being refigured as quaint pre-moderns, existing at the exploitable edge of an empire. But the costume was not conjured up *ex nihilo*. Its elements were drawn from the different cultural schemes articulated along the new frontiers. In short, these Tswana women and men did not simply don imperial designs. They opted, in the main, for a dress that defied fashion in important respects, one that configured an enduring identity at a distance from white markets and morals.

Notwithstanding local variation, this kind of clothing takes on a recognizable identity in a Eurocentric world. It is the 'folk costume' of rural peoples, of those marginalized by 'modernity', whose greatest elaboration is often expressed in the garb of women (cf. Nag 1991; Hendrickson 1986). Of course, this is not invariably the case. In much of West Africa, where élites gestured not only to Christian Europe but to the Muslim world, male dress became the more elaborate bearer of refashioned ethnic identities in colonial and post-colonial contexts. How do we account for just such differences? The answer seems to lie in the manner in which local communities are caught up in encompassing empires, a process that draws them into world economies even while they remain rooted, in important respects, in their own regimes of production and exchange. It has become commonplace to observe that, while they change existing arrangements, such processes also reinforce certain indigenous practices, recreating them as 'traditions' used to fix 'local' identities in a world of exploding 'global' horizons.

And here is the point. In the first instance, Western colonizers often set out to extract labour from men. Where this involved the commoditization of local agriculture or the establishment of plantations, both sexes were usually pressed into service. But the rise of industrial capitalism in the colonies tended initially to favour male migration to new centres. This, it is true, did not always preclude the movement of women (White 1988); but low male wages were frequently subsidized by females farming in the countryside. In South Africa, this process was so marked that the rural areas became, in many respects, female domains. Indeed, women became icons of a 'tribal' home centred beyond the reaches of modern economy, society and history.

Is it to be wondered then, that in the signifying economy of such 'modernizing' processes, 'native' women should so often come to embody 'tradition' – the latter often rooted in a newly nuanced sense of the rural? Made by colonizing forces into pre-modern counterparts of European females, they were set apart from the centres of production and 'progress' in devalued, 'domestic' enclaves. (Later, in South Africa, these would be termed, quite literally, '*home*lands'.) Here they reproduced and represented the 'tribal' essence – the cheap labour – that fuelled the economy of empire.

To underscore the point, our photographic evidence from the turn of the century shows that the clothing of the migrant male rank-and-file was limited largely to khaki jackets, shirts and trousers. This standard proletarian uniform for black males made little ethnic distinction. By contrast, the visual archive confirms that non-élite Tswana women became the prime bearers of emergent

Figure 4 'Pounding and sifting corn'
Source: reproduced from Willoughby, *Native Life on the Transvaal Border*

35

'tribal' markings of a particularly modern sort. Attesting to a generic 'ethnicity', their costume secured the rural pole of the hyphenated condition of the 'peasant-proletarian' (Figure 4): the tight-bodiced dresses of indigo cotton print, their full skirts worn over several petticoats; the appliquéd patterns of darker-blue fabric around the hem; the blankets or shawls, wrapped about the upper body at all times, except during strenuous labour; and the dark twill headscarves. Some elements of this costume were transformations of precolonial dress: blankets were worn like precolonial cloaks, and were referred to by the same term, *dikob*. In contrast, the 'hampering long dresses and innumerable petticoats' (Mears 1934: 94) and the modest headscarves clearly expressed the moral constraints and gendered norms of Victorian mission garb – at least in respect of its sombre rank and file.

This composite costume was the product of a specific conjuncture, a particular pastiche of African and European elements which captured precisely the paradoxical relation of difference and sameness that remade colonized peoples into serialized 'ethnic' populations. Characteristic of such styles – indeed, crucial to their historical meaning – is a 'conservatism', which might (as the Southern Tswana case attests) be a relatively recent feature. This is more than the marked anachronism typical of 'invented traditions'; it is a repeated invocation of the very moment of articulation that radically redefined 'local' identities in Eurocentric terms. Herein lies the essence of so-called 'folk costume' in modern Southern Africa and elsewhere.

CONCLUSION

What this history seems to reveal, then, is the complex dynamics at play in the incoporation of African communities into the European colonial world – how such communities became engaged with forces capable of recreating them as both 'local' and primordially parochial. I have suggested that we gain purchase on such global processes by pursuing their roots in the small-scale transactions that generate them. But these were no ordinary transactions, for this is a history centred on the worldwide extension not only of European Christian culture, but of industrial capitalism. Whatever mechanisms it might have utilized, colonization here relied heavily on the magic of commodities to build new consuming subjects and new relations of difference.

We have seen that the early exposure to British commodities and consumption encouraged Tswana to deploy alien objects in diverse and creative ways. But these objects were themselves embedded in forms of relations destined to transform African societies. Clothes bore with them the threads of a macro-economy; they were a ready-made means of engaging indigenous peoples in the colonial market in goods and labour. Such processes reveal, then, how the mantle of wider politico–economic forces came to rest on individual persons, redefining them as bearers of a store-bought identity.

But such processes were neither all-or-none, nor mechanical in their effects.

Changing modes of dress show that commodity culture played into existing African societies in complex ways. As the century wore on, all Tswana were confined by the rising colonial state, most being tied in some way to its cultural imperatives and its market in goods and labour. European norms of dress and comportment came increasingly to define public space in terms of an aesthetics of civility, one that positioned whole populations within a hierarchical scheme. Indeed, the restriction of black 'ethnic' identities to a diminished sphere of self-expression was central to the founding of the colonial state, which strove to monopolize the production of goods and value. As this account has shown, these were profoundly gendered and class-ridden processes, resting on novel forms of selfhood, production, beauty, and status. In recounting such histories, class is not separable from race, or race from gender.

It is within this context that we must view the paradoxical emergence of rural 'folk dress', which speaks at once of structural regulation, of selective self-expression, and of the unevenness of commoditization – even within well-colonized social fields. For while such dress evoked the moral economy of the mission, it also defied the other half of the Protestant message – the injunction to fashion new identities through increasing (if regulated) consumption. Significant features of this style would endure for decades – or rather, be actively reproduced as 'tradition'. And although it bore the imprint of Christian discipline, this costume also marked itself as anachronistic, its

Figure 5 'Entertaining friends under the baobab tree'
Source: reproduced from Willoughby, *Native Life on the Transvaal Border*

37

blanketed elegance conveying – to the metropolitan eye – an unmistakable aura of independence and reserve (Figure 5). The dress was iconic of the predicament of its wearers: it was made increasingly from foreign materials, yet it marked a locally tooled identity, elaborating in unforeseen ways on the possibilities presented by a commodity culture. The conservatism of their attire might have made rural Tswana women hostage to a discriminatory 'tradition'. But it also entailed an effort to limit dependency on the market and the fashion system, on the restless urge for advancement through endless consumption. In its more assertive forms then, ethnic dress has acted like other enclaved commodities on the margins of the modern melting-pot (cf. Comaroff and Comaroff 1992: 127 ff.). It serves to stem the force of mainstream economies and cultures as they take control of local worlds.

ACKNOWLEDGEMENTS

The title of this essay invokes the title – if not the content – of Dorfman's (1983) well-known book. Many people have responded to this material in one or another form; John Comaroff and Brad Weiss provided particularly rich insights, many of which are reflected in the text.

NOTES

1 For an extended discussion of the Nonconformist (Wesleyan and London Missionary Society) engagement with the Southern Tswana peoples, see Comaroff and Comaroff (1991); for a detailed account of the role of dress in this history, see Comaroff and Comaroff (n.d.: Chapter 5).
2 This is not to imply that Christian evangelists – even Protestants – were all alike in this respect. The link between dress, self-construction and self-improvement seems to have been especially strong among Nonconformists who stressed the methodical reform of personal habit.
3 Brad Weiss sharpened my sense of the importance of this issue.
4 See also W.C. Willoughby, 'Clothes' (Willoughby Papers, The Library, Selly Oak Colleges, Birmingham, Unfiled Notes, Box 14).
5 Some linen goods seem to have found their way to northern Tswana peoples from the east coast in the early nineteenth century, probably via Arab traders.
6 W.C. Willoughby, 'Clothes' (Unfiled Notes, Box 14).
7 W.C. Willoughby, 'Clothes' (Unfiled Notes, Box 14).
8 For a more detailed account of the African clothing market in Kimberley at the time, see Comaroff and Comaroff (n.d.: Chapter 5).
9 Such advertisements were common in papers like *The Diamond Fields Advertiser* in the late 1860s (see Comaroff and Comaroff n.d.: Chapter 5).
10 This contrasts with the situation among many Nguni peoples where, for structural reasons (J. Comaroff 1985: 30), the impact of Christianity created more clearly distinct populations, such as the 'Red' (that colour again!) and 'School' communities of the Xhosa, described by Mayer in the mid-twentieth century (Mayer 1961: 24 ff.).

2

SUGAR CANE, COCA-COLA AND HYPERMARKETS

Consumption and surrealism in the Argentine Northwest

Constance Classen

Northwestern Argentina is a potent blend of cultures, histories and geographies, of Andean civilization with European, of arid highlands with fertile lowlands, of sugar-cane fields with soft drink plants. Generations of my family have lived in this compellingly beautiful region, elaborating their own cultural history and geography out of tales of the coming of the railway and the passing of Halley's comet, of governments and guerillas, of miraculous Virgins and mysterious apparitions, of ancient love affairs and tragedies. These family tales combined the natural and the supernatural, the ordinary and the exotic, in their narratives as a matter of course, giving the stories the 'surreal' tinge characteristic of the folklore of the region. The Northwest was a place where the extraordinary was always ready to erupt in the midst of the everyday.

In the late twentieth century, one of the most surreal aspects of life in Northwestern Argentina is that produced by the influx of foreign consumer goods into the region. This influx is part of a world-wide trend towards international marketing in which products cross (and re-cross) cultures to create a global consumer culture with local variations (Barnet and Cavanagh 1994). In the 1960s the surrealist artist Leonora Carrington wrote a story describing how in the Mexico of the future one would find 'tins of Norwegian enchiladas from Japan' and 'bottles of the rare old Indian drink called cocacola' (Carrington 1989: 182). Due to the impact of global marketing, this state of surreal consumerism has now come to pass in most of Latin America. Thus, in Argentina one finds Japanese recordings of Argentine tangos and American television shows dubbed in Mexican Spanish.[1]

As a world city, Argentina's capital, Buenos Aires, has long stood at a cultural crossroads of practices and products, a South American counterpart of Paris and New York. The Northwest, however, is a traditional, agricultural region, far from the nation's capital. With its heritage of native and colonial culture, the Argentine Northwest has been an important source of symbols of national identity for the country – folk music and dances, weavings and pottery. It is here that the influx of consumer goods from the global market is most marked. This influx has been particularly dramatic in recent years as long-standing protectionist economic policies have been replaced by free market practices.

In my grandparents' time, three-quarters of a century ago, a significant portion of the goods consumed in Northwestern Argentina were produced locally, or even in one's own home. Fresh produce came loaded on the horse-drawn carts of farmers. Simple remedies for colds and stomach-aches were provided by pots of mint and rue in the patio and the aromatic wares of the herb woman. At different hours of the day street vendors sang out their merchandise: freshly baked buns, home-made cheese, feather dusters. The 'shopping centre' was the market-place, which my grandmother visited each morning at dawn to buy food for the day.

While local products were prominent in the Northwest of those years, imported goods were none the less available. In the stores there were German toys, English china and Brazilian coffee, while the theatres offered performances by renowned European musicians. Such imports, however, could usually be incorporated into the local way of life without much cultural disruption.

This way of life has not yet completely disappeared in the late twentieth century, yet the elements that survive do so in a society awash with the products and images of the global market. Street vendors continue to sell their wares; however, the wares they sell are not traditional local goods, but aspirins, cassettes, razors, artificial flowers, and posters of foreign rock stars. While a significant percentage of the population of the Northwest still makes do without telephones, the latest model Panasonic fax machines and IBM laptop computers shine in the store windows of the downtown shopping zones. While people in certain remote areas may lack running water, Coca-Cola is carted up to the most isolated mountain villages on the backs of mules.

What follows is a series of reflections on the cultural transformations caused by the modernization and globalization of the market-place in Northwestern Argentina, based on my own experiences and those of members of my family. These reflections bring out some of the 'surreal' aspects of the introduction of North American consumer culture to Argentina, from the peddling of Santa Claus in the summer to the replacement of the plaza by the shopping centre.

SUGAR CANE

When I was 15 years old I visited a sugar mill where La Mecha, the sister-in-law of one of my aunts, worked as a manager. It was harvest time, *la zafra*: the cane fields were shorn, there were trucks overflowing with cane outside the mill, and inside sweet juice ran down from the crushed stalks to be transformed into white crystals of sugar. The workers, *zafreros*, tanned and brawny, swarmed around the mill like ants on a sugar cube. After the tour of the mill was over, I had tea and sweet rich pastries with La Mecha and listened to tales of sugar –

tales as rooted in the culture of Northwestern Argentina, as sugar cane plants are rooted in the fertile earth.

The sweet sap of sugar cane has long been the life-blood of much of Northwestern Argentina. Light green fields of cane surround the cities in the summer, black ashes from the burning waste of the harvest coat them in winter. Ironically, however, while sugar is a traditional export of the region, it was itself originally an import, for sugar cane is not native to the country. The succulent plants were introduced to Argentina by Spanish colonists in the seventeenth century and subsequently cultivated in extensive plantations.

Up until the mid-twentieth century, many of the workers in the cane fields of the Northwest were kept in bondage to the plantation owners either by debt or by force. One of the most horrifying of local legends was that the plantation owners, in league with the Devil, secretly fed troublesome peons to a demonic black dog. The situation of the sugar workers – often migrants – was alleviated by legal and social reforms introduced in the 1940s. With luck and careful economy a cane cutter could earn enough in the harvest months to keep his family fed for the rest of the year.

Now many of the sugar mills, antiquated and unprofitable, are still. Instead of being fed to the demonic dog of the sugar barons, the unemployed cane workers are fed to the black dog of fiscal restraint. The fragrant scent of cane sap is replaced by the foul smoke of the tyres which the workers burn in protest outside the closed mills. For those men who do find work, wages are too low and the cost of living too high to adequately support a family.

While the sugar cane fields lie fallow in the countryside, in the cities never has more sweetness been available or consumed. The cafés are filled with people stirring sugar in their coffee, drinking soft drinks, eating ice cream. The stores are full of people consuming the metaphorical sweetness of VCRs, designer jeans, motorcycles, and other delicacies of consumer culture. After decades of political trauma and financial insecurity the large professional class of the Northwest wants all the material comforts that a stable economy and low-priced imports can give it.

Argentine folklore dictates that if you keep a package of sugar in your purse you will never run out of money, for money is sweet in Argentina – *dulce plata*. The Northwest has to sell the sugar in its purse, however, to keep the *dulce plata* flowing in, or else create another source of revenue and employment. Provincial governments in the Northwest have become major employers of the working classes, but government money in a debt-ridden economy is as much of an illusion as the perfect happiness promised consumers by advertising imagery. Without a secure financial base will not the whole fantastic sugar castle of happy consumerism in the Northwest tumble and dissolve?

COCA-COLA

The outside of the general store in the small Northwestern town is painted from top to bottom with a gaudy red and white Coca-Cola logo. Across the plaza, the white-washed façade of the café boldly advertises Sprite in giant letters. The sign posts at the intersections of the streets all display signs for Coca-Cola along with the street names (Figure 6). The implication is that beyond all signifiers, all names and directions, Coke is the only name to know or place to be.

Advertisements for soft drinks abound in the cities as well, mounted on billboards or painted over the length of apartment buildings, but there they are immersed in a forest of diverse commercial signs. In the absence of all other advertising, the soft drink logos dominate the visual landscape of many small towns in the interior of Argentina. Why, of all the elements of human existence, of all the multitudinous products on the market, is this prominence given to fizzy flavoured water?

One is reminded of how dear a commodity water is in many of the towns of Northwestern Argentina, where rain only falls regularly during the summer months. In more desperate times, trains were known to have been held up by dehydrated bandits for their precious cargo of water. The most popular of folk saints in the region is a woman who died of thirst trying to cross a desert, and whose baby was found alive, still nursing at her breast. The shrines dedicated to the 'Difunta' Correa, as she is known, sparkle with soft drink bottles filled

Figure 6 A street sign juxtaposed with a Coca-Cola sign
Source: photograph by Constance Classen

with water, offerings to quench the folk saint's thirst. Soft drinks have taken over much of the symbolic power of water, of the clear well and the bubbling spring. The image of the precious, life-giving liquid is now Coca-Cola and Sprite.

Coca-Cola and other foreign brands of soft drinks share the Argentine market with domestic soft drinks, such as the Torasso brand. While Coca-Cola presents itself in its advertising as the 'real taste' – *el sabor de verdad*, Torasso advertises itself as the 'Argentine taste', *el sabor argentino*. Ironically, however, Coca-Cola has become so embedded in Argentine life that it seems indigenous. Even its name sounds Spanish. Accustomed to living with Coca-Cola and its imagery all her life, a woman from a Northwestern town asks when I bring up the subject of Coke's status as an import: 'But isn't Coca-Cola Argentine?'

Interestingly, it is only the towns on tourist routes that are emblazoned with soft-drink ads. The signs are evidently directed as much or more at thirsty tourists (tourists are always thirsty) as at residents, though their social and psychological effects necessarily concern both. In the towns off the beaten track, soft drinks are a private affair and not a public spectacle. The buildings are bereft of eye-catching logos, the whitewashed houses shimmer in the bright Argentine sun, while residents play cards under the shade of a grape vine arbour.

SANTA CLAUS IN THE SUMMER

Christmas in Argentina falls in the summer. It is a time of stifling heat – when families leave the cities for the cooler air of the mountains or travel to the beaches of the Atlantic coast, when ice cream parlours beckon overheated passers-by with their *helados* (literally 'frozens'), appliance stores feature fans and air conditioners in their windows, and ads for sun-tan lotions with exotic names like 'Australian Gold' abound.

Traditionally, Christmas was celebrated by a family dinner followed by midnight mass. No presents were exchanged and the only 'decorations' were *pesebres*, nativity scenes which families would set up in their homes. The day for giving out gifts was *El día de los Reyes*, the Day of the Kings on the sixth of January. On the night before the sixth, the three Kings who brought gifts to the infant Jesus were imagined to ride across the sky on their camels leaving presents for children. In the morning the children – especially those who had been thoughtful enough to leave some grass and water for the camels – would find their presents hidden somewhere in the house next to their shoes. Not being tied to any season, these holiday traditions worked just as well in the summery Christmas of Argentina as they originally had in the wintry Christmas of Spain.

In Argentina today, however, North American ideas of Christmas have become increasingly prevalent. Along with, or instead of, giving presents on the Day of the Kings, gifts are now given at Christmas, an idea which local store owners are only too happy to promote. Instead of the pictures of flowers, birds and nativity scenes I remember from my childhood, many greeting cards now depict winter scenes of pine forests and villages buried in snow. Instead of the three kings with their silken robes, images of Santa Claus, incongruously dressed in winter clothing, are displayed in shop windows. If Santa Claus were to come to the subtropical Northwest for Christmas, he would surely be better off in a cool linen suit and sandals than in a heavy fur-trimmed cloak and thick boots.[2]

Northern images of Christmas have penetrated even the most remote and traditional areas of Argentina. I remember a visit I made to a humble home in a Northwestern village, high in the foothills of the Andes. Outside the cacti blossomed, the hot wind stirred up the dust, and a parrot chattered in a cage. Inside, a jolly figurine of Santa Claus stood out in the shady room. It had been placed in an aquarium, together with plants and shells, to make a kind of secular shrine. Was this, I wondered, a way of petitioning the god of consumerism for a bag of imported goodies or, more probably, just an indigenization of an appealing exotic icon?

Along with Santa Claus, the whole host of Christmas decorations has come to the Northwest: ornaments to hang on the Christmas tree, artificial pine trees to hang them on, fake snow, plastic reindeer, and so on. One look at a window display dressed in these delights makes it clear that traditional nativity scenes with their straw mangers and humble farm animals cannot compete in visual appeal with the glittering tinsel, coloured lights and shiny ornaments of the Northern Christmas. In the city streets perspiring vendors, always selling the latest gimmick, hawk inflatable rubber Santa Clauses to passers-by.

If Christmas is intrinsically associated with snow and Northernness, as it seems to have become, then there can never again be a 'true' Christmas in Northwestern Argentina, only a parody of one. Ironically, however, North-westerners are not very keen on snow, which they associate with scarcely habitable regions of the world. (The suggestion of a visit to my home in Canada for Christmas never fails to produce a shudder among my relatives in the region.) Illusions of a wintry Christmas, images of Santa Claus and cotton wool snow, amid the flowers and sunshine of an Argentine December, are apparently as much as is desired.

WORLD SHOPPING

Argentina in the 1990s, like many other countries, is up for sale to the world – its airlines, its telephone system, its minerals, its water – in a giant fire sale of national assets. The world, in turn, is for sale in Argentina, for the end of protectionist economic policies has resulted in a flood of imports entering the market. The different labels of origin on goods have turned the stores of Northwestern Argentina into international bazaars. Chocolates from Switzerland, watches from Japan, British-style furniture made in India, Middle-Eastern-style carpets made in Belgium.

As I travel between my homes in Canada and Argentina, I hardly know what to take or bring as presents any more, for the same goods are for sale in both places. To comparison-shop for goods between cities in the northern and southern hemispheres seems absurd, yet in the late twentieth-century global village it is entirely possible. My mother takes chocolate replicas of Canadian dollar coins for her great-nieces and nephews in Argentina only to find them for sale there – and at a lower price than in Canada.

Yet Northwestern Argentina, as an international bazaar, cannot compare with the nearby markets of Bolivia where everything and anything is sold for duty-free prices. Northwesterners flock to the border towns of Bolivia to buy imported goods for half what they would pay in Argentina. Chartered buses take people to Bolivia, let them spend the day shopping, and then drive them back again the same night. The trip is described as a martyrdom – the long hours driving, the stretches of bad roads at the Bolivian border, the endless wait at customs – by those who have gone, yet they go back again and again. Martyrdom is worth it for the consumer heaven which awaits: Citizen watches, Chanel perfumes, Pierre Cardin clothes. For those with lower aspirations and less money there are imitations of designer products, along with inexpensive shoes from China and second-hand clothing from the United States. My friend Luís who works in an agricultural co-operative in Northwestern Argentina boasts of having bought a shirt for a dollar in Bolivia, a shirt that indicated by its stamp that it was formerly worn by an inmate in a United States prison. (As Luís is an ardent critic of 'Yanqui' imperialism, wearing the shirt of an American prisoner gives him a kind of perverse pleasure.)

The inhabitants of Northwestern Argentina are, in general, extremely brand-name conscious, and the question of how, in a proliferation of imitation products, to spot originals is troublesome. Some manufacturers will distinguish their imitations by some minor variance from the original; for example, labelling a watch 'Citisen' instead of Citizen. Others, however, endeavour to make imitations which match the appearance of their models as nearly as possible. My cousin Cristina, a biochemist and the veteran of two shopping trips to Bolivia, says that Citizen watches have a hologram to prove that they are really Citizen watches. She's not too sure about how to distinguish real Chanel perfumes from their clones, however – how can you authenticate an odour? My present to her from Canada (via France) is a bottle of Chanel No. 5. The real thing, I assure her.

THE WHEEL OF FORTUNE

Up until the 1990s Argentina was caught in a seemingly inescapable cycle of hyperinflation. Every few years the Argentine currency would be devalued to the point where there were 10,000 pesos to the American dollar. At that time, four zeros would be knocked off the peso, new bills would be printed at the rate of one peso to one dollar, and the cycle would start over again. Hassled accountants would struggle over mammoth calculations and confused shoppers would get muddled trying to translate between the old money and the new. The saddest scenario was that of the senior citizens who watched a lifetime's worth of savings evaporate before their eyes. An aunt of mine who sold her house for a set amount of money in monthly payments, wound up receiving only pennies a month in actual monetary value after a few devaluations.

The rapidity with which the value of the peso fell meant that there was little point trying to save one's pesos for a rainy day. Cash in hand had to be turned into solid assets – food, clothes, furniture – without delay. While the value of money went down overnight, the prices in the stores went up. Indeed, the larger stores employed clerks just to change the prices on their merchandise from one day to the next, often only a step ahead of shoppers. In any case, the high cost of imported goods in a protectionist economy meant that there was little money left over to save.

The Argentine peso, tied to the American dollar and backed by gold, has been stable for a number of years now. Many of the attitudes born of hyperinflation none the less remain. Coins, for example, still tend to be regarded as trifling bits of metal which the government chooses to stamp with meaningless numbers. I remember being cursed by an indignant panhandler in Buenos Aires for giving her a handful of coins which, since my last visit to Argentina, had depreciated so much as to be worthless. Now, fifty centavos are worth half of an American dollar, a respectable sum, yet waiters will scowl when they receive coins for a tip. Nothing less than a peso note really counts as money.

Encouraged by the stability of the peso, a plethora of credit card companies has sprung up in Argentina. Advertisements showing happy consumers using credit to buy the merchandise of their dreams abound, and shop windows are papered with the stickers of all the different cards the stores accept. Even local television stations have their own credit cards.

Credit or not, however, for many people in the Northwest it would take a miracle to enable them to participate in the modern consumer society. Fortunately, a chance at just such a miracle is available to them, offered by a glittering array of lotteries, casinos, bingos and other gambling outlets. Northwesterners, like other Argentines, are more than ready to bet on that chance. It has been calculated that some 3.6 billion dollars are bet in Argentina every year, or 110 dollars per person, including children. Taking unofficial betting into account would raise this sum even higher.

With so much at stake, gamblers look for clues to winning numbers almost everywhere: in the birthdates of family members, in the predictions of fortune tellers, in the numbers printed on bus tickets. Lottery outlets display charts enabling their clients to turn their dream imagery into lottery numbers. Even the hard facts of modern life are thought to translate into lottery jackpots.

When a bomb exploded in a social services centre in Buenos Aires in 1994, lottery buyers bet massively on the numbers 17 and 56, symbolic respectively of 'misfortune' and 'a fall'.

The most important lottery in Argentina – and the top-selling commercial enterprise – is the National Lottery. There are also a plethora of smaller-scale lotteries. Each province has its own lottery. Supermarkets have lotteries. The supermarket where I shop when I'm at my home in the Northwestern city of Tucumán has a 'wheel of fortune' at the front of the store. After you buy your groceries you spin the wheel and if the number which comes up matches the number on your bill/lottery ticket you win the price of your purchases.

Television stations and shows have lotteries. Every other hour it seems one TV show host or another is picking out the winning entry of a draw for a blender, a colour television, or a new car – *cero kilómetros*. Newspapers have their own lotteries. *La Gaceta* in Tucumán quotes readers/players making statements like '*La Gaceta* lottery has given me the luck I've never had in all the long years of my life', and 'I think that *La Gaceta* lottery is wonderful because it gives people hope'. Financially-straitened Northwesterners, like so many struggling peoples in 'down-sized' economies around the world, know that neither hard work nor careful saving is likely to be enough to provide them with the good things of life, only a lucky spin on the wheel of fortune.

PASEO SHOPPING

In 1994 the first shopping centre opened in Tucumán, the largest city of Northwestern Argentina.[3] The shopping centre's name, 'Paseo Shopping', is indicative of the ambience its developers wished to evoke. The Spanish word for shopping – *hacer compras* – is not very enticing. It literally means 'to make purchases' and it suggests dry and rather tedious commercial transactions on a petty scale. One sees a harried housewife picking up bread, vegetables, maybe a bottle of wine, and then rushing home to make dinner. The word 'shopping', however, calls up visions of the American good life, of malls that double as funfairs, of stores overflowing with the newest and most desirable merchandise, and money to buy them. 'Paseo', in turn, is a traditional Spanish word for a leisurely stroll or tour of the sights. The name 'Paseo Shopping', therefore, transforms the old notion of 'making purchases' into a new image of shopping as a pleasurable leisure time activity, the modern equivalent of a stroll around the plaza.[4]

In the few months since its inauguration, it is evident that the 'Paseo Shopping' *does* function as a kind of substitute for the plaza. It is a place for families to go for an evening walk together when the work of the day is done, a hang-out for teenagers, a playground for children, a meeting place for friends.

At the same time as it fulfils some of the functions of the plaza, however, the shopping centre is dramatically different from the plaza. The plaza on a summer evening is dark, warm and moist, inhabited by mossy trees and singing birds, by shoeshine boys and itinerant vendors, encircled by the noise and bustle of traffic, the centre of a network of city streets, perhaps the site of a political demonstration or a religious celebration. The shopping centre, in contrast, is well-lit and air-conditioned, plant- and animal-free, animated only by the voices of shoppers and taped music. There are no itinerant vendors to pester visitors, no panhandlers, only the clerks and the cleaners, all official, in their place. The shopping centre is only marginally oriented to the streets or city outside: it is enclosed, self-contained, a world apart. It is a-political, a-religious, and a-temporal; open from ten to ten every day, always bright, no closing for the siesta (unlike other shopping areas). Once inside its utopian space the shopper need have no worries about hold-ups, reckless traffic, rain, muddy puddles or loose sidewalk tiles. The only danger is of slipping on the smooth, continually swept floors.

The Paseo Shopping is but the first of a series of shopping centres planned for the Northwest. With the downtown areas of cities becoming too congested to allow for easy access, the shopping centre, located in the suburbs and providing its own parking space, makes sense. Yet one cannot help hoping that the traditional store-lined streets and plazas of the Northwest, with their *joie de vivre* and bustle of activity – people off to work or school or home as well as shoppers – will not eventually be emptied by the introduction of decentralized enclosed shopping malls, as has happened to the downtown areas of many North American cities.

THE HYPERMARKET

Every year when I go back to the Northwest I find more packaged foods available on the supermarket shelves – American breakfast cereals (at seven dollars/pesos a box), canned soup, boxed ice cream, frozen vegetables. Some of the alimentary novelties have had an unusual reception. Uncertain as to how to consume the exotic breakfast cereals, Northwesterners at first ate them straight out of the box as a snack food. Later they were discovered to mix well with yogurt, and yogurt now comes packaged with its own topping of cornflakes or puffed rice.

The concept of the supermarket developed slowly in Northwestern Argentina. Until recently most people went to the bakery for their bread, the greengrocers for their fruit and vegetables, and so on. The proto-supermarkets I remember from my youth – and which one can still see in the smaller cities of the region – were generally uninviting places. The variety of products available was limited. No particular effort was made either in the design of the supermarkets or in the packaging and presentation of the goods they sold to induce shoppers to buy.

The new supermarket, however, is bright and colourful, with rows of attractively packaged goods and piles of luscious produce; unblemished apples, crisp fresh lettuce, smooth, shiny eggplants. A Disneyland of processed foods combined with an Eden of perfect produce. As the stores grow larger and larger, and the selection greater and greater, 'supermercado' seems too modest a term for such cornucopias of plenty, and a new word takes its place: 'hipermercado', the hypermarket.

The recently opened 'Hipermercado Libertad' on the outskirts of the city of Tucumán is a vast emporium of consumer goods, from food to household appliances to videos to car parts. I wander down the hypermarket's wide aisles trying to absorb all the new meanings encoded on the shelves. Avocados, once common in the gardens and patios of the Northwest but rarely seen now in the cities, are marketed in the produce section with labels that proclaim them to be *sin colestorol* – without cholesterol. A local fruit disappears from the landscape and reappears in the store as a packaged health food for diet-conscious consumers. *Empanadas*, traditional pastries of meat or corn which I remember requiring a good half-day's work – and a lot of socializing among female relatives – to prepare, are sold in the take-out section ready to be popped in the oven. Tradition is transformed into fast food.

As a place to shop in a surreal culture, a hypermarket seems remarkably apt. What particularly catches my attention, however, is the logo of the Hipermercado Libertad – a stylized image of the American Statue of Liberty (Figure 7). Liberty in the new era of consumerism, would appear to be not political freedom or the freedom of speech, but the freedom to shop, to stroll down aisles

Figure 7 The Libertad 'Hypermarket'
Source: photograph by Constance Classen

and aisles of merchandise and choose the products that are right for you. Or perhaps, the freedom to shop is what the Statue of Liberty has come to represent around the world, as people increasingly perceive the United States as one vast hypermarket of consumer goods.

THROWAWAY CULTURE

The immense increase in packaged foods available in Argentina has led to a corresponding increase in refuse (although still only a fraction of that produced by households in the United States or Canada). When I was in Argentina in the 1970s, the garbage can was a little plastic bucket beside the kitchen sink. As vegetable peelings were virtually the only waste generated, this was quite adequate.

'Recycling' in those years was an accepted way of life. When appliances broke down they were repaired, rather than thrown out and replaced by new ones. Bottles of wine or soft drinks were returned to the store for credit on future purchases. (Indeed, in many stores one had to present an empty soft drink bottle to be allowed to buy a full one – a situation which created something of a dilemma for thirsty visitors with no empty bottles to hand.) Newspapers were passed on to non-subscribing relatives. Reusable cloths, rather than disposable paper products, were used for cleaning. When my mother, grown accustomed to using tissue paper in Canada, brought a package of Kleenex with her home to Tucumán, it stood on our dining room table in its flowered box like an exotic orchid, a blatant sign of conspicuous consumption.

In the 1990s boxes of tissue paper are available on the shelves of the supermarkets in the Northwest, though in view of their exorbitant cost, buying one still seems the whim of someone with money to burn, something akin to Poppea demanding asses' milk for her daily bath. Soft drink bottles are disposable instead of returnable now – so much simpler all around. All of the enticingly and conveniently packaged foods on the shelves leave useless shells of cardboard, styrofoam, plastic or tin behind when they are consumed. My eldest aunt, born in the early 1900s, was never able to adapt to this new disposable lifestyle. When we were going through her house after her death we found a cupboard filled with old plastic yogurt containers – too potentially useful to be thrown away.

The most noticeable sign of the new boom in refuse are soft drink cans. Rarely seen in the Northwest before the 1990s, canned drinks are everywhere now, sold in supermarkets, hawked by street vendors, even dispensed by vending machines – a novelty made possible only recently by a stable currency. Empty Coke cans litter the parks and rattle across the plazas like tumbleweed. Children make toys out of them, crushing them with their feet and then walking with a flattened can under each shoe. When I ask my cousins about recycling programmes they say that, as yet, there are none. They mention enthusiastically, however, that certain schools have had competitions to see who could make the most artistic creation out of empty soft drink cans. I envision a museum of tin can sculptures created by generations of school children. Why not take advantage of the imperishability of modern rubbish and turn it into immortal art?

EL SPORTSMAN DRUGSTORE

Walking through the downtown streets of Tucumán and other Northwestern cities, one is struck by the number of English words used in store front displays. Even products made in Argentina, particularly clothing, will occasionally be advertised with English names and slogans. Given that the number of English-speaking visitors to Northwestern Argentina is minimal, these English slogans are all directed towards Spanish speakers. Their purpose is evidently not to communicate a literal message, for which Spanish would be the logical medium, but to convey an image. They carry notions of trendiness and prestige associated with the English-speaking United States. They signal that the products they refer to transcend the bounds of Argentine culture and participate in the global market-place, where English is the lingua franca.

The fact that this use of English in advertising is symbolic, rather than literal, leads to some rather interesting appropriations of English, or pseudo-English terms. A brand of artificial sweetener is named 'Slap'. A range of soft drinks is called 'Spill'. In Buenos Aires one finds boutiques with names such as 'The World's Number 1 Cigarette Racing Team' and 'Stress'. The latter accompanies its name with a picture of a coat of arms, as though indicating that suffering from stress is a desirable sign of upper-class status in the post-modern world. One shoe and clothing store in downtown Tucumán (with a branch in the Paseo Shopping) is named El Sportsman Drugstore.

The less élitist store owners will sometimes choose combinations of Spanish and English for their advertising, trying to combine down-home familiarity with American allure. One of the most popular of such linguistic hybrids is store names ending in 'landia' such as 'Radiolandia' or 'Todolandia' – the land of everything – *todo*. Among the kiosks and cafés with saints' names such as San Ramón and San Antonio in the poorer quarters of the cities, you can sometimes find a sign with the name of that non-canonical saint – San Guich – a Spanish variant of the English 'sandwich'.

CONSUMPTION, SURREALISM AND CULTURAL IMPERIALISM

The consumption of the goods and values of Western consumer culture in Northwestern Argentina is both the same and different as in North America. On the one hand, the same products, the same marketing techniques and the same advertising images can be found in both places. On the other hand, however, the Paseo Shopping is not an American shopping mall, corn flakes eaten with yogurt are not the same as corn flakes in a bowl with milk, and a *san guich* is not a sandwich.

Products entering Northwestern Argentina from abroad enter into a particular history and a specific cultural setting. They acquire new clusters of meanings – exotic, progressive, élitist, alien, wasteful and so on – within the social and economic environment of the region. Just as important to the local experience of consumer culture, imported goods enter Northwestern Argentina *without* a history. They are, in large part, cultural transplants, developed in response to North American consumer trends. Notions such as laptop computers, breakfast cereal, or shopping centres have no indigenous roots in the region, they simply appear on the scene as if materialized from a Hollywood movie. This experience of sudden materialization is enhanced by the fact that, until recently, many imports were unavailable or prohibitively expensive. As a result, there appears to be little continuity between the traditional way of life in the Northwest and the new – just a surreal juxtaposition. The latest model cars share the roads with horse-drawn carts. Street vendors coexist with hypermarkets.

Surrealism would appear to be essential to the marketing of goods in a consumer culture. All products, from electric shavers to minivans or a meal at McDonald's, are touted by their advertisers as an eruption of the extraordinary into the everyday. To promote images of Santa Claus in the summer or to advertise in English to a Spanish-speaking public in Argentina is perhaps no more odd than many of the marketing ploys used in North America.

In Northwestern Argentina, however, the surrealism of consumer society bears the mark of cultural imperialism. All that is prestigious and desirable is presented by many advertisers as coming from abroad. The home-made, the traditional and the local, by contrast, become debased and undesirable. This extends not only to particular products, but to a way of life, as products are invariably presented as embedded in a whole lifestyle. The advertisements make it clear that items such as electric shavers or imported cars belong not to the unemployed Andean sugar-cane cutter, even if he could afford them, but with the successful American businessman.

In *Cultural Imperialism*, John Tomlinson writes that, as First World goods are desired by, rather than forced upon, Third World peoples, one cannot speak of their entry into Third World markets as 'cultural imperialism' but only as 'the spread of modernity' (Tomlinson 1991: 173). To put this process in such value-neutral terms, however, is to ignore the immense power of the economic and ideological interests which forward the 'spread of modernity' throughout the world and promote the desirability of Western products and lifestyles. It is also to avoid the question of whether the desire for such high-profile 'commodities' as blond hair or round Caucasian eyes can be attributed solely to the 'spread of modernity'.

At the end of the nineteenth century the Uruguayan José Enrique Rodó expressed concern over the admiration with which Latin America often regarded the material prosperity and power of the North:

We imitate what we believe to be superior or prestigious. And this is why the vision of an America de-Latinized of its own will, without threat of conquest, and reconstituted in the image and likeness of the North, now looms in the nightmares of many who are genuinely concerned about our future.

(Rodó, 1988: 71)

Why is this vision a nightmare? According to Rodó, because countries need to elaborate their own identities based on local reality and not simply buy into foreign models, because the introduction of Northern-style materialism threatens the development of spiritual values, and because preserving a dualism between North and South makes for a healthy counterbalance of cultures in the Americas. 'If we could look into the future and see the formula for an eventual harmony [between North and South], it would not be based upon the *unilateral imitation* ... of one people by another, but upon a mutual exchange of influences' (Rodó 1988: 73–4).

Almost a century later, this ideal of cultural equilibrium between North and South America is still far from being realized. So powerful is the influence of the North on the South, in fact, that the only thing which would induce some Latin Americans to esteem their own cultural heritage over the cultural imports of the North would ironically be to see that heritage promoted as trendy and desirable in the mainstream North American media.

Yet Latin America is far from being de-Latinized. As we have seen in the examples from Northwestern Argentina, imported goods, images and terms are often reinvented within the context of their new cultural location to suit local sensibilities. Thus we find shoes in El Sportsman Drugstore, the Statue of Liberty in a supermarket and Santa Claus in an aquarium. In the long run, cultural traditions may well prove strong enough and imaginative enough in Northwestern Argentina – and elsewhere in Latin America – to selectively incorporate the products and technologies of the global market while sustaining a strong and distinct local identity.

ACKNOWLEDGEMENTS

I am grateful to family and friends in Argentina and Canada for sharing with me their experiences of, and reflections on, the development of consumer culture in Northwestern Argentina.

NOTES

1 The Japanese appropriation of the Argentine tango is discussed by Marta E. Savigliano in *Tango and the Political Economy of Passion* (Savigliano 1995: 169–206).
2 For an analysis of the globalization of Christmas see *Unwrapping Christmas* (Miller 1993).
3 Beatriz Sarlo provides a provocative description of shopping centres and the culture of shopping in Buenos Aires in *Escenas de la vida posmoderna* (Sarlo 1994).
4 It would be interesting to compare the Spanish tradition of the *paseo* with the *flânerie* (strolling or idling) of the French. On the latter see *The Flâneur* (Tester 1994).

3

PERISHABLE GOODS

Modes of consumption in the Pacific Islands

Jean-Marc Philibert and Christine Jourdan

This chapter examines the situation created by the insertion of certain Western goods into local modes of consumption in two South Pacific countries, Vanuatu and the Solomon Islands. The forms of classification and types of use to which these imported goods are subjected differ from those in place in the countries where the goods were originally produced. This lack of correspondence, which gives rise to an element of semantic indeterminacy, in turn allows for negotiations of meaning to take place, and for the relationship between commodity and consumer to be reordered according to local values.

The existence of local codes of consumption touches upon two important issues for anthropology: the first concerns what happens to the existing links between production and consumption and the reproduction of a given social order in countries which are being drawn into a single world economic system; the second, more general issue concerns the respective determining power of local and global forces in the Third World societies which anthropologists study. By virtue of their work, often situated at the junction between First and Third Worlds, anthropologists are well placed to research such questions. However, until recently, economic anthropology has paid little attention to consumption, considering it the silent and determinate partner of exchange or of production. It took the work of Appadurai (1986), Rutz and Orlove (1989), Foster (1991), Philibert (1982), Miller (1987), and McCracken (1988), among others, for consumption to be given the consideration it deserves as the place where the material is articulated with the symbolic, and the social meanings inscribed in goods are reproduced.

One of the central issues in understanding how goods cross cultural boundaries is constituted by the evaluation of material things, the determination of the value of goods, what Appadurai (1986:57) calls 'regimes of value'. Such regimes transform goods into objects of desire, or, to phrase the matter in economic terms, create utility and, at the aggregate level, account for market demand. In this chapter we are interested in what happens to goods produced according to one mode of production when they are used according to consumption practices associated with another mode of production. Specifically, we examine how goods produced under an industrial capitalist system are

55

inserted into a semantic space governed by rules of consumption that remain rooted in an agrarian mode of production.

The case studies that follow illustrate two different types of reaction of local socio-cultural systems to capitalist penetration. In the first section, Christine Jourdan explores how both local and imported goods are treated according to the same indigenous symbolic scheme in the Solomon Islands. She starts with four vignettes written from the perspective of a Westerner abroad, evoking her wonderment at some of the consumption practices she observed. She goes on to try and interpret these vignettes, by suggesting ways in which the attitudes towards things described in them would appear to be informed by a local classificatory scheme which places all objects, including industrially produced goods, on a 'nature–culture' continuum. According to this scheme, which is grounded in traditional production activities, the closer objects are to the 'nature' end of the continuum the less valuable they are, even though their production (in the case of local goods) or purchase (in the case of imported ones) may have involved hard work or financial sacrifice. The closer objects are to the 'culture' end, the more valuable they are, even if they have been acquired without effort – through inheritance or exchange, for example – and are readily replaceable. By exploring the economic and social concomitants of this particular form of classification of goods, Jourdan unravels the logic under-pinning the evaluation of traditional and consumer goods among Solomon Islanders.

If Solomon Islanders have retained an orientation towards goods which is still strongly influenced by their agrarian mode of production, the tie between production and consumption in the 'peasant world' of Vanuatu has led to a semantic space with a different layout. In the second section, Jean-Marc Philibert analyses the consumption, both private and collective, of Western goods in the half-urban, half-rural – or 'peri-urban' – community of Erakor, Vanuatu. The villagers' access to Western goods (and hence mode of consumption) is predicated on wage employment and proximity to the capital. Their actual consumption of Western goods seems nothing short of 'excessive'. This apparent manifestation of conspicuous consumption could be explained as expressing the symbolic consumption of the signs of modernity by the affluent inhabitants of an increasingly urbanized village. However, to interpret the phenomenon of consumption in Erakor simply in terms of predicted individualization of social life associated with the transition from tradition to modernity does not go far enough. For even though the desire to appear modern explains the motivation of many social actors, this, by itself, does not account for changes to the village's institu-tional structure and context.

The focus of the present analysis therefore shifts to concentrate on the impact of consumption on the ideological reproduction of the hybrid social world of Erakor, which straddles a subsistence economy and a market economy. Specifically, the analysis comes to centre on the line dividing the collective from the personal. Access to and ownership of Western goods are shown not to lead *per se* to an individualization of social life – that is, to the use of goods as markers of social identity with individuals competing with one another for status through displays of such goods. Indeed, greater participation in the market economy is shown to be a lesser threat to the ideological reproduction of this village community than poverty resulting from economic marginalization.

Both case studies explore instances of the articulation between the global market and local cultures in the South Pacific. Christine Jourdan focuses on the indigenous classification of consumer goods. Jean-Marc Philibert is concerned with the impact of consumer goods on indigenous modes of production and collective ideologies. It emerges from these two studies that systems of consumption can no longer simply be considered derivative of systems of production and exchange. Consumption, indeed, offers a unique perspective to explore the links between the material and the symbolic dimensions of social life, as well as the numerous and varied forms of articulation between local and global levels of the so-called world system.

THE CONSUMPTION OF GOODS IN THE SOLOMON ISLANDS

Ethnographic setting

The Solomon Islands, formerly known as the British Solomon Islands Protectorate, has been an independent country since 1978. The country has a relatively small population (300,000 inhabitants), a high level of ethnic and linguistic diversity (64 different languages), and a highly mobile labour force. Most of the population (80 per cent) continues to derive a living from subsistence economic activities.

The town of Honiara, the country's capital, has a population of 40,000. Created after World War II, Honiara served as the administrative centre of the British Solomon Islands Protectorate. A typical colonial town, its main purpose was to regulate the flow of goods and merchandise in and out of the archipelago, and to co-ordinate the movement of the Melanesian labour force between various islands. It is only recently, and mainly since independence, that native Solomon Islanders have become involved in the social organization of Honiara and had a significant influence on the cultural life of the town. In this new world, the young people have the cultural edge over the adults who, for the most part, are still enmeshed in village-related social activities, and for whom the world of the village – the world of *kastom* (custom and tradition) – remains the frame of reference for most symbolic and practical activities.

Much of the following analysis will be concerned with the consumption practices of one ethnic group, the Kwaio of Malaita Island. The Kwaio, who comprise some 7,000 individuals, are one of the ethnic groups that has migrated from elsewhere in the Solomon Islands to Honiara. As Roger Keesing (1982) has shown, they are more staunchly attached to the regime of *kastom* than most Solomon Islanders. Even though many Kwaio have converted to Christianity, some 2,000 of them still adhere to the ancestral religion, with its complex rules concerning sexual segregation, pollution, and so on. Except for the larger villages that are situated adjacent to mission stations by the sea, the Kwaio live in small hamlets located on lineage lands dispersed throughout the bush. They derive their subsistence from tending taro and sweet potato gardens. Alongside the subsistence economy, there is a prestige economy which centres on the production and consumption of prestige objects. The only way for the Kwaio to earn money is through finding employment on plantations elsewhere in the archipelago, or in Honiara.

Four vignettes

• It is early morning and we are walking through the bush towards the neighbouring hamlet, five hours walk away up the mountain; the path, less steep than others, has not been used for a long time. My walking companion, a young Kwaio in his twenties, leads the way. Swinging his bush-knife right and left, he slashes at the thorns and low-growing stems which catch at our legs and at the branches which scratch our faces. When the whim takes him, he steps a short way off the path and with a single slash of his bush-knife cuts off a nearby branch, which he sharpens to a spear. When he is satisfied with the point, he throws it, judges its trajectory, nods his head and, without having missed a step or altered his rhythm in the least, continues as before. I flinch with every swing of his arm as the bush-knife brings down flowers, leaves and branches indiscriminately; they fall to the ground and we tread them underfoot. I think about the number of times this is repeated every day, everywhere in the bush, and my ecological, Western, middle-class self bursts out: 'What if we folded the branches back instead of cutting them?' I get an incredulous look. 'What for? They'll grow again!'

• As we finish preparing the *motu* (stone oven), the oldest woman in our group, Mesi, points out that the fire is still too hot. If left like this, the food placed on the stones will burn rather than cook. Mesi turns away and goes towards the edge of the forest where she rips the leaves off a group of eight bushes and breaks their branches, saying, 'We need a lot of leaves. The fire must not burn our meal.' Obviously, in so doing she has damaged the bushes, of which only bare twigs and broken branches remain; it is equally obvious that this does not enter her head. I bite my tongue and say nothing, but think sadly and a little theatrically that this may be the first step towards destruction of the forest, soil erosion, and so on. Mesi is quite serene, and with calm and dexterity she puts the finishing touches to the *motu* by delicately placing her bundle of leaves on the white-hot stones.

• In Honiara, Tome and his family live in a house which they had built fifteen years ago. Made of prefabricated fibreboard panels, it is typical of the houses constructed by the local housing authority in low-income residential neigh-bourhoods. Over the years, the house has deteriorated as much under the assaults of the children as through normal wear and tear. It is now in very poor condition: rotten floors, leaking roof, flaking paint or mildewed walls revealing the lack of maintenance, even though the house is cleaned regularly, and great care is taken to sweep the floor several times a day. The house is no longer repairable; it will be torn down this summer and a new house built on the same site as the old one. The old refrigerator has found its way out to the back yard, having over the years lost everything that made it functional: the freon leaked out after the children used a knife to try to remove a fish encased in the ice covering the inside of the freezer; one after the other the racks were used as barbecue grilles; the door handle came off in the children's hands. The old stove survives, a single ring out of four still working, lit with the only remaining knob. The oven is used to store food.

• This evening, negotiations are taking place at Solo's house over the bride-wealth for his young brother Sam's fiancée. It is some weeks since Solo collected the amount of shell money (in the form of necklaces) that will be necessary for the marriage transaction to succeed, and he keeps it in a bag made for the purpose given to him by his father, carefully rolled in dried pandanus leaves. The whole bundle is placed in his family's pudding bowl, which he brought back from his native village last time he visited his home. Solo often looks over his shell necklaces lovingly: he unwraps them, rethreads them if need be, examines them again and again, and finally puts them back in their place when he has satisfied himself that everything is in order. Solo takes the same intensive amount of care of the *subi* (ceremonial club made of hard wood) which he inherited from his father and which bears a famous name. The evening of negotiation begins with a video shown on the machine Solo brought back from a trip to Hong Kong last year, which has taken its place alongside three other similar ones bought over a number of years, none of which works any longer.

The classification of goods

Until recently, the only goods Solomon Islanders used were those they made themselves. Everyone fashioned their own tools and everyday items: bow and arrows, adzes, axes, bags and mats of woven fibre, bamboo and pandanus houses, canoes, etc. Everyone made their own ritual objects, such as ceremonial clubs, for use in the ancestor cult to bear witness to the life of the lineage. Certain specialists made other goods, such as body ornaments, fine handicrafts and shell money, the importance and social value of which varied in proportion to the skill of the maker and the symbolic function of the good in the social and ceremonial life of the group. In the case of everyday items and ritual objects, the object's use-value, both practical and symbolic, governed its life; in the other case, it was its exchange value which did so. In all cases the raw materials were available in abundance and accessible to all: the virgin forest and the sea provided them, and still do.

A primary physical characteristic of all these goods was that they were disposable, an ephemeral existence being part of their very function and nature. And these goods were not only disposable, they were also easily replaceable. Whether an object was used, misused or abused was determined to some extent by its degree of replaceability, in turn defined by the place the object occupied on the nature–culture continuum. The closer the object was to the 'nature' pole, the more disposable and replaceable the object was considered to be, and the less integrated into community life. The closer an object was to the 'culture' pole, the less replaceable it was because it formed part of the social life of the group. When the object was 'natural', or, in other words, individual and situated outside social networks, it was unnecessary to maintain or repair it, as it could simply be thrown away and easily replaced. When the object was 'cultural', taking its meaning from its collective insertion and irreplaceability, it was treated with great care and often removed from the sphere of exchange.

Nowadays, the Solomon Islanders are not the only producers of the goods they use. However, the islanders seem to apply the same logic of disposability to the consumer goods they are bombarded with by the world market system as they do to their own locally produced goods. Susceptible to the allure of consumerism, the people of Honiara, the country's only town, now buy their everyday household items from shops. This incorporation of foreign goods into local households results in an important displacement of the goods' meaning. This displacement is similar to what linguists call a semantic shift. The object remains the same, but its semantic content (relationship of form, function, meaning and symbolic value) is altered. When Solomon Islanders buy consumer goods that have been manufactured by others in a foreign country for a specific use, they do not necessarily buy the purpose for which they were made along with the objects. Even the utility of a practical object may not be part of the reckoning when it is bought. Moreover, the symbolic value of objects may be dissociated from their utility because objects do not in themselves produce meaning except by connotation.

This semantic indeterminacy allows consumers to manipulate goods symbolically to construct messages about themselves through their consumption choices. A parallel may be drawn to Hall and Jefferson's study of English working-class subculture and, in particular, their description of how some English youth actively assemble selected goods into a style, often subverting the received meaning of such goods in the process. This can be done because in cultural systems, there is no 'natural' meaning as such:

> Objects and commodities do not mean any one thing. They 'mean' only
> because they have already been arranged, according to social use, into

culture codes of meaning, which *assign meanings to them* . . . . It is possible to expropriate, as well as to appropriate, the social meanings which they seem 'naturally' to have; or, by combining them with something else . . . to change or inflect their meaning.

(Hall and Jefferson 1976: 55)

It is possible for goods to be recontextualized in different symbolic spheres from those in which they were designed and produced. Consequently, it is far from certain that acquiring goods necessarily entails accepting the ideas and perceptions embedded in them at the moment of production at the start of their existence. The lack of fit between the function of the goods and their symbolic value (lost or gained) may explain Solomon Islanders' attitude to foreign goods. By dint of hard work on the plantations and financial sacrifice, Solomon Islanders try to acquire prestige goods, such as electronic keyboards, VCRs and food processors. Sometimes the purchased commodity is not actually used, because people lack the knowledge (in the case of electronic keyboards, for instance) or the means (as in the case of blenders which use too much electricity) to do so. More often, the commodity is used in excess, but is not repaired if it breaks down. This situation is described in the third and fourth vignettes in which heavily used consumer goods such as refrigerators and VCRs are shown to be junked once they are no longer serviceable. This junking may occur because, once the symbolic value of the object has been appropriated, its use value disappears and is no longer of any interest. Alternatively, it is possible that the consumer simply cannot afford to have the item repaired. At a deeper level, if the object is classified as 'natural', it would fall into the category of objects one does not repair and which will be replaced as soon as this becomes possible.

With the exception of some inhabitants of Honiara, most Solomon Islanders engage in subsistence economic activity. They are excellent gardeners and skilful fishermen. They assiduously tend their gardens, and keep a careful eye on the coral reefs which are their fishing grounds. Land tenure and reef tenure divide the various ecological zones into 'wild' nature (the sea and the forest in general), and domesticated, 'cultural' nature (gardens, the forest where people hunt and forest paths, coral reefs and fishing waters).

Solomon Islanders have great respect and love for nature when it is tamed by culture: the care they lavish on their gardens and reefs clearly demonstrates this. This has to do with the importance of the food produced for the group, and the role of the lineage and clan structures in taking nature in hand. They do not, however, have any particular attachment for wild nature, although they appreciate its bounty. Tearing off a branch, or stripping the leaves from a bush, as in the first and second vignettes, are common actions that take place outside the boundaries of domesticated nature. Aesthetic considerations, which do exist but are rarely articulated around notions such as landscape, are not enough to prevent such acts. It is the closeness of body and nature, and of memory and earth and sea brought about through gardening or fishing, that serve in a sense as the basis of an 'acculturation' of nature. Wild nature, by contrast, does not involve this inscription on the body and in the memory, and therefore does not elicit the same sentiments.

Is it labour then that makes the difference between natural and cultural objects, wild nature and domesticated nature? Is there a link between the labour one invests in objects and the care one takes of them? To some extent this is the case. However, the value of objects and the care taken of them in the Solomon Islands are only partially determined by the amount of work it takes to produce or acquire them. This is the case even for expensive imported goods. It is therefore of little consequence that dearly bought objects no longer work, or have fallen out of use. More important to an object's value is its social and ritual role within the community. Thus in the fourth vignette, Solo carefully tends and repairs the shell necklaces which play an important role in communal rituals while broken-down VCRs are left unrepaired. Ritual objects are always treated with deference in the Solomon Islands (cf. Davenport 1986: 107). Consumer goods, by contrast, are treated roughly – as are natural objects. None the less, consumer goods, as manufactured products, *are* considered somewhat more valuable than natural objects, if nowhere near as valuable as ritual objects.

In the cultural creolization that characterizes the world of Honiara (cf. Jourdan 1994a, 1994b), objects are found at the crossroads of global and local modes of consumption. The urbanites in Honiara find themselves pressured by the cultural forms and ideologies of the world system and by those from the world of *kastom*. As they are interested in participating in both these worlds, they have integrated the imported products they encounter in town with their traditional system for classifying goods in the country. This negotiation between worlds contains an element of play which should not be neglected. When young Solomon Islanders wear a Rasta hairdo, or dress like their Hollywood hero Rambo, or when their parents build houses of permanent materials instead of bamboo, they are playing at having an identity they know is not theirs. As the appropriation of foreign identities and products is, in some ways, a game, no serious attachment to those identities or products is required. When the game is over they can be put aside and forgotten.

This is all the more true given that imported images and commodities are continually being replaced – in movies and advertising in the case of the former, and in stores in the case of the latter. In the experience of the inhabitants of Honiara, a new crop of consumer goods unfailingly springs up every year, like plants in a superabundant forest. Thus, just as the Kwaio youth in the first vignette felt no qualms about cutting down a branch, shaping it into a spear, and then throwing it away, because he assumed that there would always be more branches, so do Solomon Islanders generally not feel any qualms about buying consumer goods, using them, and then discarding them? Roger Keesing (1994) has described the Kwaio as having become masters in the art of 'hunting and gathering in the urban jungle'. They have also been able to rework the ideology of Western 'throwaway' consumer culture to conform to their own ideological categories of consumption.

THE CONSUMPTION OF GOODS IN VANUATU

The second case of cross-cultural consumption examined here involves the village of Erakor in Vanuatu. Erakor is a peri-urban village, a setting which has hitherto received little attention in Melanesian studies. A key determining characteristic of such communities is that there is no geographical barrier between rural and urban areas. This makes them fundamentally unstable socio-cultural milieux. With one foot in the rural world and one in the urban, the inhabitants of Erakor make use of the social and ideological resources of both worlds without, in the end, belonging to either. Given the instability of this situation, the social reproduction of a hybrid social world such as Erakor is never guaranteed in advance, and so the dynamic interplay between cultural forms that takes place in semi-urban villages gives an added interest to the social analysis of such communities.

After a brief description of the ethnographic setting, an analysis is presented of the symbolism of consumption in Erakor, and of the relationship of consumption to identity construction and ideological reproduction. The aim of this section is to bring out the link between a particular regime of production, the ideological discourses it engenders, and the emergent mode of consumption.

Ethnographic setting

The Republic of Vanuatu, a South Pacific archipelago with a population of some 150,000 inhabitants, stretches 700 kilometres from north to south between the Solomon Islands and New Caledonia. Prior to gaining independence in 1980, the country was known as the Anglo-French Condominium of the New Hebrides, a territory that had been jointly administered by France and Great Britain since 1906.

The economy of Erakor intersects with the national economy of Vanuatu through the sale of local produce; the commercial production of artefacts; the staging of cultural events for the tourist trade; and, above all, through wage labour undertaken by the villagers in the urban area. While incorporated into the urban labour force, however, the villagers have retained rural forms of solidarity. For example, many aspects of village life, such as food production, forms of mutual assistance, fishing rights, and access to cultivable land and house sites, have not yet been turned into commodities. In other words, they cannot be bought or sold; they can only be obtained through mutual exchanges, as gifts, or inherited, for example, through membership in village household units, neighbourhoods, circles of friends, or groups of kinsmen. Villagers have also preserved in their political discourse concepts of the social order normally associated with collective ownership of the means of production. As intermittent wage-earners living on their own land, villagers practise subsistence agriculture to a greater or lesser extent. This enables them to participate in the market economy under favourable conditions by making them partially self-sufficient and providing them with a small surplus of food they can sell in town. Like all the indigenous inhabitants of Vanuatu, the villagers practise the economic dualism characteristic of Melanesian economies (Brookfield 1972: 165–7).

Erakor is the second largest village in Vanuatu with a population of roughly 1,000 people. It is a modern prosperous community situated on the island of Efate some ten kilometres from the capital, Port Vila, a town of about 20,000 inhabitants (in 1990). The people of Erakor live on their own land, an area of 1,409 hectares bounded on the north and west by a lagoon which provides them with fish and shellfish. Two of the largest hotels in Vanuatu are also situated close to the village, on the other side of the Erakor lagoon.

For most of the twentieth century, Erakor retained a peasant-type economy combining subsistence agriculture and small market production in the form of copra making and intermittent wage labour outside the village. The fall in copra prices and a sudden economic boom in Port Vila at the end of the 1960s meant that, almost overnight, the village economy became centred on newly available jobs in town. However, this economic development did not survive the 1970s' recession caused by the oil crisis and a second recession, which occurred during the period of instability that accompanied Vanuatu's accession to independence in 1980 (Philibert 1984). This economic decline was partially countered by the considerable community development that took place during the last years of the Condominium, as we shall see later. Erakor also became involved in tourism, setting up a small hotel and restaurant on an abandoned islet.

In 1983, there were 137 men and 111 women earning wages in Erakor, those wages being the source of almost all the village's monetary income. However, during the 1980s it became more difficult to find employment than it had been during the 1970s and, as a result, the 15 to 24-year-old age group was now divided into two: young people with a secondary education and steady, well-paying public service jobs, and those with little education who could aspire to nothing higher than a job as a labourer or office boy (Philibert 1984). In spite of this narrowing of economic opportunities, villagers remained optimistic about the future.

The symbolism of consumption

The arrival of Europeans in central Vanuatu around the 1870s had severe, if not always adverse, demographic, political, economic and intellectual repercussions. Unable to make sense of this unknown world within their own epistemological framework, the indigenous populations sought in the Christian religion the source of all European knowledge and power. Indeed, until the Second World War, the villagers' desire for modernity was metaphorically expressed as a transition from a 'world of darkness' to a 'world of light'. These well-known nineteenth century metaphors provided by the missionaries conveyed the passing of traditional culture now made redundant by the arrival of an entirely new world that marked the beginning of history and the chance for a 'brighter' future. 'Civilization' meant in practice a tightly integrated socio-cultural world made of modern medicine, corrugated-iron houses, clothes, the rituals and beliefs of Christianity, participation in the cash economy, new relations between women and men, and greater geographical mobility, among other things.

Being the first on their island to become Christian, Erakor villagers applied themselves from the start to mastering this new knowledge which alone could make them the equals of newcomers so powerful and so wealthy as to make islanders feel like 'rubbish men' in comparison (cf. Philibert 1992). Today, the prevailing image of development in Erakor is one of an improvement of living conditions brought about by manufactured goods. The ideal of the 'good life' in Erakor is, in fact, one of excessive consumption or over-consumption of such goods, both individually and collectively, the latter in the form of communal use of development goods (Philibert 1982).

The following definition of a well-off villager was already current in 1973: someone who owns a vehicle, a refrigerator, a gas stove, a generator, a water tank, and a lawn mower; who has a new house in corrugated iron with somewhere to shower near the house; who raises chickens and pigs; whose children go to secondary school in the capital or overseas; who eats canned food and uses plenty of curry and tomato sauce in meals (these sauces being used for meat dishes). That this ideal is taken seriously is evidenced by the fact that houses in Erakor are generally larger than in other villages and are also better equipped. In Erakor, being 'comfortably off' is thus defined in terms of the material comfort provided by goods produced outside the village. From 1971 to 1983, the tendency towards the consumption of such goods increased dramatically, as can be gathered from a consideration of the following figures on concrete houses, motor vehicles (cars or trucks), refrigerators, and television sets and videos.

- In 1971 there was one concrete house, by 1979 the number had increased to twenty, and by 1983 there were thirty-one.
- In 1971 there were fourteen motor vehicles, in 1979 there were forty-eight (including nineteen recent models), while in 1983 there were forty-four (this time including twenty recent models).
- In 1971 there were two refrigerators. Electricity and running water were installed in Erakor in 1979, with electric refrigerators henceforth replacing the more costly and less convenient kerosene refrigerators. In 1979 there were twenty-four refrigerators, which increased to forty in 1983.

- Television sets and VCRs came in after electricity became available: there were none prior to 1979, and five by 1983.

The villagers often take little care of these manufactured goods, displaying the same carelessness towards them that they show towards objects of little utility. In the use of these goods, the sumptuary, symbolic function seems to dominate. This explains why polaroid cameras and portable record players, for example, are kept even when they are no longer usable. A refrigerator that no longer works still retains its value as a sign, though it is worth less than a working refrigerator (even one that no one uses). Cars that can no longer be repaired are often kept in front of houses because their symbolic value has not completely disappeared.

During the colonial period, possession of manufactured goods indicated social success in the white world for villagers who laid claim to status of '*évolué*' in the colonial system. There was also considerable community development during this period. A water supply was brought into Erakor and running water installed in a good number of houses; a power supply was provided, new roads were built, as well as a new concrete town hall and community centre linked by telephone with the capital. Erakor can be said to have indulged in a conspicuous consumption of development goods (the manifestation of a resolutely modernist discourse) at this time. This modernist discourse was the latest manifestation of the historical role the villagers allotted themselves of 'showing the way' of the future to other ni-Vanuatu.

Consuming the signs of modernity

Erakor villagers massively invested their economic gains of the 1970s in consumption. Yet why did goods from the industrial world become the signs of the villagers' cultural identity? The 'overconsumption' of the people of Erakor cannot be explained by reference to a preoccupation on the part of the villagers with material comfort, for many of the goods they buy are, to outsiders, of marginal utility. For instance, refrigerators are mostly used to keep drinking water cold and are sometimes only started prior to a visitor's arrival. The food villagers consume requires little to no refrigeration: various tubers, green leaf vegetables, rice, canned fish, fresh bread baked daily, tropical fruits, etc. Fresh fish is eaten when someone has gone fishing; the little meat consumed is either bought fresh in town or frozen from the village co-operative store. In a similar fashion, the houses that have electricity do not turn the electric lights on every night, preferring instead the soft glow of a hurricane lamp.

The answer is rather that the goods are valued for their symbolic significance as agents of cultural change and social power rather than for their actual utility. The goods link village culture with what is perceived to be the dominant culture of the world outside. The consumer goods so conspicuously displayed are material proof of the social equality between villagers and Europeans, since they signify equal competence in the modern world. At the same time, they mark the villagers' superiority over less progressive natives in other islands of Vanuatu (Philibert 1982).

'Overconsumption' can also be explained in terms of the behaviour of affluent people deprived of the means of political self-assertion. Until independence, Vanuatu political power was concentrated in the national administration and in the missions, leaving villagers without much scope for political action. Consequently, it is as if the villagers had transformed their blocked political desires into a symbolic discourse in the form of conspicuous consumption. Overconsumption then became a sort of sublimation of political conflict – and at the same time a dramatization of social reality – whose effect was to imbue manufactured goods with a potent symbolic value which made them suitable for defining the village's cultural identity in the modern world (Philibert 1982: 92).

The number of permanent houses in Erakor, which rose from twenty in 1979 to thirty-one in 1983, in a community of 130 households, serves to illustrate the process of identity construction through consumption of the signs of modernity. A concrete house has great symbolic value in Vanuatu for a variety of reasons. The colonial administration, ostensibly for public health reasons, has long urged people to build more 'salubrious' concrete houses in lieu of their traditional dwellings. Furthermore, obtaining the mortgage which makes it possible to build such a house demonstrates a mastery of the institutions of the market economy. Lastly, having such a house reveals a high level of ready cash needed to buy the proper furnishings for each single-purpose room: kitchen, bedrooms, dining-room, and so on. Aside from furniture, the living-room, for example, must have decorated shelves, curtains in the windows, artefacts of the kind produced for tourists on the walls, and plastic flowers in glass vases. The traditional house has not, however, disappeared. In fact, well-off villagers living in the height of modern comfort are now having small traditional huts built in their yards, where they sit on mats on the ground, in the fashion of the poor, and drink kava (*Piper methysticum*).

The consumption of symbolism

Erakor is a hybrid community in the sense that two economic rationalities are juxtaposed there: a non-market rationality applying to the village domain, and a market rationality for the domain outside the village. This economic dualism means that, while villagers believe they are still living in a rural world, in a significant way they already belong to the urban world, so geared are the village's economy and social life to wage labour and other activities in town. Collective rights in the village domain still exist, and these are principally actualized through agricultural activities, and governed by communal structures such as the kinship system and the village council.

Although the national labour market has divided the village into the employed and the unemployed, resulting in disparities of available income, the traditional practice of subsistence agriculture continues to support an ideological discourse which denies the existence of social differentiation within the village – or rather, offers a social context in which such differences have no significance. This remains true despite the number of changes which have taken place within the village agricultural system. For example, as a result of population increase, there is no longer enough cultivable land for the slash-and-burn horticulture practised in Erakor and little or no undivided land remains, most of it having passed into private ownership. Some villagers, among both the employed and the unemployed, have stopped gardening altogether, while some no longer have access to house sites in the village (Philibert 1988).

There are now only a few collective representations to separate the social arena of the village from that of the town. The village's communal ideology became what it now is during the colonial period, when village people closely observed the colonizing Westerners and developed the ideological tools they needed to understand the newcomers and, at the same time, to rethink themselves in an intercultural context (Philibert 1982). The present communal doctrine, therefore, emerged from the melting-pot of strategies adopted by several generations of villagers as they adapted to a Europeanized world. The same selection process is at work today, in the present social context, as villagers develop an awareness of how their past works to preserve the collective logic underpinning village social relationships. It is important to emphasize the context in which this collective memory has been formed, given that the native definition of traditional and modern worlds took shape within power relations which varied considerably over a hundred years of colonial history (Philibert).

The consciousness of villagers is explored here by postulating a collective imaginary shaped around a series of oppositions. These oppositions are between inside the community and outside, between a subsistence economy and a market economy, between collective and private ownership of the means of production, between a sense of communal indebtedness and private indebtedness, between interacting with the external world as a member of a community and as an individual, between time experienced in a rural setting and an urban setting, between membership in a kinship unit and membership in a household, etc. Each new generation strikes a shifting balance between this set of oppositions, while the shape of the structure has remained so far intact.

In Erakor the fashioning of individual and collective identities has clearly become dependent on a large consumption of manufactured goods. The emergence of a class of 'nouveaux riches' in the village is not seen, however, as necessarily leading to the creation of 'nouveaux pauvres'. Villagers think it natural to acquire goods which provide a higher level of personal comfort if they have the means to do so, without considering that higher personal consumption might harm community life by reducing the share contributed to the community. Nor does this material comfort excite the envy of those less fortunate. If it did, the well-off would have to hide their wealth to avoid the risk of witchcraft, the usual revenge of the powerless and deprived in Vanuatu, but there is no evidence of their doing so. Indeed, quite the contrary, as the repeated purchase of new cars and motorcycles show.

In fact, what we are seeing is the incursion of consumer behaviour into the domain of the personal or the unreciprocal. Manufactured goods bring comfort and greater well-being, values which are understood to belong to the personal, rather than the collective, sphere. For this reason people consider that nothing is taken away from the collective domain by acts of consumption which are individually indexed. One can therefore never be criticized for having too many consumer goods. The collective logic is still anchored in village pre-capitalist forms of production and access to village means of production, while the consumption of manufactured goods escapes this logic, as if the foreign origin of such objects places them outside the social domain of the village. The villagers are apparently not aware of being in competition with one another through the conspicuous consumption of the object-signs of modernity. On the contrary, they deny that consumption has any such function, considering the fulfilment of their 'wants' through the acquisition of imported goods to be nothing more than a matter of 'good sense'.

There is abundant evidence of a progressive individualization of social life taking place in Erakor. Local collective solidarities have been eroded at the level of production for, as the village economy has become integrated into the national economy, the villagers have turned to wage labour to provide for their needs. In a socio-cultural world as unstable as this Melanesian village, there is no one dominant ideology, no triumphant hegemonic principle. Village production continues for the moment to sustain collectivist discourses and provide a context of social equality in the village community, while the acquisition of Western goods (most of which, incidentally, are actually made in the Far East) is placed in the domain of individual consumer practices.

While it is true that Western goods, products of a superior technology, have great prestige in Erakor, this attraction in itself does not alone account for the high levels of consumption of them. Nor can this consumption be explained in terms of an adherence to a 'universal code of recognition' (Adam 1980:158). We must rather seek to understand the displacement of the traditional logic of village consumption towards a personal dimension which, in turn, stimulates the commoditization of consumer habits. To put it another way, we must show how these goods come to occupy a gradually emerging ideological space, while collective consumption behaviours associated with public events such as a christening or marriage, now considered less convenient, disappear.

The consumption of a collective idea

It would be a mistake to consider the market and non-market dimensions of the village economy as mutually exclusive, one being governed by a collective, the other by an individual logic. In fact, the market system subsidizes village sociability and supports the symbolic production of the Erakor community as those involved in paid employment use their income to participate in public activities. Paradoxically, it is the poor, the people who are marginalized in the market sector and thus forced to limit their productive activities to the village domain, who are undermining the communal dimension. It is they who, for lack of financial means, are unable to meet the requirements of a social regime made costly by the prescribed public rituals which mark the acquisition of new social statuses. For example, young Erakor men have started to cohabit in the village with women coming from other islands, rather than marrying Erakor women, while the most socially mobile among the latter now live in town with well-off urban dwellers. Unable to fulfil village social expectations and obligations, the poor are undermining the collective dimension by asserting their social identity as individuals, rather than as members of large social networks based on age, friendship or kinship.

The Melanesian dual economy model will continue in Erakor as long as a corporate social ideology survives. However, this model is becoming more and more of a fiction. Village-based production activities are being progressively marginalized, to the point that they will soon serve no other purpose than to provide social protection for villagers without access to wage-earning jobs. In other words, those village economic activities will no longer produce a community life, merely the idea of a community, for individuals engaged in market-type economic activities in town.

There is transpiring in Erakor a repositioning of social activity: activities which in the past had a communal or reciprocal aspect, because they pertain to the village domain, are now being reclassified as belonging to the personal domain, and are thus subject to a more flexible code of consumption and a less restrictive style. This happens when a growing number of villagers are unable to conform to the collective, public and necessarily more costly model when they look for a spouse, a place to live, an economic activity, or forms of reciprocity, and so on. The result is an impoverishment of the village 'liturgy', of the share accorded to the public rites which nourish the ideology of a community of mind and interests.

CONCLUSION

This chapter has examined the interplay between different logics of production and consumption in two small and peripheral countries of the South Pacific. In the Solomon Islands, imported goods are placed in a classificatory scheme still closely allied with the indigenous logic of production and this affects the way such goods are appraised, at least as measured by the ways in which they are used and discarded. Although Western goods clearly inspire desire, their worth is not primarily determined by their purchase price. Among rural Solomon Islanders, who liken the wealth of consumer goods found in the towns to the bounty of nature – both seeming endlessly reproducible – this cultural evaluation takes precedence over price alone in determining value. In this case, it has the odd effect of reversing the expected polarity between manufactured goods and those locally available by denying the scarcity of the former.

The Vanuatu village of Erakor stands for a different moment in the engagement between village social systems and the global economy. We are also dealing here with a community marked by socio-cultural instability: in the hybrid social world of a peri-urban village, no explanation running along traditional versus modern lines will do. The villagers' logic of consumption is still partly shaped in an ideological space emanating from a communal system of production grounded in reciprocity. However, the ownership, transaction, and evaluation of manufactured goods are increasingly escaping this logic to become reassigned to a new category, that of the personal, because social activities previously requiring a communal *imprimatur* no longer need such form of approval. Paradoxically, this phenomenon owes less to reasonably well-off villagers who are successfully engaged in the market economy than to village poor unable to afford costly public rituals.

We consider that in all societies a link exists between the system of production and forms of consumption. This is not to say, however, that practices of consumption are determined by the functional requirements of a system of production. The link between consumption and production exists not only at the base level of economic structures, but also at the level of social forms and culture.

All modes of production, whether capitalist or pre-capitalist, create social oppositions in the process of appropriating labour. A great deal of ideological work is consequently needed to paper over such social divisions and fractures. This use of ideology affects 'regimes of value' (Appadurai 1986) in at least two ways: first, it partially determines the components of social identity, such as sex, age, valuable knowledge, division of labour, power, etc.; second, by virtue of being closely linked to identity construction and thus to the role assigned to material goods in such a process, it is in part responsible for the semantic space which gives things their meaning by inserting them into a semiotic chain (Philibert 1989). Although such ideologies are found in all societies (Pouillon 1975; Philibert 1986), we can expect those associated with an agrarian mode of production to be different from the 'commodity fetishism' found under capitalism.

The central issue raised in this chapter was the determination of value, or more precisely, what turns manufactured goods into the object of local desire. We have tried to show how this process of evaluation takes place in an

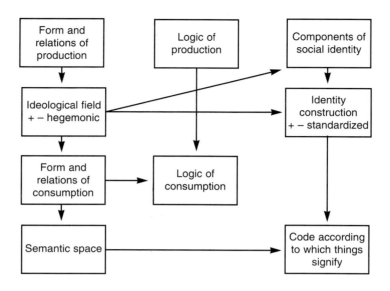

Figure 8 The cycle of consumption in the Pacific Islands

ideological field shaped in part by the activities of production – a one-dimensional field among the Kwaio, a two-dimensional one in Erakor. This ideological and cultural field 'produces' different sorts of subjects by determining the components of social identity. It is also closely connected to 'regimes of value' by shaping identity construction and thus the position of various goods in this process. In the case of Erakor, the consumption of Western goods has undoubtedly contributed to the individualization of social life, but what any particular goods come to mean and how desire for them arises is not a straightforward matter. Goods do not signify in and of themselves: their meaning comes from their position in a chain of signifiers. In Erakor, it is the shrinking of collective forms of consumption that has created space for individual efforts and money to be expended on the acquisition of manufactured goods, now seen as a matter of personal choice. Figure 8 gives an idea of the direction of the total process.

The study of consumption, not as a tributary of systems of production or of exchange, but as the place where the material and the symbolic dimensions of social life meet, will reveal many ambiguities such as those presented here. The focus has been, in one case, on the cultural dimension of the evaluation of goods and, in the other, on the social context of this process. Both approaches reveal varied types of accommodation between local systems and the world system that are too often ignored by world system theorists – the effect of which is to deny many indigenous groups the agency that is rightly theirs and the historical role they have played in the making of their present-day world.

ACKNOWLEDGEMENTS

Jean-Marc Philibert carried out fieldwork in Vanuatu in the peri-urban village of Erakor from 1972 to 1973 and again in 1979 and 1983 – a total duration of some twenty-four months. He would like to thank the Social Sciences and Humanities Research Council of Canada for the research funds that made these fieldwork trips possible. His special thanks go to the people of Erakor for having tolerated an anthropologist's professional curiosity for so long. Christine Jourdan has been working in Honiara, capital city of the Solomon Islands, since 1981. She is grateful to the people of Honiara for their kindnesses and patience towards her, and to the Social Sciences and Humanities Research Council of Canada for financial support. Both authors wish to thank Jane Philibert for her invaluable assistance.

Part II

CONSUMING THE 'OTHER'

4

COOKING THE BOOKS

Global or local identities in contemporary British food cultures?

Allison James

At the side of the main road to Alnwick which runs through the lonely, windswept moorland of north Northumberland a sign catches the eye. Swinging forlornly from its white wooden post it advertises, in the silence of this landscape, the Carib-Northumbria restaurant. These words signify an intriguing pairing, heightened by the painted palm trees which adorn the sign set amongst that so English scene of fields where sheep safely graze. In Northampton, a Midlands town once thriving on the proceeds of the shoe industry, now displaced by warehousing and commuting, an Indian restaurant has been refurbished. Its Taj Mahal-like windows, fabricated from painted plywood placed over plate glass, strike a discordant note among a straggle of plain shop fronts, small businesses from video hire to home brew. Its claim, proudly advertised, is full air-conditioning. It is as if the heat of an Indian summer can be experienced – literally, rather than just figuratively – inside. Together with the Indian cuisine this contrives to simulate, for the customer, a momentary taste of India in central England. It is, however, short-lived. The meal's finale brings with it a swift and abrupt relocation: placed on the saucer, alongside the bill, lies a gold-wrapped sweet. Described on its wrapping as an 'After Curry Mint', it mimics – perhaps mocks – the seeming sophistication which the After Eight Mint, in its dark brown envelope, lent to the English suburban dinner party of an earlier era.

Such juxtapositions and mixing of cuisines, times and locations are many and manifold in form, lending anecdotal support to the suggestion that we are all in the process of becoming creolized. Take a further example: the traveller on British Rail's first class Pullman service could until recently enjoy a 'cosmopolitan dinner' from the Dishes of the World series which features food 'from India, the Middle East, China, Greece, Italy, Scandinavia and France' (*Intercity*, November 1991). A suggested menu begins with Dim Sum with Hoisin Sauce from China, is followed by Duck and Mixed Berry Sauce from south-west France and ends with Tiramisu from Italy for desert. The food, described as 'sophisticated but fun', seems somehow a fitting menu for the 1990s.

However, this observation leaves unquestioned the different ways in which

77

particular individuals may embrace, or indeed reject, this culinary variety and the meanings with which they may imbue such post-modern menus through the act of food consumption. In exploring these issues, therefore, the relationship between food and cultural identity is central and raises a number of interconnected questions. Using England as a case study, I ask whether, in the context of an increasingly (global) international food production–consumption system and a seemingly 'creolized' world, food still acts as a marker of (local) cultural identity. If food is literally for thinking about identity – 'you are what you eat', 'one man's meat is another man's poison', and so on – then does the confusion of culinary signposts, exemplified above, signify the loss of the markers of distinctiveness which separate Others from ourselves? Or, are contemporary food practices registering a modified English cultural identity? Is Hannerz correct in his assertion that:

> . . . [an] openness to foreign cultural influences need not involve only an impoverishment of local and national culture. It may give people access to technological and symbolic resources for dealing with their own ideas, managing their own culture in new ways.

> (1987: 555)

If so, what kinds of cultural changes might be being marked (marketed) in Britain? What new forms of identity might we be confronting through the recent appearance of the Chinese Pizza?[1]

This chapter seeks tentative answers to some of these questions. Through an exploration of the ways in which English food is variously imaged in academic and popular writings about food, it will show that subtle distinctions in food practices shore up different, sometimes conflicting, statements about identity and how, through these discordant meanings, attention is drawn to the temporal flow through which identities come into being. Consumption practices are seen here therefore as precariously flexible, rather than fixed and constant, markers of self and of identity.

IDENTITY AND CONSUMPTION

That food acts as a marker of cultural identity has long been noted within anthropological work on social classification, suggesting that food consumption practices are seemingly unequivocal indicators of cultural difference (Douglas 1966; Bulmer 1967; Lévi-Strauss 1962). It has been argued that acts of consumption register ideas of edibility through delimiting conceptual boundaries around that-which-can-conceivably-be-eaten within any particular culture, which is but a selection made from all-that-it-is-possible-to-eat. Through this, cultural differences of identity are mapped out: we eat horsemeat they don't; they eat grasshoppers we don't. Indeed, the very concept of 'foreign' food – which has become increasingly popular in Britain and about which I shall have a great deal more to say – derives from the marking out of difference:

'foreign' food is food from abroad consumed at home, food of the 'other', strange and unfamiliar. Shared patterns of consumption thus mark our difference from others and mapping, as they often do, on to other signs of difference – from the organization of domestic space through to the division of labour and concepts of sexual intimacy – food consumption practices provide confirmation of wider differences between cultural orders (Tambiah 1969; Leach 1964; Douglas 1975: 249 ff.).

And yet, despite this confident mobilization of food as a stable and enduring marker of cultural identity, a certain fickleness characterizes the way in which food consumption practices shore up concepts of cultural identity. As recent work on food systems has shown, historically, there has been a constant interchange between cultures in relation to food consumption (Mintz 1985; Goody 1982). Trade, travel, transport and technology have all played their part in facilitating a considerable exchange of consumption practices. This brings into question, therefore, the very notion of 'authentic' food traditions, raising doubts as to the validating role food might have with respect to cultural identity. For example, as Goody (1982) notes, it was not until the end of the nineteenth century that olive oil became an indispensable ingredient in Provençal cooking. Before then it had been but marginal to that particular food tradition. Similarly, pizza and pasta – now regarded as the most 'Italian' of Italian foods (but fast becoming the most global of global foods) – were originally only to be found in Italy's southern regions. Likewise maize, now regarded as a staple, 'traditional' food in many regions of Africa, is not an indigenous plant. Introduced by the Portuguese in the sixteenth century, and originating in America, it became known as Turkish wheat in Britain, Spanish corn in France, Sicilian corn in Italy and 'foreign' corn in Turkey (Tannahill 1973: 205). As Tannahill observes:

> Among history's many ironies is the fact that a cheap food designed to feed African slaves on their way to America should have resulted, in Africa itself, in a population increase substantial enough to ensure that the slavers would not sail empty of human cargo.

> (1973: 205)

Such links, Goody (1982: 36) notes, provide a salutary lesson for those attached either to the holistic or to the timeless view of culture. They also de-emphasize conceptions of society linked to the isolated and bounded nation-state (Featherstone 1990b: 2) and, in so doing, re-emphasize the need for a reflexive concept of culture which takes account of its temporal and spatial minglings (Hannerz 1990: 239).

None the less, within the popular imagination firm conceptual links tie whole cultures to particular cuisines, as the titles of contemporary cookery books make clear: *Far Eastern Cookery* (Madhur Jaffrey), *Chinese Cookery* (Ken Hom) and *A Book of Middle Eastern Food* (Claudia Roden). One interesting question which I shall pursue, then, is what counts as 'traditional' food in contemporary British society and how are images of 'tradition' used to prop up, relocate or dissuade allegiances to particular local identities against the backdrop of increasingly global, potentially homogenizing, cultural processes? Similarly, how is 'authenticity' invoked, and by whom and for whom?

A second cautionary note must be sounded. Although food clearly does mark out distinct local cultural identities, despite its globalizing tendencies, at the same time consumption practices work to fragment the idea of a unitary local culture. A plurality of *intra*-cultural identities are simultaneously registered in acts of food consumption. Again, this has been well documented. For instance, during rites of status passage, special kinds of food will be eaten and commonly consumed foods may become temporarily taboo for the initiates undergoing transition to a new social identity (Richards [1956] 1982). Similarly, it has been noted that age and gender both shape consumption practices (Charles and Kerr 1988) and that the gift of food can cement social relations just as the withholding of food can negate them (Ortner 1978). And *all* of these processes of staking out diverse identities might take place within the confines of a single 'authentic' food tradition or cuisine.

Thus, the abundant referencing of identity through food consumption practices contains excluding, and often contradictory, statements about cultural identity. Mobilized in different social contexts and at different times through particular food items, fine lines of discrimination are revealed, markers of difference which are used to distinguish the Self from other selves in everyday life: what you eat may tell me that you are a young/old/male/female/high status/low status/sick/well kind of person. At the same time, these identities may also testify to, or indeed become submerged by, a wider cultural referencing: that you are a Jew, a Muslim or a Hindu, or that you are also African, French or British. And on still other occasions, the food that you choose to eat might tell me that you would see yourself (and wish to be seen by others) as Scottish – haggis and mashed neeps on Burns night – rather than British, as a city dweller and sophisticate, or more specific still as a Londoner or Aberdonian or, indeed, through the regular consumption of jellied eels, a true East Ender.

Paradoxically, therefore, food provides a flexible symbolic vehicle for self-identity, precisely through the invocation of sets of '*inflexible* cultural stereotypes which link particular foodstuffs to particular localized identities' (James 1993). Given the present context of a global economic culture where, for the affluent West at least, the international food system ensures access to a spiralling diversity of foodstuffs, this chapter asks whether food can retain its role as a signifier of identity. If so, how are new foods and new identities made mutually reflective? If not, what cultural sense is being made of this potentially endless diversity of culinary markers within particular locales? What strategies of consumption (and production) are being brought into play and how are they being used to constitute the Self in society (Friedman 1990)?

RECENT CHANGES IN BRITISH FOOD PREFERENCES

With respect to contemporary English society these issues are particularly pertinent for, since Elizabeth David first published her book about Mediterranean cooking in the 1950s, there has been a marked change in English food preferences (Mennell 1985). The cookery columns in women's magazines of the 1950s, which provided cooking hints and tips in recipes for traditional family food, were augmented, and later displaced, by a more sophisticated food journalism in the 1960s. This brought to the conservative English palate the tastes and textures of 'foreign food' and, from the mid-1970s radio and television programmes began to take food as a serious topic for discussion and reflection through the broadcasting of regular features on food and drink. In recent years these have been supplemented by more specialist series focusing on particular 'foreign' cuisines such as those of India, China, Spain and Provence. This reflects an interest in the consumption of foreign food which looks set to continue. In 1991, for instance, chicken tikka masala, chilli con carne and lasagna were the best-sellers in Tasks precooked food range (*Sunday Times*, 23 September 1991) and, in 1993, it was reported for the fast-food sector in Britain that Indian take aways now outnumber fish and chip shops. That so British of British institutions appears to be in terminal decline (Mintel International 1992).

However, although these trends might seem to bear witness to an undeniable internationalization of English taste buds, the extent to which such shifts in consumption practices can be taken as a reliable index of a more global sense of identity remains unclear for there are also signs of an opposite movement towards a more localized, even parochial, taste in food. Evidence for this is legion in the weekend pages of the quality British press. The consumption of food, increasingly positioned for their relatively affluent readership as a leisure activity rather than simply as a nutritional necessity, is now a mark of culture, rather than simply a cultural marker. This can be seen, for instance, in the *Guardian* newspaper's launch of the Big Cheese Club in 1993 to mark the renaissance of artisan cheese-making in Britain and in the foodie writers' celebration of quintessential English food: 'Baked goods encapsulate all the best qualities of traditional English cookery: simplicity, robustness, and forthright use of fine ingredients' (Ehrlich, *Guardian*, 9 October 1993). Do such shifts in attitude suggest, therefore, that the consumption of 'foreign' food has been a mere stepping out of role, a 'liminal' taste experience, which, through the contrast it presents, has reaffirmed a sense of what is truly English? Is there a reinvention of tradition occurring whereby English food is, ironically, becoming a mark of *British* cuisine? Or, instead, is a new form of English food emerging, a new authenticity represented by the Anglicization of curry with chips?

To consider these questions I draw on Hannerz's (1990) discussion of cosmopolitanism. In this he emphasizes the importance of recognizing the subtle differences masked by concepts of world or global culture and suggests that these ideas be understood in terms of the 'organization of diversity rather than by a replication of uniformity' (Hannerz 1990: 237). Adapted for the food domain, Hannerz's discussion usefully distinguishes four contemporary food trends, described here in terms of overlapping discourses. In the first, the increasingly transnational character of food is emphasized. No longer limited to particular locales, foodstuffs are seen to have an international, increasingly homogeneous, character. Diversity and difference in cuisines are consciously played down or understated. Second, and in seeming direct contrast, there is an urgent emphasizing of the heterogeneity of cuisines, of their cultural diversity, of the fine distinctiveness of particular local food stuffs and of the peculiar and special experience of eating food within its own locale. A third trend vociferously defends the local, is truly anti-cosmopolitan, while the fourth acknowledges the gradual creolization of food, the mixing of cuisines as of cultures, redolent in the idea of curried pasta, lasagna with chips and vegetarian haggis. But, distinct though these different trends in cosmopolitan tastes are, they none the less share in a wider commonality: each refracts in different ways the motifs of authenticity and tradition and, in so doing, the relationship between food and local forms of identity is constantly restated and reaffirmed in the face of more global claims.

DISCOURSE 1: GLOBAL FOOD

The appearance of the big 'M' for McDonald's in the streets of Moscow, as well as those of London, bears witness to the globalizing of fast food. During 1984–8 McDonald's increased its franchising by 34 per cent and, in 1988, its outlet in Belgrade, Yugoslavia, was serving over 6,000 customers per day (Finkelstein 1989). Coca-Cola and other kinds of snack food have been similarly successful and, for Sargent, show without doubt that

> food cultures are becoming more and more homogeneous as Western food conquers the world. Behind the standard-bearers of McDonald's and Coca-Cola, fast foods, snack foods, processed foods, food gimmicks and soft drinks are on the march. They have swept through North America and made inroads into Britain and parts of Europe.
>
> (quoted in Finkelstein 1989: 46)

But such food imperialism is not, I suggest, purely a matter of taste. It is also a matter of meanings: embedded within the hamburger or fizzy drink are images of identity waiting to be consumed, identities which are dependent on the form and presentation of the food itself.

In the majority of chain restaurants, for example, novelty and surprise are kept at a minimum. World-wide, the decor and menus of chain restaurants will be familiar and recognizable, with only minor accommodations made to the local context and even interactions with the consuming public will be routinized, domesticated and mundane:

> The training of restaurant personnel, as set out in the 600-page McDonald's staffing manual, includes suggestions for specific conversational exchanges. Greeting the customer is important: 'be pleasant, not mechanical' which means employ a convincing smile. Other suggested comments include 'Hi, I'm here to serve you', 'Come and visit us again'.
>
> (Finkelstein 1989: 11)

Through this standardization of consumption experiences the uniqueness of the Self is played down, making the identities on offer similarly safe and conventional. Traditionally cautious in their eating habits with a taste for plain food and with robust appetites (Mennell 1985), for the English the appeal of these fast-food outlets lies in their framing as family eating establishments. For the young, they are places to go alone for informal, classless food consumption at any time of day or night. The pleasures gained from eating a Big Mac derive, therefore, from its very uniformity, its lack of difference in a heterogeneous world culture. The global is made manageable, is rendered knowable: 'the diner knows exactly how to order the foods and what s/he will receive whether in Tulsa or Tokyo . . . and the interest food can generate in different cultural practices and social styles is retarded' (Finkelstein 1989: 47). This global, homogenized identity imaged in such fast-food outlets is thus reassuringly *local* in feel, encompassing in a foreign land or urban cityscape a wide diversity of individual consumers. It is food from home at home and a place to locate or anchor the Self when abroad.

Elsewhere the ubiquitous burger may mean precisely the opposite. Embracing one particular local identity (American) in a global context this food may, for example, enable consumers to take on, momentarily, a more transnational, differentiated identity and lifestyle through taking in the authentic taste of America. A new convert to McDonald's in Beijing described this experience:

> I love it. I love the milk shake, I love the Big Mac, I love the apple pie, I love . . . .
>
> (Gracie, *Guardian*, 24 April 1992)

A few yards from Chairman Mao's mausoleum, McDonald's Beijing outlet does good business: 'outside, the queues are shepherded through a maze of railings and gates, tripping over each other in their eagerness to taste "real American food" ' (*Guardian*, 24 April 1992).

Thus, in the capital cities of Eastern Europe and the newly industrializing centres of the South, fast food may offer a route into a new globalized identity, made possible through the very homogeneity of fast-food outlets world-wide. But, simultaneously, those acts of consumption may also reflect and refract more local conceptual frameworks: being able to 'buy into', literally consume, an American–global culture, may be a measure of an individual's status and prestige in terms of more traditional and localized meanings (Hannerz 1987). Or, these same local identities may, by contrast, be reflected in the *rejection* of the global burger: 'After one perfunctory nibble, a portly middle-aged man threw down his cheeseburger in righteous indignation and declared: "This is not a patch on Chinese food"' (*Guardian*, 24 April 1992).

The homogenizing of food across the globe through the fast food revolution has not, therefore, produced a comparable set of homogenized identities. Indeed, as Chase notes (1992: 68), in Istanbul the penetration of Western fast-food chains has led to an *increased*, rather than decreased, local culinary complexity through the revival of traditional Turkish snack foods which offer similar contemporary, 'grazing' experience at half the price. Global food has therefore yielded subtly different experiences and outcomes. It has simultaneously encouraged the expression of sameness *and* difference, universalism *and* particularism (Robertson 1992), re-authenticating local identities in a global context.

DISCOURSE 2: EXPATRIATE FOOD

Following Appadurai's suggestion that in the global cultural economy 'media-scapes . . . help to constitute narratives of the "other" and proto-narratives of possible lives' (1990: 299), in this section I focus upon one contemporary and highly popular food narrative: the story and dramatic enactment of Peter Mayle's escape from the English climate and cuisine to that of Luberon mountains in the Provençal region of France. The book is the realization of an advertising executive's dream in more than one sense: it was Mayle's dream to relocate to France, a dream shared by many other English middle-class couples (Hattersley, *Guardian*, 8 March 1993), and a dream which became a dream of an advertisement for the promotion of the French lifestyle. With *A Year in Provence* selling over one million copies, the publishers have already sold more than 500,000 copies of its successor, *Toujours Provence*. But what accounts for the book's appeal, given that the televised version of this dream was panned by the critics and Mayle's account of Provençal life refuted by other inhabitants of rural France (Seel, *Guardian*, 26 February 1993)? The answer, I suggest, lies in the identity it offers the reader, an identity mediated for the most part through food.

The book traces one whole year in Provence, beginning and ending with a meal. New Year's Eve is described as taking place in a restaurant and the following Christmas sees the Mayles dining in the kitchen. The intervening pages are no less concerned with food, constituting for the reader a seemingly complete menu for Provençal life and providing a taste of what it is to be French or, more specifically, to take on a Provençal identity. January sees 'foie gras, lobster mousse, beef *en crout*, salads dressed in virgin oil, hand-picked cheeses, desserts of a miraculous lightness, *digestifs* . . . a gastronomic aria' (Mayle 1990: 2). February brings snow, 'lamb stuffed with herbs, *daube*, veal with truffles and an unexplained dish called the *fantaisie du chef* (1990: 36). And so to March and on through the year, each month a new dish and a new taste of Provence, until November. Described by Mayle as 'good eating weather' we are introduced to:

> ... a crisp oily salad and slices of pink country sausage, an *aioli* of snails and cod and hard-boiled eggs with garlic mayonnaise, creamy cheese from Fontvielle and a home-made tart ... the kind of meal that the French take for granted and tourists remember for years.
>
> (1990: 181)

By this time Mayle sees himself as 'being somewhere between the two', that is between being a Frenchman and a tourist (1990: 180). And it would seem that this changed identity has been largely accomplished through ingesting Provençal food. He has quite literally been reconstituted by it: at Christmas, which in Mayle's Provence is dominated by food – by 'oysters and crayfish and pheasant and hare, pates and cheeses, hams and capons, gateaux and pink champagne' – the Mayles feel finally 'at home' (1990: 188–97).

Thus, for this expatriate-cosmopolitan (Hannerz 1990), food is not used to invoke memories of home, as in the colonial era (Powdermaker 1967: 98–9), but instead to offer a certain and steadfast route to a new local (Provençal/provincial) identity. Unlike the anthropologist, a fellow sojourner abroad and for whom going native is an anathema, Mayle does not lust after cream cakes and ham sandwiches as Barley does in his foreign field (cf. Barley 1986: 119, 183–4). Neither is he beset with a yearning for home, unlike Lévi-Strauss who, despairing in his *Tristes Tropiques*, conjured up a distinctively French-sounding meal from the local ingredients he had to hand (1974: 323):

- humming birds (which the Portuguese call *beija-flor*, kiss flower) roasted on skewers and *flambés* with whisky
- grilled caiman's tail
- roast parrot *flambé* with whisky
- *jacu* stewed with the fruit of the *assai* palm tree
- *mutum* (a kind of wild turkey) stewed with palm buds, accompanied by a sauce made with Brazil nuts and pepper
- roast, caramelized *jacu*

No. Mayle's bingeing is a progressive and welcomed re-orientation of the Self, a deliberate taking on of a new local identity in a foreign land. His description of a French blood-donor session makes this abundantly clear:

> In England, the reward for a bagful of blood is a cup of tea and a biscuit. But here, after being disconnected from our tubes, we were shown to a long table manned by volunteer waiters. What would we like? Coffee, chocolate, croissants, brioches, sandwiches of ham or garlic sausage, mugs of red or rose wine? Eat up! A young male doctor was hard at work

with a corkscrew, and the supervising doctor in his long white coat wished us all *bon appetit*.

(Mayle 1990: 93)

Mayle literally gives part of himself to France in exchange for the authentic taste of France and an identity as a Frenchman.

Indeed, for us stay-at-homes, Mayle is offered to us as a cultural broker. He is to be our guide to Provence:

Meet his friends and discover his favourite places as he tells you where to stay, what to see and, his favourite subject, where to eat. We'll help you create the taste of Provence at home with Mireille Johnston's recipes and Oz Clarke's wine guide.

(*Radio Times*, 6–12 March 1993)

Ostensibly, of course, the book is not about food at all. It is about an Englishman abroad, hoping to divest his English identity. But as an expatri-ate-cosmopolitan figure who has eaten *à la Provence*, Mayle can tell us 'what it is *really* like to live in Provence'. Described by the critics as 'bitingly funny about local rural *mores*' but none the less retaining a 'warm enthusiasm for local life and landscapes' Mayle's book is offered as 'advised reading for anyone planning to move to Provence'.[2]

What the book provides, therefore, is a claim to authenticity, and an authenticity authenticated through pages of gastronomic detail. Humble patrons and peasant-like café owners, ordinary people, steeped in ordinary, traditional Provençal food dish up a traditional Provençal life to a global-literate audience. This is not the Parisian way, the sophisticated chic of a more cosmopolitan France. Indeed, Mayle quickly distances himself from this identity, a reminder of his own former life as an advertising executive (1990: 127–30), in a passage remarkable for the almost total *absence* of food:

We could have been in Paris. There were no brown weathered faces. The women were fashionably pallid, the men carefully barbered and sleek. *Nobody was drinking pastis*. Conversation was, by Provençal standards, whisper-quiet. Our perceptions had definitely changed. At one time, this would have seemed normal. Now it seemed subdued and smart and vaguely uncomfortable. There was no doubt about it; we had turned into bumpkins.

(1990: 128 [my emphasis])

But the Mayles are relatively wealthy – indeed, cosmopolitan-bumpkins who can afford to choose to disdain the French élite and side with the peasantry. Pastis is for Provençal, for heterogeneity and for a French identity fragmented by the same motifs of locality – age, region and social class – with which Mayle's own Englishness is or used to be (Bourdieu 1984). But, now, as an expatriate-cosmopolitan, Mayle has the leisure and competence to dally with French versions of his Self (Hannerz 1990).

And it is food which provides the vehicle for this pleasuring, as it does in the pages of foodie magazines and on the television screen for those Brits who would wish to be seen as similarly cosmopolitan. For example, the British Broadcasting Corporation has in recent years offered its viewers comparable cultural food guides: personal introductions to the intricacies and subtleties of 'foreign' cuisines have been given by Madhur Jaffrey (Far East and India), Ken Hom (China), Keith Floyd (France and Spain). For the reader, the pages of magazines such as *Good Housekeeping* and *Good Food* are replete with recipes and detailed descriptions of the food and wine to be found in 'foreign' fields. They too image the localness of particular 'foreign' countries and offer up 'foreign' lifestyles for the consumer. Under the caption 'travellers' tastes', in 1993 regular readers of *Good Food* could have learned about Greek food in April, Indian meals in May and Tunisian cuisine in June. For a middle-class, or aspiring middle-class, readership with enough time and money to cook out these fantasies, these popular magazines and television programmes provide, like Mayle's book, the route to a culinary, expatriate cosmopolitanism (Hannerz 1990).

Such claims to authenticity and tradition are common to much contemporary food writing and food journalism (cf. Levy 1986; Davidson 1988). The foodie writers seek and find, as Mayle does, the marks of authenticity in diversity, in the small scale and in local artisanal modes of production. Differentiation is celebrated through the quality and authenticity of local food traditions, world-wide. For instance, in their book about Mediterranean food, Scaravelli and Cohen (1987) discourse on rice. To reproduce their recipes authentically they make the following suggestions:

> For Italian rice dishes we recommend that you use an Italian rice (Arborio is the best).... For Spanish dishes use rice from Valencia but, if unavailable, use Italian rice. Italian rice is also suitable for French dishes, although if you can obtain rice from the Camargue, use it .... Turkish rice dishes are best made with basmati, Carolina long-grain or parboiled rice. For Greek rice pudding use Carolina short-grain or Italian rice and for other dishes use parboiled or Carolina long-grain rice.
>
> (1987: 18)

This presents a stark contrast to the homogenization of food achieved within the globalized discourse and yet, curiously, shares part of its dominion through its celebration of locality. Here, then, is a resistance to both globalization and creolization as forms of cosmopolitanism. This is not a familiarity with a global, homogenized food culture but, rather, a global familiarity with the subtle distinctions of spice and herb which differentiate between regional specialities across the globe. Thus Davidson's (1988) discussion of Asian food begins with a description of the food traditions of Laos, which he insists are distinct from those served in neighbouring China, Vietnam, Cambodia, Thailand and Burma, and which make 'the cuisine of the Lao people truly distinctive' (1988: 198).

DISCOURSE 3: FOOD NOSTALGIA

A variation of the celebration of locality in a global context is to be found in the food heritage/nostalgia industry, a sentiment expressed in a recent newspaper report. Referring to a prosecution brought by the trading standards department in Northumberland over a Stilton cheese, tradition and authenticity are marshalled to defend local interests in the face of global threats to standardize cheese production:

> A mature Stilton cheese, whose mites and maggots were such that Daniel Defoe said spoon was needed to eat them has won a legal battle over hygiene . . . . The small residents were essential to genuine Stilton said Adrian Williams, solicitor for Safeways supermarket, rather than evidence of careless cheese-handling. He accused the trading standards officers of ignorance. 'Here is a product which has been English to the bone from the 1700s onwards,' he said. 'It has had mites on it ever since.' The bench dismissed the case. Peter Pugson, chairman of the UK Cheese Guild called the decision 'a victory for English commonsense' and offered the standards department a place on the guild's diploma course.
>
> (Wainwright, *Guardian*, 4 October 1991)

In 1993, the *Guardian* newspaper again made an appeal for authenticity and tradition in relation to food consumption:

> When was the last time a good piece of British cheese wrapped itself around your tastebuds? Have you ever made the acquaintance of the spritely Cheshire made by the Appelby family; the majestic mature Lancashire of Mrs Kirkham; the Irish Cashel Blue; the beguiling Spenwood or the infinitely beguiling Wigmore; or the imperial Stilton from Colston Bassett?
>
> (Fort, *Guardian*, 9 October 1993)

It was argued that the disappearance in the 1960s of such cheeses as the Blue Vinney of Dorset does 'not reflect well on the performance of the Dairy council, and [speaks] much of the malign influence of large commercial concerns' (Fort, *Guardian*, 9 October 1993). Like the newspaper's yearly endeavour to find a truly British sausage, often locally produced in small rural communities, the Cheese Club offers those who join the opportunity to sample traditional British cheese. Members can purchase rare artisan cheeses, dispatched with tasting notes to guide them in their consumption. Other foodie magazines provide similar services, putting their readers in touch with mail order outlets for regional specialities.

This renewal of interest in local, regional produce can be seen as a reaction to the seeming internationalization of contemporary British cuisine:

The British, it seems, have got the food they deserve. Having shamefully neglected our own traditional dishes for 40 years, we now have a flashy, meretricious cuisine based, for the most part, on ersatz imitations of Mediterranean foods, unrelated to any even in our own history.

(Boxer, *Sunday Times*, 22 September 1991)

According to contemporary foodism, traditional British food is plain and robust, the family food of farmhouses and firelight:

I love British breads, which are as memorable in their own way as the best Parisian baguette. Like many people, however, I'm even more enthusiastic about the little titbits that get eaten with tea, coffee, drinks or children's glasses of milk . . . the realm of quiet afternoons and weekend breakfasts. In short, they represent home life – and home cooking – at its best.

(Ehrlich, *Guardian*, 9 October 1993)

But dishes such as steamed puddings, pies and pastries are also emerging out of their glorious domesticity. Gill, for example, notes that sticky toffee pudding is fast becoming the 'black forest gateau of the 1990s' (*Sunday Times*, 17 October 1993). Similarly, the appearance of bread and butter pudding and tripe on the menus of the more fashionable restaurants indicates a revival of English food in defiance of the trend towards more global food cultures.[3] There is, then, within this discourse, a considerable resistance to heterogeneity in terms of food from across the globe, and an insistence on the distinctive homogeneity of local food traditions.

However, access to the contemporary public celebration of authentic English cuisine may be limited. Simplicity and tradition may often only be bought outside the home at expensive London restaurants and exclusive clubs or rural retreats such as the Hertfordshire restaurant, described by Fort as 'an architectural oddity set in an exquisite, small, wooded valley' with its own kitchen garden growing 'beetroot and carrots, and lettuces galore, and great perfumed borders of herbs, trimmed apple tress and cordons of pears, and all manner of good and healthy stuff' (*Guardian*, 9 October 1993). Like the food of the expatriate discourse this food is not food for mass consumption. The money necessary to purchase traditional English cheeses or the time required to cook authentic teacakes and muffins means that the diversity of identities which localized traditions of food and eating celebrate may, ironically, be enjoyed only by the well-heeled few. As Fort muses, 'it [is] a good thing for cooking in this country that the traditions of Eliza Acton and Dorothy Hartley and adventurous, middle-class rural Britain [are] still alive and flourishing' (*Guardian*, 9 October 1993). Thus, like Mayle's version of Provence, the multiple identities that such foods potentially embrace in their acknowledgement of diversity are illusory. These foods may simply recreate, reorder or sustain older class divisions (James 1993).

DISCOURSE 4: FOOD CREOLIZATION

First published in 1989, Mayle's book has been heavily promoted ever since and, accompanying the TV serialization, the *Radio Times* magazine focused on 'Peter Mayle's Provence' for three consecutive weeks. Feature articles about Provence introduced the reader to 'Mayle's Provence' and in a feature article, 'Mayle's People', we made acquaintance with Jean-Luc, Mayle's greengrocer and a local restaurateur. Jean-Luc epitomizes authentic Provençal food in declaring 'war on the modern fruit and vegetables'. His market garden boasts '150 kinds of vegetables' and '60 sorts of herbs' (*Radio Times*, 13–19 March 1993). Jean-Luc is in the food heritage business, preserving Provençal identity through its food specialities: he grows his unusual vegetables 'out of respect for the land, and in apology for what we have done to it' (*Radio Times*, 13–19 March 1993). Thus, 'with the help of Provençal cookery writer Mireille Johnston' we were enabled to recreate this gastronomic Provence in our own homes (*Radio Times*, 6–12 March 1993). Week 1 saw recipes for appetizers, Week 2 those for main courses, and Week 3 the desserts.

As a symbolic mediator for the distrusting, fearful ordinary English – who dare not travel too far, who are as unadventurous in their diets as in their lives, whose stomachs recoil at drinking local milk (Mayle 1990: 105) – Mayle's cosmopolitan role was clear: he was to serve as a cultural guide, leading us carefully through the labyrinth of ways in which, if not becoming truly Provençal, we might at least take on a momentary French-like identity and 'become a cosmopolitan without going away at all' (Hannerz 1990: 249). For a day, with a meal, the reader could 'create the taste of Provence at home' (*Radio Times*, 6–12 March). Claims to authenticity and tradition abounded, as the step-by-step instructions revealed how to cook up a new and convincing Provençalness. We were given 'local tips and recipes', with ingredients carefully calculated and balanced, so that we might simulate being in Provence where: 'onions, courgettes, aubergines, tomatoes and peppers are filled with many different ingredients, depending on what is at hand or in the garden' (ibid.). Week 2 told us that 'the true flavours of Provence are found in the markets, from sun-ripened tomatoes to fresh, fragrant herbs. Many of the dishes are based on the local principle of "make something with nothing"' (*Radio Times*, 13–19 March 1993). Most dishes are served with a final drizzle of olive oil, that so traditional and indispensable ingredient which, as noted above, was only 'authenticated' at the turn of the century (Goody 1982).

But in Week 3 the pudding recipes signalled the end of this gastronomic adventure, the end of our dalliance with French ways and a return to a more puritanical, traditional English style. Of the two desserts on offer only one smacked of French food; the other seemed to be more English in its appeal.

Described as 'sinfully sweet', this pudding recalled the 'naughty but nice', puritanical Brit consumer for whom the eating of food is traditionally more a necessity than a pleasure (Mennell 1985; James 1990). In Mayle's Provençal world no food could be seen as sinful.

This subtle shift to an English-like Provençal cooking bears witness to a new culinary trend within British society: creolized food (Brown, *Sunday Times*, 9 May 1993). This rejects authenticity and, through exploiting the heterogeneity of food, is gradually giving shape to a new homogeneity. Creolized food appears in many guises, providing for the consumer a global experience of consumption often within a single meal if not on a single plate. One London café exemplifies this trend in consumption, describing its food as 'a sophisticated and mouth-watering mélange of the East with the West, illustrating the culinary style that has evolved in the UK over the past 30 years' (ibid.). Here the food is a cultural blending, reflecting the mixing of decor styles which envelop the diner: 'they cut down on ghee and chilli in Indian dishes, and . . . they Indianize thoroughly western dishes such as burgers, tuna and lamb chops' (*Sunday Times*, 9 May 1993).

Such mixing of tastes and cuisines might simply be seen as a response to local conditions where authentic ingredients may be lacking. For the exiled or labour migrant, whose personal circumstances may precipitate a journey across the globe, memories of home may linger, to be recreated in new localities through the medium of food. However, the proliferation of creolization of food traditions in England represents, I suggest, more than simple utility or an accident of history. It is a new mark of Englishness for, although decried by champions of the expatriate and nostalgia food discourses, creolized food represents in many ways an accommodation of the traditional English attitudes to food and consumption. As Mennell (1985) notes, an emphasis on the importance of saving both time and money has traditionally shaped English attitudes to food. Thus, even on the foodie pages of the *Good Food* magazine and the *Sunday Times*, which empathize with food smacking of authenticity and tradition (Discourses 2 and 3), can be found recipes for meals that can be made in minutes and tips to avoid wasting time. Convenience foods, readily embraced by the English in the 1960s as a short cut to better food, are in the 1990s enabling us to spice up plain English mince with a spoonful of pesto, a jar of ragout, or a bottle of cook-in-sauce. It is a way to 'get posher nosh by cheating means' (Mennell 1985: 260).

But it is also a reflection of English distrust. The mass bottling of Italian sauces and packeting of fresh pasta has enabled the English to sojourn abroad on a culinary package holiday. They can have home plus foreign food, just as in the package holiday the tourist travels for home plus sun (Hannerz 1990). And yet, this discourse does not stand alone. It sits alongside the others, sometimes sharing in their concerns. In October 1992, for example, *Good Food* contained a feature on ready-made pasta sauces, recognizing that 'Italian cuisine is beloved by the British, but the fasta the pasta the better' (October 1992). And yet, just six pages previously, we had simultaneously been encouraged to 'forget that trip to the trattoria' and find 'Italian inspiration at home' through making 'authentic risotto dishes' and Italian breads (October 1992).

CONCLUSION: DISCOURSING ON FOOD

In contemporary England, then, four discourses of food shape both local and global identities, with each laying claim to a particular kind of cosmopolitan identity through their different evocations of the motifs of tradition and authenticity. And yet, through their shared and overlapping themes, these discourses constitute an arena of choice for individual consumers. In embodying identities in a multiplex fashion, they offer ways of embracing Otherness, of confronting the global through localized, even personal, food styles and, conversely, a way of living a local life with and through global imagery. Thus, the exotic fruit now routinely available on supermarket shelves may be used casually to enhance a traditional English fruit salad – a careless cosmopolitanism invoked through ignorance or choice. Alternatively, these fruits may be carefully selected and deliberately employed, to recreate authentic 'local' tastes at home, by the food gourmet, the new immigrant or the politically exiled.

The globalization of food is not, therefore, just a matter of the movement of food stuffs between nations; nor is it simply the amalgamation or accommodation of cuisines. It is a complex interplay of meanings and intentions which individuals employ subjectively to make statements about who they are, and where and how their Selves are to be located in the world.

ACKNOWLEDGEMENTS

Draft versions of this chapter were read at the ASA conference in Oxford 1993 and the University of St Andrews, Department of Anthropology, 1994. My thanks to all those who, through their comments and queries, helped me think further about these ideas.

NOTES

1 That the idea of such a creolized food makes us laugh arises out of its positioning as an anomalous food stuff. Like the joke, it represents, literally, a play upon form, a disorder (cf. Douglas 1975: 90 ff.).
2 These quotations are taken from the cover of the paperback volume.
3 Yet, of course, such fashionable 'artisan' foodstuffs may be well known and enjoyed by ordinary people in the locality. This reflects the complexity and heterogeneity of meanings which food can have.

5

COFFEE BREAKS AND COFFEE CONNECTIONS

The lived experience of a commodity in Tanzanian and European worlds

Brad Weiss

The history of colonial and neo-colonial relations as they are experienced in Northwest Tanzania is intimately entwined with coffee. Efforts to develop and expand coffee production in Haya communities of this region have been the concern of a wide array of international and local agencies – from turn-of-the-century missionaries who introduced new varieties to Haya farmers to contemporary Field Extension Officers (*Bwana Shamba*) who promulgate new cultivation techniques. Coffee is also a substantial medium through which Haya men and women concretely experience their relation to the wider world of international markets and commodity exchanges. Fluctuations in the price of coffee (in recent years, less in flux than in precipitous decline) bring home the marginal position of rural Haya farmers relative to the global economy.

Yet, in spite of the fact that the flow of coffee as a commodity and the ever-expanding international market seem increasingly to appropriate and incorporate communities like the Haya into an encompassing order of values, there are also important disjunctures in this process. For example, many Haya men and women said to me: 'We Haya grow this coffee, we harvest it, and then we sell it to you in Europe. But what do you Europeans do with it?' This uncertainty about the ultimate use of Haya produce should raise important questions about the values of a 'global economy' and the extent to which it effectively integrates regional worlds. This query is also indicative of the extent to which coffee continues to be produced and consumed – and hence imbued with values – within Haya communities in ways which are quite distinct from the presuppositions of a global economy. The purpose of this chapter is to explore the dynamic relation of certain regional, national, and transnational meanings of coffee, and to demonstrate how an investigation of the varied interpretations and uses of this product can provide critical insight into the nature and significance of colonial and post-colonial encounters.

My research on coffee forms part of a larger research project on the semantic dimensions of commodity forms in Haya communities from the perspective of lived experience. This perspective focuses on the integration of material forms, commodities among them, into the wider socio-cultural processes through which the Haya construct a lived world. The lived world of the Haya is an order of concrete spatial and temporal relations that is both *imbued* with cultural meanings and serves to *direct* creative cultural activities. To inhabit a world in this way – to construct its orientations in the course of ongoing collective action and interaction – is, at the same time, to objectify the values that guide, restrain, enable, and motivate the agents of these actions. The significance of commoditization processes and the value of particular commodity forms can only be understood, I would argue, in relation to such encompassing socio-cultural processes of action and objectification.

This emphasis on lived experience poses a direct challenge to a long tradition of anthropological analysis that proceeds from a classification of different types of objects and exchanges, and then attempts to elucidate the different practical contexts in which they figure, as well as the symbolic characteristics and qualities attributed to them. The now classic distinction between gifts and commodities, for example, has become emblematic of contrasting orders of economy and sociality (Gregory 1982; Taylor 1991; cf. Carrier 1992 for critique of this essentialist distinction). Moreover, this division provides a teleological model of cultural transformation, as (to use Gregory's terms) the 'reciprocal dependence' of social agents transacting the 'inalienable objects' of a highly personalized gift economy progressively gives way to conditions of 'reciprocal independence' between agents transacting wholly 'alienable objects' in an impersonal economy of commodities. The position I develop in the following pages eschews any such presumed distinctions between 'types' of goods, relationships, or exchanges, to focus on the concrete social practices through which material forms are integrated in social life, and thereby become endowed with specific local values and meanings. In this way, the presence of alternative objects and transactions introduced by processes like commoditization need not be understood as distinct from, or an anathema to, meaningful practices and personalized relations, but as cultural transformations which entail distinct symbolic qualities and potentials for constituting a lived world.

Cultures differ in their assumptions about the ways in which value is generated and secured through the flow of goods. A detailed examination of a single transnational commodity, such as coffee, which has differential meanings in interpenetrating worlds of transaction, provides a means of comparing these various ways of objectifying value.

COFFEE PRODUCTION IN KAGERA

While the kingdoms (*engoma*) of Buhaya (now the Kagera Region of Tanzania) were highly stratified hierarchical systems, since the turn of the century class differences (and the processes of production and commoditization that enable them) have emerged principally in relation to the intensive growth and marketing of coffee.[1] The potential for producing and marketing coffee for cash in this region was first exploited by the White Fathers. *Arabica* varieties of coffee were first introduced in 1904 as a part of their missionizing project. Planting and marketing coffee as a means of providing cash for individual Haya landholders to pay taxes was first made compulsory in 1911 (Curtis 1989: 89). In addition to the agricultural development of this cash crop, Haya coffee marketers contributed to the expansion of commoditization while reaping tremendous profits from the early boom in coffee prices (ibid.: 72). As Haya farmers began to grow and market *arabica* as well as indigenous *robusta* varieties on a commercial scale, coffee exports from the region increased steadily, from 234 tons in 1905, to 681 tons in 1912 and over 12,000 tons in 1939.

Coffee remains the single greatest source of income for the vast majority of Haya households (Smith and Stevens 1988: 557). Moreover, coffee is, and has long been, central to the structure of class relations in Kagera. This claim is well illustrated by the fact that an overwhelming percentage of the coffee grown in Kagera today is marketed by an extremely small percentage of the total number of 'farmers' (*wakulima*, the Swahili term used by coffee co-operatives for its members) who sell coffee to the co-operatives.[2] The development of these extreme class divisions was facilitated by the marketing system that flourished in Kagera in the 1920s.[3] Haya coffee traders (known colloquially as *wachuluzi*, from the Swahili *kuchuluza* – 'to trickle down') were able to make substantial profits by paying out advances to coffee farmers strapped for cash between harvests. The marketeers would thereby receive the right to harvest and market the farmer's coffee crop, often at a rate of two to three times the amount of the cash advance. With independence and the eventual implementation of 'African Socialism', such marketeering became illegal, but (as the contemporary co-operative records indicate) continues to thrive as a black market. Indeed, the system has become more nuanced and volatile with its illegalization. Market-eers will now offer advances based on the harvest of a single tree, for example, or advance the price of a given number of 'bowls' – *bakuli*, a standard measure of coffee that must be paid to the marketeer at harvest. In the 1980s, a decade with widely fluctuating currency rates, marketeers could realize a return of up to ten times the amount of their advance. Many coffee farmers that I spoke to, however, preferred the assurance of cash in advance from the black market, to the ever-delayed and occasionally non-existent payments offered by the state.

The black market in coffee, then, is most effective in taking advantage of the need for ready cash. Those who have access to cash are able to purchase the prospective coffee harvests of their clients who cannot wait for the state's payments. In this way, control of the annual procedures (and proceeds) of coffee cultivation is cut short in favour of the immediate requirement of money. These practices have interesting implications for economistic theories of social transformation. For example, it has been argued that the development of commerce has a 'disenchanting' effect on cultural forms of temporality, as the

commodity form, especially money itself, makes possible a 'rational calcula-
tion' of future outcomes (Bourdieu 1979: 17). In Haya experience, however,
money seems to confuse and distort temporal processing itself. This propensity
of money is well expressed in a phrase the Haya commonly use to describe the
evanescence of their economy: *Ebyo mbwenu ti bya nyenkya, n'ekibi kya mpya* –
'The things of today are not those of tomorrow, that's the evil of money'. It is
not, therefore, the rational calculus of money that 'forecasts' the future, but the
potential of the money form in relation to the commoditization of coffee that
makes that future intractable.

The expansion of coffee production throughout this century should not be
taken as evidence of whole-hearted support on the part of Haya men and women
for cash-cropping activities, or for colonial and post-colonial forms of
commoditization. In the 1930s, for example, rural farmers openly resisted
'innovative' agricultural policies and techniques designed to stave off coffee
blight, saying *Twaiyanga*! ('We refuse!') to allow agricultural extension officers
on to our farms (Curtis 1989: 220 ff.). Some Haya men and women I knew were
thankful for the marketeers providing them with access to cash in times of
crisis; others, however, told me that the traders were called *wachuluzi* because
they made tears (not profits) 'trickle down'. The expansion of cash-cropping
coupled with reluctance (and occasional hostility) towards adopting its very
means, indicate that the production of coffee in Kagera did more than provide a
source of monetary income to Haya farmers and traders: it transformed the very
signs and practices through which Haya communities constitute the world
they inhabit.

COFFEE AND SOCIALITY

In order to appreciate the ways in which transformations in coffee commerce
entailed transformations in the meanings and values of Haya socio-cultural
activity we need to understand the place of coffee in the *pre*-colonial culture and
political economy of the region. *Robusta* coffee grown in Haya communities
was an important crop – as well as an important trade good – in this part of
Africa throughout the nineteenth century. Coffee was transacted between
polities – especially from Bahama kingdoms to Baganda in the north – in
exchange for bark cloth and ivories.

Most scholarship has asserted that coffee in the Haya kingdoms was held as a
royal monopoly (Austen 1968: 95; Curtis 1989: 54; Hartwig 1976: 111), but
there is also evidence to suggest that coffee was harvested and transacted by
Haya commoners for their own purposes. Individual coffee trees were also
strongly associated with both the well-being of those who cultivated and
inherited them, and the productivity of the family farms on which they were
situated. A person's *amagala*, their 'life-force' was bound up with their coffee, to
such an extent that the death of a coffee tree was an omen of its owner's death
(Hyden 1968: 82).

Robusta coffee cherries were dried and cooked with spices to be offered as informal gifts to friends and guests – much as they are to this day. These cherries (*akamwani*, a diminutive of *amwani*, the Haya term for any coffee) are prized as a masticatory, and are chewed in the course of the day as a small snack, much as betel and kola nut are taken in other parts of the world. Moreover, such coffee cherries were central to Haya rites and relations of blood-brotherhood, since (according to my own informants) the two seeds within the single pod provide an agricultural icon of this assertion of common clanship (cf. Beattie 1958). Coffee, then, was and continues to be central to a number of everyday and ceremonial practices that facilitate the construction of Haya sociality.

The ways in which coffee transactions figure in the creation of Haya sociality, and especially the spatial dimensions of this creative process, further suggest important links between coffee as a cash crop and a masticatory. *Akamwani* is often used in rites that serve to establish and secure a recognizable place. In house opening ceremonies, for example, the propitiant will often toss coffee cherries in four directions: in front of her, behind her, to her right, and to her left. I was also told that a person preparing for, or returning from, a long trip would toss *akamwani* in these cardinal directions in order to secure the journey.

These ritualized uses of coffee are exemplary of practices called *okuzinga* – 'to bind, or surround' (cf. Weiss 1996). As the direction of the rites suggests, the binding achieved by this action implies the creation of certain spatial orientations. To begin with, the rites serve to establish a *central* position relative to which the four directions are co-ordinated. The propitiant, that is, defines a centre that lies at the intersection of these directions, and in this way secures, or 'binds' that position. However, as the fact that these rites are often performed in recognition of a long-distance journey indicates, this secured centre is a relational place. The centre bound by these rites creates a relationship between different places: between the 'here' defined by these acts and the distant destination of the trip, and between the 'inside' position at the intersection of these directions and the regions that lie beyond and 'surround' them.[4]

These spatial orientations also have implications for the significance of the coffee that is used to produce them. *Akamwani*, as I have indicated, is among the most pervasive substances in Kagera, and figures in manifold acts of exchange and encounter. When, for example, guests arrive in a Haya household the host or hostess will, almost immediately, offer them some coffee to chew, and if none is available hosts usually apologize for their lack of hospitality. Suffice it to say, these coffee cherries are the quintessential Haya 'objects for guests', and their transaction continues to mark the establishment of a vast array of social relations, from simple neighbourliness to inheritance and installation practices. The many contexts in which coffee cherries figure suggest that they are a medium that helps to realize and objectify a relationship and *contrast* between 'insiders' and 'outsiders'. As 'objects for guests' the use of coffee is premised on the difference between insiders and outsiders, while such tokens simultaneously attempt to overcome that difference by mediating between insiders and outsiders.

The tensions and paradoxes posed by this fusion of intentions – the fact that coffee transactions conjoin through separation – are worth considering in greater depth for they reveal crucial connections between coffee produced for export and coffee cherries cooked for local purposes. The act of presenting coffee to guests, for example, is made to 'represent' a Haya meal. Most Haya households offer coffee cherries to their guests in a small woven plate which is covered by some twisted strands of papyrus. Similarly, a plate of bananas offered as a common meal is also covered (but by a banana leaf) when it is served. Guests take the papyrus and stroke their fingers with it prior to picking up coffee cherries. This is called 'washing' – *okunaba*, the same verb used for cleaning one's hands prior to taking a meal.

These similarities between serving a meal and serving coffee, however, can also be seen to throw into relief the ways in which these two activities are different. As Haya friends often told me, you offer guests coffee because coffee can never fill them up – it is, thus, unmistakably distinct from good food. Haya meals – at which (if successful) thoroughly *filling* food is offered – are consumed only by members of a household, behind closed doors, and definitively separated from neighbours and other more distant outsiders (cf. Weiss 1992 and Weiss 1996). Eating a meal in these ways demonstrates the integrity and self-sufficiency of the household that is able to provide for itself; yet coffee cherries can and should be offered to guests because they are not filling. The point of this contrast is that coffee can establish both connections and separations in social relationships. In effect, the use of coffee in such instances works to transform outsiders into *guests*, a gesture that asserts a relationship, but definitively not an *identity*, between those who give and receive. This dialectic of intimacy and distance, relatedness and separation, is also demonstrated by the fact that a man's father-in-law is the stereotypic recipient of coffee as a guest in one's home; affinal relations embody the kinds of ambiguities characteristic of the contexts in which coffee is offered.[5]

COFFEE MARKETING IN KAGERA

Negotiating tensions between intimacy and distance, insiders and outsiders, in terms of both sociality and spatiality is also a feature of coffee *marketing* in Kagera. There are, for example, concrete connections between coffee as a commodity form and the system of roads and automotive transport that link this commodity to a wider political economy. At all levels of the local political economy, among both wealthy coffee entrepreneurs and poor cultivators, the transport system is inextricably linked to coffee as a commodity form because, in everyday parlance, cars and lorries are what might be called a 'standard measure' of coffee volume. That is, when speaking of an amount of coffee produced for sale to the state-run co-operatives, the Haya with whom I spoke would always refer to, for example, 'one lorry', or 'three cars' of coffee as a measure of total volume. The use of cars and lorries as standard measures indicates that the very logic and means of commoditization have certain spatial implications that are embedded in the concrete forms (i.e. the automotive means referred to) through which this historical process is evaluated. Cars and lorries as units of measurement make clear the fact that coffee as a commodity is *defined by* its movement from more local relations to distant ones.

Other aspects of the spatial form of coffee production and transaction in Haya lived experience demonstrate the links of commoditization to sociality. To begin with, coffee trees are always planted a good distance from the house that lies at the centre of a Haya farm (*ekibanja*). Banana plants (*engemu*) that provide the daily staple for almost all Haya households are, in contrast, planted throughout the farm, including among the coffee trees. Those banana plants most prized for preparing meals (as opposed to snacks, or sweets) are planted in the immediate vicinity of the house. Indeed, the best banana plants are said to thrive in the areas adjacent to a house where, according to the farmers I spoke to, they can share in the intimacy and productivity provided by the warmth of an active household.

Agricultural policy in colonial Tanganyika, and later Tanzania, has discouraged inter-cropping of coffee with bananas. Haya farmers are encouraged to plant new coffee trees by themselves, on a separate plot of land within the family farm (Rald and Rald 1975). This technique is now known as *kilimo cha kisasa* in Swahili, 'modern farming', but it has certainly not been widely adopted in most Haya villages. Keeping coffee trees at a distance from a house, yet interspersed with banana plants, allows Haya households to maintain the tension between intimacy and distance characteristic of coffee transaction. Coffee trees planted among bananas lends to them qualities of close association and attachment that are characteristic of a household's relationship to its staple crop. Yet, their simultaneous distance from the centre of the house equally embodies the *distance* that coffee, as both a food for guests and a crop intended for transport, connotes.

Interspersing coffee trees with bananas rather than rigorously segregating the two also points to the fact that the distinction between the two different kinds of coffee – the cash crop and the masticatory – is ambiguous. *Arabica* varieties of coffee must be sold to co-operatives, as only *robusta* varieties can be prepared as *akamwani*. However, even *robusta* coffee can, and indeed, *must* be marketed through the state's co-operatives.[6] Integrating *robusta* coffee trees into the landscape of the family farm can be seen, then, as a way of exerting control over the ultimate purpose of the coffee crop. When *robusta* cherries are harvested in and among the other produce of the farm, some can be diverted for use as *akamwani*, while the rest is prepared for the co-operatives. Again, these spatial arrangements allow for an interpenetration of purposes, an ambiguity that connects with, and is in some ways created by, the connection between cash crops and *akamwani*.

COFFEE AND THE WESTERN WORLD

The ways in which coffee trees are located and cultivated on household farms in Kagera speak to the kinds of connections this particular commodity establishes between local, regional and international worlds. In order for Haya farmers and families to control the effects of this cash crop, there is, I have suggested, a simultaneous attempt made to incorporate the coffee trees into certain intimate dimensions of domesticity and sociality on the one hand and, on the other, to keep them removed from the centres of everyday productivity so as to ensure some sort of independence and integrity. Thus, just as coffee is situated in the lived world of Haya communities, coffee also situates those Haya communities with respect to the wider world of which they are a part. It is a medium that is intrinsically translocal.

The coffee produced by Haya and other 'Third World' farmers also figures prominently in the social imagination of the Europeans and North Americans who are among its consumers. For these consumers it is also the case that coffee formulates and comments on experiences of the interconnections between regional worlds. Coffee provides a substance at once stimulating and sobering that carries with it a taste of the 'exotic' from which it originates. In particular, coffee consumption, like the use of other imported or 'domesticated' foodstuffs, from tea and sugar to pineapples and bananas (cf. Schivelbusch 1992; Sahlins 1988; Schama 1988; Mintz 1985; Austen and Smith 1990), has important implications for the meaningful and material order of class relations in the West, and for the implication of global relations in the construction of those relations. One crucial forum, for example, in and through which this order was concretized in Europe was the coffee-house, which Schivelbusch describes as '*the* site for the public life of the eighteenth-century middle class, a place where the bourgeoisie developed new forms of commerce and culture' (1992: 59).

As a public focus of 'commerce and culture', these eighteenth-century coffee-houses are especially notable for the ways in which they contributed to the development and definition of socio-cultural practices that constitute 'the public sphere' of bourgeois society (Stallybrass and White 1986: 94 ff.). Conducting business in an atmosphere conducive to 'civil' discourse became a hallmark of these institutions. The emblematic example of these commercial and cultural possibilities is Lloyd's coffee-house, established at the end of the seventeenth century (Schivelbusch 1992: 49-51). Lloyd's not only trafficked in a prized medium of overseas commerce, but was especially popular with its agents – shipowners and captains, merchants and insurance brokers. The discussion of trade news characteristic of this clientele promoted the development of a news service that published 'Lloyd's News'. Indeed, coffee-houses in the early eighteenth century often housed offices of journalism, thus concretely linking cornerstones of the public sphere, mercantile commerce and print capitalism. Lloyd's interest in commerce beyond the sale of coffee and newspapers eventually led to its establishment as the renowned institution we know today as Lloyd's of London.

The coffee-house is a crucial institution, not simply because it was the place where commercial interests and public discourses developed, but because it was an especially appropriate site for inculcating the dispositions characteristic of the emergent public sphere through coffee consumption itself. As both a consumer good and a sobering drink, coffee contributes to the constitution of bourgeois selfhood, and the forms of subjectivity that are embedded in the public sphere. Clear-headed rationality, alertness, and restraint were often cited as the (Protestant) virtues of coffee, a 'wakeful and civil drink' (Howell, quoted in Stallybrass and White 1986: 97), virtues that were explicitly contrasted with the unseemly, 'rude', even corpulent, pleasures of ale. Coffee, then, becomes what it remains in many ways in the culture of advanced capitalism, both a sign *of*, and instrument *for* achievement, energy, invigoration, and effort – all essential features of the 'civilized' self. Through the short, sudden burst of energy and concentration it supplies, coffee is the original therapy for the micro-management of bourgeois personality.

Coffee further permits these attitudes, motivations, and dispositions to be objectified in the capitalist reconstruction of time, as 'coffee breaks' become means of temporal reckoning that are routinized in labour practices. Using coffee to mark and *make* time in this way thereby fulfils a capitalist fantasy, providing a respite from work undertaken for the sake of work itself – and thus the direct conversion of 'leisure' into 'productivity' – made possible through the medium of a highly desired, commodified stimulant.

Further, coffee being a commodity, these meanings, experiences, values, effects – in a word, tastes – with which it is imbued, are explicitly situated in the articulation of regional worlds. Coffee not only defines and characterizes critical new features of public interchange, it enters into these interchanges as an unmistakably international commodity. For example, the very word 'coffee', like *café* and *kaffee* (as well as the Swahili term *kahawa*), is derived from *qahveh*, the Turkish pronunciation of the Arabic *qahwah*.

It is also clear that coffee is marked as a distinctly foreign good, one that is differentiated, marketed, and indeed known through a symbolic code of internationalism. Variety, as it presents itself to the coffee consumer, is not formulated in terms of flavour, age, heritage, or botanical stocks, but of countries of origin. These selections and varieties correspond to what James in the previous chapter, 'Cooking the Books', has described as 'an urgent emphasizing of the heterogeneity of cuisines' that is one increasingly characteristic dimension of the globalization of consumption. The internationalism of coffee – especially for the connoisseur – reflects, as James says, 'not a homogenized food culture but, rather, a global familiarity with subtle distinctions . . . between regional specialties across the globe'. Whether downing a cup of Java, or lingering over a mug of Kenya AA, the coffee drinker always selects from among an array of place names that gives him or her a place

101

in an international world of goods. The sensibilities of coffee drinking in the West, whether the desired effect is one of distinction, or camaraderie, are therefore inherently cosmopolitan. The social life of coffee – as commodity, stimulant, and lexical item – 'grounds' the forms and practices of the public sphere, and the subjective dispositions of its habitus, in a wider transnational nexus of signs and transactions.

PRODUCING DOMESTIC SENSIBILITIES

The modes and objectifications of sociality and selfhood embedded in coffee are not restricted to the public sphere, but come to pervade the cultural practices of Western capitalism as coffee itself becomes pervasive. In Germany, which first developed a market for *arabica* in Kagera, coffee became especially important to the development of bourgeois domesticity and, from the mid-eighteenth century onwards, linked that domesticity directly to the Prussian nation.[7] As the colonial plantations of France and Holland were the main sources of coffee in Europe during the eighteenth and nineteenth centuries, the state imposed stiff taxes on coffee to curb the flow of Prussian funds to these colonial powers. Eventually, chicory, grown by 'good German peasants', was developed as a coffee substitute.

This alternative beverage, chicory, lent new meanings to class relations in Germany, as those who cultivated aristocratic tastes continued to brew what became known as real 'bean coffee', while the petty bourgeoisie suffered the indignities of blackened chicory. Moreover, Prussian tax collectors and customs officers in the nineteenth century were popularly known as 'coffee sniffers', an indication of the kinds of intimate scrutiny to which even household relations were subjected. This popular appellation is a testament to the fact that aromatic distinctions between 'bean coffee' and chicory, colonial imports and their domestic counterparts, became central to connections between domestic intimacy and class distinctions. It further reveals the contradictory role of the state in promoting and fostering the development of privileged consumption within a domestic enclave through the intrusive policing of domesticity itself.

Without further research into the final destination of Haya coffee exports in the early twentieth century, it is difficult to say with certainty what its consequences were for colonial experiences of consumption. Still, the place of coffee in European and American social life – of coffee-houses in commercial enterprise, 'bean coffee' in the context of Prussian class relations, and coffee-breaks in the workplace – does suggest certain parallels with Haya concerns. In each case, forms of distinction in publicly recognized social status are demonstrated through the exchange of a medium that carries with it connotations of both familiarity and strangeness. Given these potentials and parallels, it is interesting to note that immigrants to America, especially immigrants from the peripheries of German colonialism within Europe (i.e. Czechs and

Poles) took great pride in having a pot of coffee perpetually brewing on the stove – a source of prestige none could have hoped for in Europe at the time (Levenstein 1988: 106).

These possible connections of coffee production in Kagera to metropolitan households exemplify the ways in which, as the Comaroffs have noted, 'colonialism was as much about making the centre as it was about making the periphery. . . . And the dialectic of domesticity was a vital element in this process' (1992: 293). For just as Haya farming communities use coffee to negotiate their local position in a global economy in ways that have been constrained, but never simply determined, by the forces of the global market, so, too has the presence of coffee – a colonial and post-colonial commodity – in Europe and North America recast dimensions of the public and the private through the practices and experience of the cosmopolitan consumer.

This chapter has explored a series of dialectics, domestic and otherwise, that are characteristic of the production and consumption of coffee. As a central feature of both economy and everyday experience, coffee is a substance that embodies articulations within and across local and global orders. In the construction of class relations, social space, and even bodily intimacy, coffee provides a medium through which connections and disconnections, conjunctures and disjunctures, can be recognized and acted upon. While it is important to appreciate these broad parallels between Haya- and European-lived experiences of this commodity, it is also important to recognize the range of equally seminal differences. Thus, the links that coffee establishes both between rural Haya communities and urban European communities, and within each of those communities, are forged very differently. For example, coffee contributes to the bourgeois forms of selfhood I describe through the cultivation of inner states. Sobriety, work discipline, and self-control are valued cognitive and affective states produced through, and experienced as, an individual's attempts at self-improvement.

Haya consumption of coffee is also concerned with selfhood and identity, in so far as aspects of the self, such as marital, clan and residential status, are constituted through transactions involving coffee. Yet the coffee itself produces these Haya forms of selfhood less through the production of inner states than through the ways in which coffee transactions allow persons effectively to differentiate themselves from those with whom they transact. In other words, coffee contributes to Haya forms of the self through the kinds of *relationships* it institutes with others. These persistent differences in Haya and European understandings of coffee as a medium of sociality and selfhood demonstrate that the increasing globalization of commodity forms does not entail the homogenization of cultural values and practices. It can no longer be presumed that global forces like commoditization lead inevitably to the eradication of specific local meanings, no matter how ostensibly powerful and seductive commodity forms might appear.

Most studies of colonialism and commoditization focus on the agency and symbolic creativity of metropolitan communities – who either impose their vision and values on passive consumers, or extract values and construct meanings from the otherwise inert 'raw materials' provided by the (Third) world's producers. My analysis of coffee has instead demonstrated that coffee 'producers' can also be 'consumers', and that the meanings of *both* production and consumption are mutually constitutive and transformative – for coffee diverted from the world market in order to be prepared as an offering to an affine has obviously had its significance both defined and altered by being treated in this way. In short, the differing trajectories of coffee as a valued object demonstrate the difficulties of neatly distinguishing between producers and consumers, and suggest that the connection between production and consumption is less a clear-cut sequence in economic practice than a multi-stranded and reflexive cultural process. Clearly, *akamwani* offered to an affine and café latté sipped at a food court are not the same substance; but just as plainly, examining coffee as gift and commodity, or cash crop and fine food, as we have done, reveals a complicated dialectic of Haya and European symbolic constructions of the material world.

ACKNOWLEDGEMENTS

The research upon which this chapter is based was made possible by a Fulbright-Hays doctoral dissertation fellowship. The Tanzanian National Institute for Science and Technology (UTAFITI) enabled me to live and work in Tanzania. I am also especially grateful for the tremendous generosity of Severian and Anatolia Ndyetabula. An earlier version of this chapter was presented at the annual meeting of the African Studies Association, Toronto 1994, and has benefited from the comments and questions of that audience. I must also give thanks to David Newbury, Ralph Austen, Katie Bragdon, Bill Fisher and Julie Corsaro for their valuable comments, as well as to David Howes for his editorial work. I am solely responsible for any remaining errors.

NOTES

1 Just over one million Haya live in the Kagera Region, located in the north-west of Tanzania. The Haya form a part of the Interlacustrine socio-cultural area, that includes (among others) the Ganda and Nyoro in Uganda to the north, as well as the indigenous peoples of Rwanda and Burundi to the west and south-west. Haya villages (*ekyaro*) in the rural areas of Kagera, the primary site of the research on which this chapter is based, are composed of a number of family farms (*ekibanja*), which are also places of residence. All the farms within a village are situated immediately adjacent to one another, so that the village as a whole is a contiguous group of households on perennially cultivated land. These residential villages are dispersed across, and clearly contrast with, open grassland (*orweya*). The primary produce of Haya family farms are perennial tree crops, bananas that provide the edible staple, and coffee that provides the main source of money. While coffee remains the most significant (albeit declining) source of cash income in Kagera

today, this cash is filtered through the Haya community in an informal economy (*biashara ndogo ndogo* in Kiswahili) of marketing local produce, beer, household commodities, as well as new and used textiles and clothing at local weekly markets.

2 My data for an admittedly small number of co-operatives suggest that less than one-quarter of the overall number of 'farmers' sell over three-quarters of the total volume of coffee marketed in Kagera. In my sample, of 122,342 kgs of coffee marketed by co-operatives with a total of 481 members, the 97 members (20.1 per cent of membership) marketing the highest volumes of coffee sold 91,823 kgs, or 75.1 per cent of the total volume. This figure, moreover, is skewed by the fact that those who market the greater volumes of coffee are much more likely to be registered as members of several co-operatives. Therefore, the 97 memberships cited above represent many fewer *individuals*, each of whom has multiple memberships. This, in turn, means that an even smaller percentage of individuals controls this share of coffee volume.

3 See Curtis (1989) for a detailed discussion of Haya entrepreneurs in this period.

4 When these rites are performed for ancestral propitiation they also establish a spatial connection between the places of the living and the dead.

5 It could further be argued that the very purpose of blood-brotherhood, again facilitated by coffee cherries, is to mollify potentially hostile relations through an intentionally fabricated intimacy.

6 According to my Haya informants, all coffee is considered the property of the state and must, by law, be sold to co-operatives for marketing. Preparing *akamwani* is a petty, if pervasive, offence.

7 The following discussion of coffee in Germany is taken, in large part, from Schivelbusch (1992: 71–9).

6

SELLING GUATEMALA

Maya export products in US mail-order catalogues

Carol Hendrickson

For over fifteen years I have worked in Guatemala, focusing largely on the subject of Maya weaving and local representations of social identity through dress. About seven years ago, I started clipping and collecting advertisements published in the United States that had something to do with the Maya – ads that contained images of Maya people or Maya-made objects, as well as ones with items that looked as though they might be Maya or that claimed to be inspired by Maya designs. My collecting activities got a substantial boost when a colleague whose name is travelling the 'kula circuit' of mail-order catalogue lists began giving me stacks of these advertisement-books.[1] Among the thousands of objects being sold, I was surprised to find quite a number of products from Guatemala. About the same time, I was teaching from Marianna Torgovnick's *Gone Primitive* and Sally Price's *Primitive Art in Civilized Places*. As a class assignment, I had students locate and talk about representations of 'primitive' objects in the media and, not surprisingly, a number of advertisements were brought in for discussion. At that point I decided that I should look more seriously at the Maya ad-images I had collected.

As Torgovnick (1991: 18–23) and Price (1991: 1–6) characterize the term, Maya products in US mail-order catalogues count as 'things primitive' in the Western world. In keeping with popular contemporary understandings of the primitive, objects are described as being produced in small isolated communities without the benefit of tools and technologies found in other realms (namely the 'West', another term that begs for consideration). In order to fit this bill, Guatemalan mail-order goods are regularly described as coming from small communities – 'village' is, in fact, the preferred term. Thus, for example, Totonicapán, a municipality with a total population of over 62,000, is described in a CARE catalogue as 'a tiny village in Guatemala' (2: 22).[2] Furthermore, words that are rarely used to refer to landscapes in the United States are employed to distance and exoticize the geographic point of origin of the objects. The term 'highlands' is the most common (the redundant 'high altiplano' is also used in one instance [Oxfam America 1992–3: 4]), though a couple of companies have made use of the eco-favourites 'rainforest' and 'jungle' (cf. Torgovnick 1991: 22). In fact, all of these ideas are combined in a text describing a silver necklace and earrings from Cobán (a municipality with over 42,500 people), which claims: 'handmade in a tiny town high above the Guatemalan rainforests' (Signals spring/summer 1993: 22). Finally, the lack of technological sophistication in production methods further emphasizes the idea of the primitive. This idea is conveyed with adjectives such as 'handwoven' or 'handcrafted' and explicitly stated in passages such as: 'Amid an area devastated by civil war, a group of impoverished women from Las Minas, Guatemala are producing beautiful woven garments and table settings with nothing other than the primitive Mayan technology of the backstrap loom' (Save the Children holiday 1993: 37). The accompanying photographs of backstrap looms, intricately-knotted fringes, and irregularly shaped designs formed by tie-dyed threads supply further information on pieces that are seen as visually complex, distant in origin, and yet so 'simple' in their production that they can be made at home with little more than sticks and string.

While some of the characterizations of products strike me as 'just a little "off"', in Torgovnick's (1991: ix) words – especially when compared to what I know from Guatemala – that, of course, is not the point. As Torgovnick sees it, the term 'primitive' is 'by nature and in effect inexact or composite: it conforms to no single social or geographical entity and, indeed, habitually and some-times wilfully confuses the attributes of different societies' (1991: 22). While this characterization does not seem to fit the Guatemalan–Maya material exactly – after all the pieces have very specific geographic and/or cultural labels – it is true that the terms used to describe individual objects can be all over the map, so to speak. (Recall the use of the term 'jungle' that I mentioned earlier.) What is more, while the Maya objects for sale in the United States may be tied in a buyer's mind to their foreign points of production, the meanings and uses of these goods have generally been reframed within the space of a catalogue in anticipation of the knowledge, desires, and lifestyle of the new consumers. Thus, what might be first and foremost a belt in Guatemalan contexts (and even here I hesitate because uses and meanings of objects in the highlands are certainly not static or narrowly defined and their users not purely Maya; nor is it uninteresting to Guatemalans how these objects are used abroad) in the United States may become a pair of suspenders or a dog collar and leash. In a similar reframing of issues, Guatemalan textiles get paired up with political and environmental issues of varying specificity. Indeed, as Micaela di Leonardo points out (1990: 534–5), many of the societies producing objects that so closely conform to Western notions of the 'primitive' are 'peasant' in traditional social scientific terms. However, what di Leonardo takes as a misuse of terms, I understand to be 'a second-generation view of the subject', using Price's characterization of a contemporary understanding of 'primitive art' (1991: 4), one removed from the definitions of academics but alive and well in the realm of popular culture.

In *Gone Primitive* Torgovnick asks, 'Will postmodernism end Western lust for things primitive?' and responds in the negative with the comment that:

the evocation of the primitive is bound to become ever more wilful, ever more dependent upon striking a deal – based on mutual pretense – satisfactory to both partners who participate in its creation: the 'them' so much more like us now, and us, often garbed in clothing and living amid objects that evoke 'their' traditional forms of life.

(1991: 38)

'Our' (re)presentations of 'their' traditional forms of life, like those of their handwork in the catalogues, are translations of uses and contexts of use. I want to turn now to a consideration of some of the key themes that arise from the catalogue images and/or written text, but first I want to say a word about my methodology and the goals of this chapter.

I can only estimate that I have looked at over 350 mail-order catalogues since 1991. From this group I have located mailings from over forty companies that contain merchandise that I would label primitive in Torgovnick's sense. These sell 'authentic', handcrafted products and/or 'look-alikes' inspired by ancient or contemporary primitive designs. Within this group, twenty-eight companies sell at least one product with the label 'Guatemala' or 'Maya' attached to it; and within the Guatemala/Maya group I have focused on the twenty-seven that sell textiles and other sorts of 'craft' products. (This excludes one company that only sells Guatemalan coffee.) The companies in this group of twenty-seven range from dominant, mainstream, for-profit, mail-order merchandisers like L.L. Bean and Victoria's Secret (where explicit political and educational messages are non-existent) to international, non-profit, development-oriented organizations like Oxfam and the Paraclete Society (which use catalogues as politico–educational as well as marketing tools). An organization like the One World Trading Company is an extreme case of this latter sort (specializing in Guatemalan products and striving to educate its clientele on the social and political ills of that country), while Robert Redford's Sundance mail-order catalogue employs a kinder, gentler approach to educating its customers. Originally focused on the theme and products of the American West, in the early 1990s Sundance expanded its offerings to reflect 'a diversity of cultures, traditions, and artistry' – including the Maya – because it 'found that the same spirit of creativity and pride in handcrafted workmanship is shared by artisans internationally' (spring 1993: 2).[3] Here, as in other places, the Maya get lumped as Indians or natives or, even more generally, natural-craftspeople-and-kindred-spirits (if not blood relatives) to similar types around the world.[4]

What I did next was to examine the texts and photographs describing and surrounding the Guatemalan products and draw from them key themes. I am interested in particular words used (or not used) in discussing the products, recurrent phrasings and images, explicit or implicit references to social and political issues, ties between the Maya or Guatemala and other social groups or areas of the world, and links among these issues that take place via the product. I realize that there are substantial differences among the catalogues, ones that relate to but do not necessarily completely coincide with the profit-to-non-profit continuum. As Carrier (1990) points out, the differences can be seen to fall along two important axes. One has to do with the degree to which catalogues elaborate on their images of the products beyond a basic material description, whether this is in words or pictures. At one extreme, Carrier sees catalogue companies providing a 'simple portrayal of their wares, their significant technical features, and their prices . . . [without] the objects in use or in association with different sorts of people' (1990: 696). Of the material I collected, the text (but not the picture) of a skirt sold in Victoria's Secret (spring 1991: 89) most closely adheres to a strict product-oriented description: 'Patterned (99) sarong style skirt, in soft Guatemalan blanket cotton. Waist has elastic insets. S,M,L. JM430-025 Reg. $88. Sale $49'. The picture in this case does not give real information on Guatemala, but its use of a fashion model, leg bared above the knee, provides a particular gendered image of how the prospective buyer can imagine herself in the clothes (cf. Young 1994). At the other extreme, Carrier sees catalogue companies that, by virtue of word and image, 'tell with images of specific people and of personalized social relation-ships'(1990: 697). It is in this more socialized sphere of presentation that Carrier sees another axis of meanings come into play, one that has to do with 'differences in the class, culture, and gender imagery that advertisers invoke in their publications' (1990: 696). (To this list I would add issues of race, age, and politics, all of which play out in important ways in the Maya–Guatemalan cases.) For Carrier, however, these differences in presentation work toward a more unified goal: he sees catalogues functioning to convert alienated commodities into possessions with personal identities all their own (1990: 693). Leaving aside the issue of how consumers themselves appropriate mail-order merchandise, Carrier focuses on the 'imagery of possession' in the catalogues themselves, claiming that 'if the imagery . . . in these catalogues does make the objects advertised seem less impersonal, then those who buy them will be acquiring things that fit their notion of "possession" more closely than would things that were not wrapped in this symbolism' (1990: 702).

Carrier's argument reminds me of a point made by Michael Taussig in his discussion of fetishism, animism, and post-capitalist animism as related phenomena. Taussig argues that:

> 'fetishism' as Marx used that term in *Capital* . . . refer[s] to the cultural attribution of a spiritual, even godlike, quality to commodities, objects bought and sold on the market standing over their very producers. He could just as well have used the term 'animism'. Under capitalism the animate quality of objects is a result of the radical estrangement of the economy from the person; no longer is man the aim of production, but production is the aim of man, and wealth-getting the aim of

production... *Post*-capitalist animism means that although the socio-economic exploitative function of fetishism... will supposedly disappear with the overcoming of capitalism, fetishism as an active social force inherent in objects will remain. Indeed it must not disappear, for it is the animate quality of things in post-capitalist society without the 'banking' mode of perception that ensures what the young Marx envisaged as the humanization of the world.

(1993: 98–9)

While the 'banking' mode of exchange certainly lives on in the world of mail-order catalogues, it is a common tack in the sale of Guatemalan goods to emphasize the people behind the creations, their spirit in the goods, the spirit *of* the goods, and the 'touch' between people via handmade objects.[5] My goal, then, is to locate a set of visual and verbal images that predominate in the catalogues, images that are constructed by the sellers to enliven the goods and convince the buyer that it is the product that has the active capacity to create a social relationship across cultures. While these themes are not absolutely uniform in all the examples (nor any one theme necessarily found in each product description), I believe that they are common enough across the lot to make this examination worthwhile.

At this point, my analysis focuses more on the verbal than the visual dimensions of the advertisements. When I started this investigation, I thought that there was a great deal more play going on in the written texts than in the images, with obvious links to current social issues in the West and to commentary on the primitive and so-called traditional arts and crafts. The visual images in the catalogues seemed unremarkable and out of touch with the new wave of commodity images that I saw in some of the more expensive print campaigns appearing in fashion and news magazines, images that demand new ways of 'reading' and products that gain meaning from 'opaque and ambiguous ads' (Goldman 1992: 3). Instead, the catalogue images appeared to be examples of the transparent frames of advertisements from an earlier era, ones that exhibited straightforward representations of objects pictured alone or used in obvious ways, and that called upon predictable 'reading' skills.

I recognize now that the 'realist' images have encoded within them a large number of cultural assumptions associated with documentary photography (or drawing, in one instance) and that some link with the representation of the primitive in Western photographic history (cf. Feld 1982: 233–6; Lutz and Collins 1993). Some images, for example, present products with no models, no props, and, often, only the background colour of the catalogue page. Others have models wearing the pieces or items laid on chairs, tables and floors, some with background scenery and others, again, with just the background colour of the page. In a few instances, there are also shots taken in Guatemala that illustrate production techniques or give a general sense of the place of origin of the goods. All of these sharp-focus, no-nonsense photographs of the merchandise, producers and places of production help document the existence of the objects, their pedigree as made by 'real Indians', and/or their visual-material qualities. The different photographs and accompanying texts can also be seen as referring to two vastly different worlds that are then used by the catalogue company to move their products from a sphere of production into a different sphere of consumption. Let me explain.

One of the worlds that is created by images and text is 'out there' and unknown to a good percentage of buyers. (I can only guess that the majority of potential purchasers have not visited Guatemala and, even among those that have, a brief trip may only have reinforced the foreignness of the place.) This other world is constructed by the occasional use of photographs taken in Guatemala and, more commonly, by the textual material describing the producers of the goods, their history, where they live, and other personalizing details. These photographs and verbal descriptions enlarge the knowledge of potential consumers and draw them closer to the situation of the Maya: they also animate the products and create a social relation between producers and buyers in order to move the object closer to the sale.

Products, thus imbued with an aura of another world, are then moved into the everyday world of the prospective buyer (or, at least, some version of what a prospective buyer might like that everyday world to be). Photographs that show models and text that gives 'practical' information (sizes, price, etc.) suggest use values for the items, work to establish compatibility with consumers (e.g. 'it will fit me and make me look good'), and enable readers to determine if they can afford a piece. Photographs, in particular, are important in establishing the immediacy of these items – their tactile qualities, their 'there-ness' – which makes the next logical step, the purchase, not only desirable but somehow 'natural'.[6]

In the rest of this chapter, I map out some of the key themes encoded on Maya–Guatemalan products in mail-order catalogues. In doing so I hope to point out the creative capacities of advertisements, their appeal to and power over consumers, and the energy and insight it takes to 'read' commodity images in a cultural/political way.

INTIMACY AND FAMILIARITY

Intimacy and familiarity with the products and their producers come in various forms: the objects cuddle up to you or are introduced in such specific detail that you need to buy them to continue that relationship. In some cases the use of first and second person pronoun helps: suspenders, for example, are 'handwoven for you' (CARE volume 3: 24) and the little figures on Worry Doll belts and pins say 'Tell us your worries and we'll whisk them away' (Seasons spring 1993: 7). The companies marketing the goods *care* for the objects, the people who produce them, and you as a customer. In return the people whose goods are being marketed give us the gift of their insights on life. A Pueblo to People catalogue opens with a 'Dear Friends' letter and the observation that 'Huichol, Quiche, Mam, Cakchiquel, Kekchi, Tzutuhil, Quechua [the middle five groups are Maya] – through their crafts they share with us some of their vision of the universe' (summer 1991: 2).

Objects are also described with cultural and geographic specificity: you get to know the people, places and production processes in the comfort of your own home. A fairly widespread practice is to identify the product with its place of origin. For example, you can buy 'Nebaj suspenders, hat, and bag' (Daily Planet early spring 1995: 23), a 'San Lucas Village Moon Vest' (Smithsonian spring 1993: 54), a 'Todos Santos duffel' (Sundance fall 1992: 15), 'Cotzal shawl' (Oxfam America 1992–3: 11), or 'Toto Ikat Pillows' (CARE 3: 28).[7] In this way you are provided with a map of the highlands and given a sense of familiarity with the origin of the object. Co-operative efforts, an idea that resonates well with a Western concept of indigenous 'community and earth-connectedness' (Pueblo to People summer 1991: 2), are likewise named and their work described: for example, the Aj Quen Co-operative (Oxfam America 1992–3: 10), the Asociación Maya de Desarrollo (Paraclete Society International 1992–3), and Los Artesanos de San Juan (Pueblo to People spring 1993: 2).

As I mentioned earlier, in a few instances, photographs of colourful Guatemalan scenes – young girls at Lake Atitlán (Oxfam America 1992–3: 5) or a weaver at a backstrap loom (Oxfam America 1992–3: 10; Pueblo to People summer 1988: 8) – accompany the product images and introduce the shopper to the producers (usually labelled with the more honorific terms 'craftspeople' and 'artists') as well as the world in which their products are made. Though the specific items being sold usually do not appear in these country images, the sense none the less is that the prospective buyer is drawing closer to some real understanding of the production and social processes made material in a bag, shirt or place mat.

AUTHENTICITY, TRADITION, AND UNIQUENESS

While the words 'authentic' and 'genuine' are virtually absent from the product descriptions, the spirit of these concepts is reflected in the photographs and the accompanying texts. The words 'tradition' and 'traditional' are repeatedly invoked, as in: 'Guatemala has a rich tradition of weaving', used in the description of a placemat and napkin set (CARE volume 2: 9), and 'traditional village motifs', used to describe a vest (Smithsonian spring 1993: 54). A claim such as 'hand-loomed by Central American craftsmen whose skills have been passed down from generation to generation' (L.L. Bean spring 1991: 32) makes a roughly equivalent reference to tradition, but personalizes and dramatizes it with the idea of generations of skilled artisans. Reference to age and continuity also secures this notion: for example, an apron is described as 'woven in the highlands of Guatemala by descendants of the Mayans' (CARE volume 2: 8) and a pillow with designs 'based on traditional patterns woven for centuries by the Chimaltenango Indians of Guatemala' (CARE volume 2: 23). These words elicit visions of a past – a common territory for advertisements, according to Berger (1983: 130) – as well as distant places where life is different . . . thick with history and rich with traditions.[8]

The products are also frequently described as 'unique' or 'one-of-a-kind', with some descriptions using multiple adjectives to stress this: 'It's definitely distinctive, and its individually woven centerpiece makes each one unique' (Sundance fall 1992: 15). These references to uniqueness call to mind several related topics: (1) the irregularities and slight variations that mark handcrafted work – explained in one catalogue as: 'Handmade means unique . . . No two items are exactly alike' (Paraclete Society International 1992–3), (2) the cultural pedigree of the craftspeople and the link between the creators' heritage and the singular statement of handmade objects, and (3) the relationship of these pieces to works of fine art – as in 'a unique piece of art' (Daily Planet early spring 1995: 36). In addition to these characteristics of the object, some catalogues also pledge to do their part to preserve the distinctiveness of a people and a product. The more socially-oriented of the catalogue companies market goods so that the people who produce them can retain their culture, a livelihood and health: for example, a passage in a brochure from the Paraclete Society states that 'the weaving project was requested by Jakaltek families wanting to protect local designs and weaving traditions' (1992–3). A Sundance catalogue, on the other hand, offers 'childhood favourites in cowboy patchwork: a unique teddy, made in Guatemala [of patchworked fabric] exclusively for Sundance' (fall 1992: 44). In this instance, the catalogue text associates the singularity of the foreign product with the exclusivity of the supplier. What is left unsaid is the fact that the purportedly unique objects must be made many times over to supply the hundreds of customers, each ordering his or her 'unique piece of art'.[9]

Some might argue that these 'traditional', 'unique' pieces offer US consumers a real alternative to the overwhelming imitation in their lives in an America with 'no origin or mythical authenticity' (Baudrillard 1988: 76; cf. Bruner 1994: 397). Others, however, make a more positive assessment of these consumers' condition, recognizing people's active search for and recognition of values and history in specific social contexts (cf. Bruner 1994). Taking this position, I would argue that while perhaps not representing 'our' history and tradition, the Maya objects none the less allow buyers to contemplate and appreciate a set of values related to their own. It seems to me that most of the catalogues foster this experience of cultural reflexivity . . . an inward contemplation, with a possibility for recognition and change. Among the subset of catalogue companies that explicitly address social issues 'out there', there is the additional encouragement to think of others and to support people living in another culture with a purchase.

LEISURE, PLEASURE AND PLAY

The association between Maya products and the consumer's leisure time or casual lifestyle is not uniform, but I think that it is an important theme. Colours described as 'bold' (CARE volume 3: 30) and 'vibrant' (Sundance fall 1992: 29) mark these products as belonging to the Western sphere of recreational activities rather than work (cf. Sahlins 1976: 186–8). Adjectives like 'festive' (Eddie Bauer Home Collection February 1993: 47; Signals spring 1994: 21C) and 'easy to wear' (Maya Jones Imports 1993: 3) also contribute to the theme.

What is more, there are verbal and visual associations with leisure, a casual lifestyle and youth (see Figure 9). A young, barefoot woman in a 'comfy jumpsuit' models what is described as a 'funky headband . . . . A great, cool look' (Daily Planet winter 1992: 10). A photograph in an L.L. Bean catalogue shows a young woman with a bicycle in the country, dressed in shorts, a T-shirt, and a 'handwoven Guatemalan vest' (spring 1991: 32). And Sundance catalogues show a 'cowboy patchwork blanket' made from Guatemalan fabric thrown over a paddock fence, with text describing a night spent sleeping under the stars and under the blanket (spring 1993: 36). (A cowboy would probably be in a work mode in such a situation, but presumably the person who purchases the blanket would not.) In addition, domestic settings for Maya-made products are suggested in a few instances by photographs of products draped on wooden dressers and wrought-iron beds (CARE volume 3: 24–5; Sundance fall 1992: 19).

Class elements emerge more or less ambiguously within this leisure frame. Some settings – for example, a table with table runner, flower arrangement and wine glasses – are modest but hint of a cultured lifestyle as well as a knowledge of tasteful, high fashion display (e.g. Oxfam 1992–3: 4), while other photographs leave open the question of whether the setting is a vacation home or someone's permanent rustic residence. Class and leisure issues, I would argue, are expressed differently within frames geared to youth. Daily Planet employs younger adult models often posed in unconventional postures, such as seeming to dangle from vines on a 'rainforest' page (winter 1992: 10–11). They are playful – smiling, gesturing and hugging – and they are also set to travel, vicariously through their purchases or in earnest in their photojournalist's vest and Guatemalan cargo pants (winter 1992: 6).

The subject of leisure in these catalogues – not unemployment, but a freedom from care – is also tied with pleasure: the pleasure of seeing beautiful handmade objects, the joyful anticipation of possible ownership and use of socialized possessions (in Carrier's sense), and, in some cases, the pleasure of helping others through a purchase. Play is also important here, not only in the sense of the leisure activities that are part of the catalogues' presentations, but also the creative play going on in the catalogue pages among cultures, time frames and causes. I return to this subject in the section on cultural bricolage,

Figure 9 'The blazing colors of the Central American rainforests'

but first I want to consider how very serious issues of human rights and survival enter into the merchandise world.

THE COMMODIFICATION OF POLITICAL–SOCIAL CAUSES AND CONCERNS

Roughly a third of the catalogues I have identified as selling Guatemalan products express concern for the lives of the producers, and these concerns are tied to 'the sell'. For example, marketing strategies that link environmental issues to products are popular today. However, while there is the occasional tie between, say, a Guatemalan product and the mention of rainforests – for example, what the *Daily Planet* catalogue labels its 'Fabulous Jungle Jumpsuit and Ikat Pants: Direct from the rainforests' (early spring 1994: 29), it is more common to find Guatemalan goods on the same pages with other, more 'genuine' rainforest items than immediately tied to these ecological issues. In fact, Guatemala has a basic problem when it comes to using a rainforest marketing strategy: the Maya who produce the export goods generally live far from the areas considered rainforest.

This is a small point that, I think, could be easily overlooked if it were not also the case that for the past fifteen years (if not for the past five hundred years) the Maya have been seen as victims of internal violence and prejudice. This means that the repression and struggle of Guatemala's indigenous peoples often, but by no means always, take over as the dominant political motifs associated with the products. As I mentioned earlier, there are whole catalogues and companies devoted to marketing goods made by victims of the violence and harsh economic conditions in Guatemala or Mesoamerica. These catalogues have explicit political missions often expressed in an abbreviated way in their names, such as Pueblo to People, One World Trading Company, and The Paraclete Society – with the word 'paraclete' said to be from a Greek term meaning 'advocate' (*Chicago Tribune* 15 November 1992) – and in more elaborate ways in mission statements and other commentary accompanying the mail-order products. In these instances, photographs that document the more violent realities of the people involved are virtually never used.

At the other end of the political–social spectrum are companies that exhibit only a passing awareness of Guatemala and the Maya – indeed, they use those names to help market their goods, but make no mention of current affairs or claim to be aiding the people. Companies in this category include such mainstream giants as L.L. Bean and Eddie Bauer, as well as smaller places such as Northern Sun Merchandising (which bills itself as selling 'products for progressives'). Other companies 'in between' show relatively little awareness of specific problems, but rather have a generalized orientation toward social causes. The proceeds from the Daily Planet and Sundance, for example, support various arts and social concerns.

Somewhat ironically, a significant subset of the catalogues I have been examining present the harsh economic and political realities of Guatemala in the same space that they encourage the products' use for the much wealthier foreign consumers' leisure activities. This seemingly impossible task, however, is only one of the balancing acts accomplished within the catalogues. Issues are played off against one another (in the most serious sense of the word 'play') to create a multi-functional, multi-vocal and multi-cultural display: I discuss this under the label 'cultural bricolage'.

CULTURAL BRICOLAGE

Some catalogues avoid country-specific, political agendas yet still have their cultural messages to sell. Instead of describing situations of past or present conflict, these may build on more positive notions of transnational and transcultural affinities among peoples. In an article on 'Authenticity', Richard Handler draws parallels between nationalist and culturalist ideologies and writes that 'cultures, in our common sense, are the individuated entities of world society, just as, in our commonsense understanding of political reality, nations are the individual actors of international or world politics' (1986: 2). Nations have cultures that define them and make their boundaries meaningful. This idea gets played out in mail-order catalogues in terms of a country-label like 'Guatemala' virtually always signalling that the product is made by Maya – *is* Maya – rather than any of the other 4.5 million people who live in the country.

A problem arises with this equation, however, if you allow that some segment of 'their' national population is oppressive, that 'we' of European descent bear some responsibility for the processes of domination and coercion in the New World, and that, in general, a certain segment of the world population has lost its 'spiritual connection with Mother Earth' (Pueblo to People summer 1991: 2). Because of this split between ethnically and spiritually-endowed 'haves' and 'have-nots', boundaries get reshuffled and groups emerge that are transnational and transcultural. A couple of examples illustrate these group formations: in Pueblo to People, an opening letter states that '"Indian" is such a strange word, its very origins an error.... All it really means is "those who were here before us and still remember who they are"' (1991: 2). The Sundance catalogue embraces an even wider range: 'More and more, we seek to complement the art of Native Americans and western craftspeople with examples from around the world, trusting that the diversity of cultures, traditions, and artistry will enrich our catalogue as it does our lives' (spring 1993: 2).

In some cases, not only is merchandise from different cultures and nations brought together and sold side by side, but products from one are characterized in terms of another. For example, crocheted berets from Guatemala come in 'rasta colours' (Northern Sun Merchandising fall/winter 1992–3: 30); a 'painter's jacket' of Guatemalan tie-dyed cloth is cut 'kimono-style' (Oxfam

1993–4: 34); and a Guatemalan shirt 'evokes the art of the American South-west' (Wireless early summer 1993: 30). Ties with the western or south-western US seem to be particularly popular. A blanket pieced from various Guatemalan fabrics is described as follows:

> Cowboy Patch Blanket. Our thick patchwork quilt's scores of colorful hand-woven Guatemalan fabrics recreate the spirit of the west. With a simple black and white reverse, this treasure will be at home on the range or in your home.
>
> (Daily Planet early spring 1994: 35)[10]

In a few instances, these cross-cultural themes also get played out with the models, some of whose features mark them as 'non-white' and 'ethnically other', though not particularly 'Guatemalan' (cf. the Paraclete Society cata-logues as well as recent mailings from Pueblo to People).[11]

The degree to which catalogues indulge in this cultural bricolage seems to depend on the sort of 'ethnographic authority' being constructed in the pages of the catalogue. As Torgovnick (1991: 23) points out, the authority to make claims about 'primitives' is validated in various ways in late twentieth-century scholarship, and the same, I would say, is true in the mail-order business. Catalogue appeals for political causes may convincingly employ a narrow focus on academically-defined ethnic groups, nations, or regions, while appeals for a more spiritual, popular understanding gain force by blending cultural references and constructing groups according to what are seen as similar sensitivities and/or historically distant ties.

CONCLUSION

The mail-order catalogues and the merchandising strategies I have just discussed are playful as well as serious. They often bring to the attention of consumers new information and insights, and often work to establish a relationship between producers and buyers; yet, at the same time, the catalogues limit and organize consumer knowledge in order to make a sale. For the catalogues that promote more than 'mere' merchandise – for the ones that go beyond the products and relate significant information on their producers as well as promote political issues – there is also the question of effecting change through the marketplace ... celebrating the 'active social force inherent in objects', about which Taussig writes (1993: 99), but still within a 'banking' frame: upholding local traditions while catering to Western tastes, and defining consumer support for causes in terms of market 'votes' (equating support with dollars spent).

In the case of the Guatemalan products sold through mail-order catalogues, consumers sometimes *are* made more aware of the situation in that country and Maya *do* earn money from these businesses. However, in each case Maya causes need to be tailored to sell to foreign audiences, and individual products cannot become too connected with the horror of the country of their origin. Furthermore, to my knowledge, financial arrangements and product control (thread quality, colour schemes, uniformity of size, etc.) are generally not in the hands of the local producers but, rather, organized and determined by local or international third parties. This situation, however, seems to be changing by degrees as 'they' become 'so much more like us now' (in the words that I quoted from Torgovnick earlier) – so much more educated and market-wise – and 'we' in the West continue to be seduced by their objects and the images of 'their traditional forms of life'.

ACKNOWLEDGEMENTS

I want to thank Dana Howell for her seemingly endless offerings of catalogues and comments, without which this paper would never have been written. I would also like to thank David Howes for his insights and encouragement on the rewrite of what was originally a paper delivered at the 1993 meetings of the American Ethnological Society. Thanks also to Kate Ratcliff for her helpful suggestions on the penultimate draft.

APPENDIX: LIST OF CATALOGUES WITH PRODUCTS LABELLED 'MAYA' AND/OR 'GUATEMALAN'

Art Institute of Chicago: holiday 1992–3; 1993/1994
L.L. Bean: spring 1991
CARE Package Catalogue: volumes 2, 3
Carroll Reed: spring 1995
Company of Women: holiday 1993
Daily Planet: winter 1992; summer 1992; fall/winter 1992; spring/summer 1993; fall/winter 1993; holiday I 1993; early spring 1994; late spring 1994; fall 1994; fall/winter 1994; holiday I 1994; early spring 1995
Eddie Bauer Home Collection: February 1993
Maya Jones Imports: 1993
Miller Stockman: winter 1991
Mystic Trader: 1994
Northern Sun Merchandising: fall/winter 1992–3
One World Trading Co.: spring/summer 1988; fall/winter 1988
Oxfam America: 1992–3; 1993–4
Paraclete Society International: 1992–3; 1993–4
Pueblo to People: summer 1988; spring 1989; summer 1991; spring 1993
Red Rose Collection: fall 1991; holiday 1991; early spring 1993
Save the Children: holiday 1991; holiday 1993
Seasons: spring 1993; spring/summer 1993; summer 1993
Signals: spring/summer 1993; summer 1993; early spring 1994
Smithsonian: holiday 1992; spring 1993; holiday 1994; summer 1995

Solutions: holiday 1992 (coffee)

Sundance: fall 1992; winter 1993; spring 1993

Trade Wind: fall/winter 1992 (This 1992 catalogue was mailed again in 1994 with a new letter.)

Tweeds: 1990

UNICEF: fall/winter 1994

Victoria's Secret: spring 1991

What on Earth: autumn 1992

Wireless: early summer 1993; summer 1993; fall/winter 1993; fall/winter II 1993; holiday 1993; early summer 1994; early spring 1995

NOTES

1 In *Advertising Fictions: Literature, Advertisement, and Social Reading*, Jennifer Wicke points out that advertising arose concurrently with the novel in the nineteenth century (1988: 1), and that advertisements first appeared in the front of books. Contemporary mail-order catalogues might not be literature in any conventional understanding of the term, but they certainly take on qualities of the genre with themes organizing different pages or sections (chapters?), progressions of themes/narratives from page to page, and the involvement of central characters (often the owner(s) of the business, but also others – as in the frequent appearance of unnamed models and various 'we's' and 'I's'). Illustrations (photographic or otherwise) that do not seem to relate directly to the price tag of the products may add to the feeling of 'story' rather than 'sales'.

2 Note that a number of the catalogues selling 'authentic' Guatemalan products use less-than-authentic place names because of inappropriate Spanish orthography. Totonicapán appears as 'Totonicapan' in the CARE catalogue: in other catalogues Atitlán appears as 'Atitlan', Patzún as 'Patzun', while other terms are hypercorrected (e.g., 'Nebáj', instead of Nebaj, and 'jaspé' [tie-dyed threads], instead of jaspe). Other spellings have compounded problems: for example, 'San Antonio de Aqua Caliente' for San Antonio Aguas Calientes (What on Earth autumn 1992: 40). Jane Hill (1993: 162) writes on similar orthographic failures in the use of what she calls Nouvelle Southwest (US) Anglo-Spanish.

3 Since I first wrote this paper, Sundance has taken another marketing turn. Guatemalan goods are now completely absent from the catalogue. In his fall 1994 opening letter, Redford talks about the common heritage of all craftspeople, yet he mentions only groups who live or lived within what is now the United States – 'the ancient Anasazi' and 'potters and sculptors working in their studios in New York or Santa Fe' (1994: 2). While a number of the Sundance pieces hail from places far removed from the Southwest (e.g. India, Bali, and Egypt), their other-worldliness is not emphasized. In fact a unifying theme seems to be the products' adherence to a colour aesthetic in which muted 'earth tones', especially an array of browns, predominate. This makes the more colourful Guatemalan pieces that they used to market now seem out of place.

4 Purveyors of catalogue merchandise are certainly not the only ones with a habit of lumping diverse people under broad labels. Roseberry (1991: 56) notes that writers on the moral economy of peasants – people with an explicit interest in promoting a new theory of consciousness – none the less 'treat the peasant or artisan past in unambiguous, uncritical terms', drawing examples uncritically from a variety of societies and different historical moments.

5 A good example of 'the spirit *of* the goods' appears in a Trade Wind catalogue. It states: 'the idea that clothing can have a life of its own has been common to Mayan weavers for centuries' (1992: 2).

6 Berger tells us that the colour images of advertisements, like oil paintings of earlier years, 'play upon the spectator's sense of acquiring the *real* thing which the image shows. In both cases, his feeling that he can almost touch what is in the image reminds him how he might or does possess the real thing' (1983: 141). Taussig could add that 'the eye grasps at what the hand cannot touch' (1993: 183).

7 The use of Toto, the local term for Totonicapán, further emphasizes a familiarity with the place.

8 This phrasing has its roots in L.P. Hartley's statement: 'The past is a foreign country; they do things differently there' (quoted in Lowenthal 1990: xvi). For the case of Guatemala and Maya handwork, however, I would rephrase the idea: 'Guatemala is both the past *and* a foreign country; they do things differently there; and we want to buy what they do/make.'

9 Note also that the medium by which we know of these unique works of art depends on mechanical reproduction (cf. Benjamin 1969).

10 A virtually identical blanket appears in the Sundance catalogue. It remains a 'cowboy patchwork' (complete with scenario for its use) though explicit mention of the West is lost:

> Cowboy patchwork blanket. A cowboy sleeps under the stars – and his favorite patchwork blanket. Ours is made of brightly colored, handwoven Guatemalan cotton patches, reversing to a single striped fabric. Each blanket is unique, with variations in the weave.
>
> (Sundance spring 1993: 36)

11 These multi-cultural models generally do not look like they are professional mannequins.

Part III

CONSUMPTION AND IDENTITY

7

NEGOTIATING IDENTITIES IN QUITO'S CULTURAL BORDERLANDS

Native women's performances for the Ecuadorean tourist market

Mary M. Crain

During the late 1950s, tourism was increasingly promoted as a viable development strategy for many Third World nations, with many international agencies arguing that it constituted a passport for development. Subsequent literature, however, espouses a much more critical view of the role of international tourism in Third World contexts, arguing that touristic practices often mirror colonial relations and reproduce relations of inequality, as distinctions based on gender, race and class frequently divide Third World touristic workers on the receiving end from their foreign 'guests' (cf. Crick 1989; Enloe 1990; MacCannell 1989). Similarly, the structural contrasts which underlie touristic practices, such as those of work versus play, suggest patterns of domination, as an industry which provides relatively unskilled and low-paying jobs for some, often serves as a playground and as a site of pleasure for others.

According to Dean MacCannell (1989) contemporary tourism constitutes a modern ritual, one that is analogous to the performance of sacred rites in pre-modern societies and it entails the Western subject's search for 'authenticity' in 'other cultures', 'other places', and 'other historical periods' (cf. also Urry 1990). While the search for authenticity may be only one of many motives underlying touristic practices, what is also pertinent to the case to be considered here is the role of tourism as a 'commodity-sign', operating within circuits of consumption which organize social life and produce meanings in contemporary post-industrial societies. Today, practices of consumption constitute one of the means by which social groups construct diverse identities and selves (cf. Bourdieu 1984; de Certeau 1984; Hebdige 1979; Urry 1990; Fiske 1989). Touristic consumption frequently relies on gender differences, on culturally constructed notions of 'femininity' and 'masculinity', in order to establish meanings, that make the touristic experience appealing to diverse audiences (cf. Enloe 1990: 32). Ethnic tourism often proceeds by appropriating

125

non-Western cultural forms, objects and peoples, and recoding them for public consumption. In the process of this recoding, 'native traditions' are inevitably disassembled and rearranged, in order to ultimately recreate an apparent semblance of 'authenticity'. Such semiotic appropriations, which frequently emerge in touristic contexts, are often artificial, aesthetic purifications of 'tradition' (cf. Clifford 1988). This reworking of ethnic attributes is well-captured by MacCannell's term, 'reconstructed ethnicity', which refers to 'the maintenance and preservation of ethnic forms for the persuasion or entertainment . . . of a "generalized other" within a white cultural frame' (1992: 168).

The preceding comments inform my discussion of the emergence of various forms of 'ethnic tourism' in highland Ecuador during the past three decades. To illuminate this shift towards tourism, conceptualized as a 'discourse of development', I turn to a consideration of one touristic venture in particular, an undertaking that linked Native American women in the highland community of Quimsa in the Ecuadorean Andes, with employment in an international tourist hotel in the nation's capital. This case sheds light on the manner in which relations of inequality underlie touristic practices, as I demonstrate that aspects of the unfree servile relations characteristic both of the colonial era and the subsequent hierarchical hacienda system in Quimsa provided a symbolic model for the contractual labour relations established between these Indian women and the management operating the luxury hotel. Thus, my analysis points to certain correspondences between the experiences of contemporary ethnic tourism and the experience of colonialism (cf. Rosaldo 1989).

Arguing that gender and ethnicity be regarded as performative constructs (cf. Carr 1993; Taylor 1994), this analysis illuminates native women's calculated enactment of their identities in a manner which resonated with dominant stereotypes regarding 'Indianness' circulating in metropolitan Quito. I attend not only to the ability of 'the powerful' to reconfigure subordinate identities, but also to the agency of native women, who, while drawn into unequal relations not of their own choosing, were not passive subjects but actively reshaped hierarchical relations to their advantage. They accomplished this via a self-conscious representation of their gender and ethnic identities in the urban setting, a new self-fashioning designed to win them favours and extend their employment opportunities in the urban marketplace.

Finally, I pose the question of why, given specific contexts and particular audiences, these indigenous women might pursue essentializing strategies, by engaging in practices of 'reverse orientalism'. However, before exploring these issues in greater detail, I provide a brief ethnographic background. The following pages describe traditional agrarian relations in Ecuador and delineate significant political changes occurring during the 1960s, and subsequently, which opened a space for various touristic ventures.

TRANSFORMATIONS IN TRADITIONAL AGRARIAN SOCIETY AND THE EMERGENCE OF TOURISTIC VENTURES

During the late 1950s, the area of the northern highlands, which encompasses the community of Quimsa, was dominated by vast haciendas. A large peasant population, living close to the subsistence level, was attached to each of these properties. The labour-power of the entire peasant family was subject to the landlord's appropriation. Peasants worked four to five days per week as tenants on estate land in exchange for rights to a subsistence plot (Crain 1989). During the close of this decade, there were frequent public debates regarding the first agrarian reform bill which called for changes in this highly stratified land tenure system. This legislation aimed to release Indians from these labour obligations and require landowners to begin paying wages and to redistribute some of their land to former tenants. Mounting demographic pressures as well as a scarcity of land within the peasant sector created a tense social climate. Many estate owners were fearful that their own property might be subject to either land invasions, or, to state expropriation, on behalf of impoverished peasant communities.

It was during this particular historical conjuncture that a remaking of the Ecuadorean landscape occurred, in which touristic ventures became one of the prominent features in the northern highlands. For example, in the context of impending agrarian reform and shifting investment strategies, several hacienda owners sold the bulk of their estates, retaining only a small core area of land surrounding the large manor house of each hacienda. The latter space was converted into 'hosterías', country inns, slated for 'ethnic and historical tourism'. Modern conveniences, such as central heating and indoor plumbing, were installed in these old colonial homes and rooms refurbished to receive a foreign clientele. Quito-based travel agencies promoted packaged tours to these sites in which guests were provided with a feel for pre-existing colonial relations, with Indians serving sumptuous feasts in extensive formal gardens (cf. Neave in *Elle* 1992). Many features characteristic of a traditional working hacienda, such as the small chapel and the bullring, were left intact. For example, at the Hosterías Cisne and Capuli, local Indians were hired both as artisans to exhibit their handicrafts, and as entertainers, who performed native songs and dances typical of the region, for guests in the interior courtyard of each of these inns.

Alongside this conversion of several of the large estates, certain Indian communities became targets for touristic development during the end of the 1950s. Thus, in the Native American community of Otavalo, renowned for its indigenous textile production, the national government began promoting its Saturday morning market for tourists. By the 1970s, the Peace Corps had established textile co-operatives and offered technical assistance to native artisans. They suggested experimenting with new styles that would prompt tourists to purchase local products (Walter 1981). Today, the steady stream of tourists and development agents who make a pilgrimage to Otavalo, either to acquire native handicrafts, or to stimulate production, is matched by the outward flow of native Otavaleños themselves. As shrewd entrepreneurs, the Otavaleños have travelled for centuries in international commercial circuits successfully marketing their goods (cf. Salomon 1973).

In yet another instance, which I want to examine more fully here, Sr. Rodríguez, an influential Ecuadorean politician and prominent landowner in the community of Quimsa, promoted 'luxury tourism' as an innovative development strategy, designed to provide economic alternatives for land-poor peasants whose families were bound by relations of debt peonage to his estate, the Hacienda La Miranda. Wanting to avoid the creation of a tourist attraction in the rural home community (as occurred in the cases of the hosterías, and in nearby Otavalo), this élite notable was intent on relocating a portion of the now surplus Indian population which was heavily dependent on his resource base. He assumed the role of cultural broker by fostering contacts with the owner of a large luxury hotel under construction in Quito and eventually secured employment for twenty Quimseñas in the tourist trade at the Hotel Rey. His initiative stimulated the first widespread out-migration of peasants from Quimsa.

Adept as an interpreter of Indian culture, Sr. Rodríguez translated native traditions into a 'language' that the hotel management was able to understand. He was also knowledgeable regarding the aesthetic tastes of the North American and European touristic audiences who would frequent the Hotel Rey. From an aristocratic Ecuadorean landowning family, he had held various political positions of national and international prominence. All of these experiences familiarized him with the lifestyles of 'the rich and famous' and enabled him to formulate certain assumptions regarding the preferences of this new class of tourist. Ideas about native culture figured prominently in all of his formulations, and he sought to tailor Quimseñas gender and ethnic identities to conform to 'stereotypical images of Indianness' which would appeal to cosmopolitan audiences, both foreign and Ecuadorean nationals.

Sr. Rodríguez persuaded the hotel owner that a backdrop of 'Indianness' would be beneficial for hotel culture and he suggested that the natives from his hacienda could form part of the hotel's staff. During his consultations with the hotel owner, he argued that native women should be given preference for hotel jobs over native men. Partially as a consequence of the 'forced acculturation' imposed under colonialism, an experience imposed more directly upon native men than native women (the former were obligated to leave their communities and abandon some of the visible trappings of Indian identity), Sr. Rodríguez claimed that native women were the repositories of the essence constituting 'Authentic Indianness'. In promoting his strategies of 'ethnicity-for-tourism', he favoured native women as the main vehicles for the representation both of 'exotic otherness' and 'racial difference' at the hotel (cf. MacCannell 1992: 158).

Other gender ideologies also influenced Sr. Rodríguez' assessment, as he regarded the entrance of native women into the professional hotel trade as a logical extension of the gender-prescribed roles of these women in the rural sphere. Associated metaphorically with 'the inside', Quimseñas were responsible for the maintenance of domestic space, both in the peasant compound and in the households of the rural élite. Under traditional tenancy relations, 'servicio' (domestic service), performed at the colonial manor house of the Hacienda La Miranda, was defined as 'women's work'. Unmarried peasant girls as well as some senior women were obliged, on a rotational basis, to undertake domestic chores, such as washing, ironing, sweeping, and cooking, from dawn until dusk. In Sr. Rodríguez' estimation, native Quimseñas were 'naturally' predisposed to perform such taxing manual labour, and their facility at undertaking repetitive tasks, combined with their nimble fingers, demonstrated in their vocation for handicrafts, made them highly suitable for their new assignments as waitresses and hostesses at the hotel. During their service in his household, Quimseñas had also received intensive instruction regarding personal cleanliness and the values of self-discipline and deferential comportment, codes of conduct which would prove beneficial upon their arrival at the hotel.

Finally, generational and aesthetic factors were also at stake, and influenced the selection of hotel employees. More than half of the female servants Sr. Rodríguez initially dispatched to work in Quito were attractive, adolescent girls, of seventeen to twenty years of age. These young women had parental attachments, but were without families of their own. Selected to cater to the whims of the hotel clientele, the 'youthfulness' and 'unmarried' status of these girls only accentuated their 'availability', and gave rise to rumours regarding their promiscuity.

THE HOTEL REY AS CULTURAL PRODUCTION

In 1959, twenty indigenous Quimseñas were ordered to leave their homes and go to Quito to begin paid service work at the luxurious Hotel Rey (pseudonym). Escorted to Quito by the Rodríguez family, they were instructed to work under the management in order to prepare the hotel for its inauguration the following year. Just as 'the muchachas', Indian girls who served as domestics at the Hacienda La Miranda, had lived periodically in the servants' quarters within the confines of the manor house, in order to ease their transition to urban life, the Quimseñas were initially assigned 'live-in' arrangements at the hotel.

A member of the Inter-Continental hotel system, a multinational chain of luxury hotels, the Hotel Rey was completed in 1960. A towering monument to modernity, and the largest luxury hotel of its kind to be constructed in the 'new Quito', it was conveniently located along one of the wide thoroughfares spanning the cosmopolitan capital, away from the crowded, winding and dilapidated streets of the old colonial city centre. While the hotel projected a progressive modern exterior, ensconced within its corridors, particular spaces, objects and tasks were allocated to the 'bearers of tradition': that élite service corps of native women hailing from the community of Quimsa.

The Hotel Rey depended on the visual alterity provided by native women in order to establish a corpus of meanings that underscored its distinctiveness *vis-à-vis* a range of competing hotel establishments. During the initial years following the foundation of the Hotel Rey, none of the other hotels in Quito followed suit by hiring native Ecuadoreans as part of their permanent staff. One of its managers proudly commented to me regarding the exclusive ambiance encountered solely at the Hotel Rey:

> We strive to offer our guests a certain feel for a genteel way of life. In more common hotels one may not encounter the 'gente de categoría' (people of certain pedigree) that you find here. Among our clientele, both foreign and Ecuadorean nationals, are those who can appreciate certain distinguishing features, that minute attention to details that makes our hotel stand out as unique. Beyond a doubt, the warmth and hospitality of our cheerful women of Quimsa, arrayed in their folkloric apparel, enrich the hotel environment, adding a colourful, personal dimension to all of our services. And for any of our guests who may be unfamiliar with our nation's ancient heritage, the Quimseñas' presence provides them with an instant lesson regarding Ecuadorean history.

It was not just the Quimseñas labour but, above all, the cultural meanings they embodied that were appropriated by the hotel. The incorporation of the Quimseñas underscored the hotel management's desire for capturing such coded differences as 'the rare' and 'the exotic'. Quimseñas were the 'authentic' cultural products conspicuously exhibited to demonstrate the hotel's high standards of taste. As an ideological construct deployed in this hotel discourse regarding native women, 'authenticity' carried connotations of 'cultural purity' and 'timeless tradition'. Following the logic of the narrative recounted by the hotel manager, Quimsa women, as persistent reminders of Ecuador's pre-Hispanic heritage, were neither coeval with the hotel management nor its guests, but were located in some remote primeval time situated in a distant past (cf. Fabian 1983; Little 1991). Their daily presence evoked images of rusticity and a slower way of life rooted in the quaint peasant village. Such imagery provided a point of contrast with the dynamic hustle and bustle of a modern business and touristic enterprise such as the Hotel Rey. Differences in the gender, racial and class background of the Quimseñas stood in stark contrast to the hotel's predominantly upper-class, male clientele.

Daily operations at the Hotel Rey depended on a gendered and racial division of labour in which the visibility of the native female body was particularly salient. In 1982, the number of Quimseñas employed by the hotel had risen to 30 but this was out of a total hotel staff of approximately 300. Thus, Quimseñas constituted a relatively small, but highly visible, 'folkloric' component of the hotel's entire staff. While men in the community of Quimsa have long since abandoned traditional dress and replaced it with Western apparel, Quimseñas have been more inclined to conserve native dress codes. Therefore, in the home community, it is not men but the native women, with their elaborately embroidered blouses, layers of billowing skirts, and imitation gold beads that wrap the full length of their necks, who constitute the highly charged visual signs of ethnic identity. However, while on duty at the hotel, the 'authentic dress' Quimseñas were required to wear did not conform to any of the everyday dress codes commonly encountered in the rural community. Instead, 'authentic dress' as mandated by the hotel management, was an aesthetic purification of tradition. It most closely approximated the extravagant, regal dress that only wealthy Quimseñas can afford, an attire reserved solely for festive occasions in the home community. At the hotel, this festive 'uniform' was combined with the starched white apron, that once indicated Quimseñas' status as 'servants' on the haciendas.

Quimseñas were concentrated in the hotel's two restaurants and adjacent bars, while all other jobs undertaken by women, which were less subject to the male tourist gaze, such as that of the chambermaid, were reserved for non-Indians. In each restaurant, Quimseñas worked as hostesses and as 'saloneras' (waitresses). The former welcomed and seated customers while the latter were responsible for serving the finest cuisine and beverages. They could be found both high and low, in the bowels of the hotel and in its upper extremities, as several staffed the basement coffee shop, known as Café Cocha, while others worked in the deluxe 'Mitad del Mundo' (Middle of the World) restaurant. The latter was perched on a pinnacle – the top floor of the Hotel Rey – and was often encased in billowy clouds that on a rainy day wove fibrous threads around it, like cotton candy.

Quimseñas could also be seen on the ground floor of the hotel, plying their silver carts and trays down the long corridors and into the large meeting rooms, where national and international business deals were often hammered out and press conferences occurred. They served coffee and tea in several of these salons whose walls were decorated with elaborate tapestries. While laden with Indian motifs that exuded an ethnic flavour, such tapestries were not designed by Indian artisans but were the exclusive productions of Marisha Ott, Quito's doyenne of tourist and ethnic art.

By the 1970s, three men from Quimsa joined the hotel staff, and they were also concentrated in the restaurant trade.[1] In contrast to the native women, however, who were privileged as part of the hotel's visual display, the men's labour was unmarked and hidden. Employed as cooks and pastry chef, these men were confined to the kitchen, and thus no mandatory ethnic dress code was imposed on them.

PERFORMANCE OF AN 'AUTHENTIC' SELF

Many of the women working at the hotel, whom I first interviewed in 1982, actively denounced the period of servile relations and their forced migration to the hotel. They resented their uprooting from their home community and all the other coercive measures that formed part of their initial entry into the hotel trade, where, upon arrival, they were compelled to provide services for 'others'. Their recognition that relations of inequality governed this transition are highlighted in the testimony of Mama Juana: 'We went from being servants in the 'Big House' of the patron to become servants in the biggest house of all, the Hotel Rey, and there we passed our time in Quito, attending to all the foreign patrons.'

Despite feelings of estrangement upon their arrival in an anonymous urban setting where no other 'paisanos' (villagers from the natal community) resided, their training at the hotel and subsequent experience in cosmopolitan Quito provided these women with an exposure to new ways of life – unknown to the majority of Quimseñas who remained in the village – and eventually led to the constitution of new subjectivities. This recomposition of Quimseña identity conflicted with traditional definitions of 'femininity' and undermined patriarchy's control over the behaviour and movements of these peasant women (cf. Ong 1987; Crain 1994b). Despite the prevalence of hierarchical working conditions, as professional wage-earning women in the nation's capital, Quimseñas experienced greater mobility, as well as a new sense of self-respect and personal autonomy that empowered them. Such a refashioned construction of self contrasted with the extreme forms of personal dependency that characterized the lives of many female peasants of their parents' generation, who were tied as tenants to the Hacienda La Miranda.

Indigenous peasants from neighbouring communities maintain that Quimseñas are more readily accepted by white Quiteño society than they themselves are. Both envious and at the same time disparaging, these neighbours claim that urban Quimseñas are reputed to be 'loose women', who are both aggressive and flirtatious. They are also admiringly labelled 'mujeres vivas', women who are shrewd and streetwise, and therefore not taken advantage of by anyone.

Quimseñas are aware that the commoditization of their gender and ethnic identities constituted part of the Hotel Rey's successful marketing scheme, deployed to entice tourists. Just as the hotel, pursuing the counsel of Sr. Rodríguez, appropriated visual images of their 'Indianness' and utilized them as an aesthetic scheme, designed to advance its own commercial agenda, Quimseñas have resorted to a series of counter-appropriations that advance their own interests. For example, Quimseñas actively appropriate the history of the Hotel Rey and weave this history into their own labour narratives. As the only members of the hotel's current staff who were present during the hotel's inauguration and who have actually resided within its premises, they often refer to themselves as 'the founders' of the hotel, and they proclaim their 'labour rights' to employment there. In the words of Doña Aneta, a hotel employee for almost thirty years: 'We opened the doors of that hotel in 1960. We breathed the very life into it. Because of that, we will always have our rights, they can't deny us our jobs at the hotel.'

Having established a socio-economic niche that is currently reserved for them alone, Quimseñas have been able to monopolize the bar and restaurant trade at the Hotel Rey. They have also aggressively promoted the sale of their artisanal products to hotel guests, and continue to solicit customers for their handicrafts beyond the premises of the shop. Furthermore, senior Quimseñas have fought to maintain their steady jobs at the hotel and have not been replaced by younger women. To date, no non-Quimseña has ever been hired to work in these spaces.

Urbanized Quimseñas have also wielded their influence beyond the confines of the hotel, by securing service positions for close relatives in the homes of élites, both in the nation's capital and abroad. New forms of self-representation have emerged in conjunction with the experience of deterritorialization. Labour narratives, such as the preceding one, as well as stories regarding their illustrious association with the Rodríguez family, are pronounced every time Quimseñas seek employment or attempt to market their products. As 'border crossers', Quimseñas are currently engaged in 'the sale of self' in an urban setting in which they mediate between diverse zones of cross-cultural inter-action. Their identities take on an increasingly hybridized form, and they undergo subtle shifts depending on the particular context, urban Quito or rural hacienda, and the presence or absence of 'dominant others' within these contexts (cf. Bhabha 1994; Kondo 1990; Scott 1990). Facing stiff competition both from Indian and mestizo women, who are also in search of employment in the nation's service industries, Quimseñas realize the importance of construct-ing a public identity among élites that calls attention to their 'exclusivity' and 'fashionability'. Thus, in their public presentation of self, they tactically manipulate appearances for their own ends by laying claim to Sr. Rodríguez's name and fame as part of selfhood and a politics of identity. They also deploy the 'cultural capital' they have accumulated as a result of their service at the deluxe Hotel Rey, to persuasively influence élites as to their superiority as employees, and hence, their desirability.

Quimseñas are cognizant that prospective employers are not only buying their labour, but are also procuring emblems that bestow prestige since, by employing many Quimseñas, élites demonstrate that they exercise a monopoly over certain signifiers of caste and class in Latin America, such as a cultivation of idleness and a disdain for manual labour. Quimseñas have acquired a fine-tuned appreciation of upper-class lifestyles and tastes, and they enact stylized performances that reveal their familiarity with these life-worlds. In their 'on-stage performances' addressed to future employers, they emphasize their 'ethnic difference' as 'indígenas' (indigenous peasants), as an aesthetic pref-erence which they presume that such élites desire, through exaggerated displays that essentialize 'Indianness'. At the same time, however, Quimseñas are aware that even many worldly, upper-class Ecuadoreans continue to associate 'the indigenous race', and native women in particular, with physicality, proximity to the natural world, as well as sloth. Thus, Quimseñas also downplay the negative connotations of their ethnic and gender differences by emphasizing their superior social status, manifested in their intimate historical ties with the households of aristocratic Ecuadorean families. Such intimacy, commonly expressed in the idiom of kinship, is suggested in the following remark: 'As servants in the Casa Grande of Sr. Rodríguez we were all part of one large family.'

Acutely aware of the élites' obsession with the acquisition of 'the authentic', as opposed to their abhorrence of 'the imitation' or 'the fake', Quimseñas exacerbate this preoccupation during interviews with prospective employers by staging performances of their own authenticity. These performances are often a parody of élites' expectations regarding what an 'authentic Quimseña servant' should really be like. Although the majority of individuals of indigenous descent who left the rural highlands and migrated to Quito in search of jobs were quick to shed the visible attributes of 'Indianness' to avoid racial discrimination in the urban context, Quimseñas, because of their putatively higher social status, have often acted otherwise by reasserting markers of their ethnic identity.[2] Although the cultural boundaries demarcating a unique sense of Quimsa as a community have gradually weakened (the results both of out-migration and the invasion of global media images), a more self-conscious construction of ethnic identity as a rhetorical strategy has emerged, particularly *vis-à-vis* non-Indian audiences (cf. Crain 1991; 1994a). Thus, in their encounters with prospective employers, Quimseñas pay careful attention to an outward show of appearance by dressing to produce an 'authentic look' that will meet with élites' approval, such as promenading in the Hotel Rey uniform or wearing their finest native festive dress combined with a starched white apron. Such dress codes are maintained for the benefit of potential employers even though the total cost of native dress is increasingly prohibitive – currently at least three times greater than that of Western dress.

That this presentation of an 'authentic self' is a performance, one strategically designed to prove their identity to élites, is made clear by the fact that it is a context-bound construction of their ethnic and gender identities. 'Off-stage', relaxed in the privacy of their own homes in Quito, or during a return trip to Quimsa, these same women may on occasion adopt the much cheaper Western style of dress, such as polyester stretch pants made in Taiwan and a T-shirt with an Iowa State logo stamped on it – the latter bequeathed to them by a Peace Corps volunteer or, nowadays, marketed by multinationals (cf. Scott 1990).

The 'authentic dress' and acquiescent demeanour of one of the Quimseñas, whom I accompanied during a job interview, mirrored the essentialist stereotyping of Indian culture perpetuated by the Hotel Rey more than it conformed to any of the contemporary codes that govern either dress or behaviour in Quimsa today. In Quimsa such codes are frequently subject to subtle modifications and, therefore, 'reinvention' (cf. Clifford 1988). Cognizant, however, of the élites' concern for the expression of a unique self as a tactic for securing jobs, Quimseñas launch into discourses about threats to their own 'authenticity' that, they argue, also constitute threats to the reputation of élites, as the latter are anxious to maintain a monopoly over all things considered 'authentic' and 'rare'. Thus, they warn élites that there are Quimseña 'imposters' roaming the streets of Quito who have surreptitiously gained entrance into the domestic service trade.

Quimseñas explain that because 'they' are in such high demand, and thus not always readily available, Indian girls from other communities disguise themselves as Quimseñas in order to acquire the jobs in upper-class homes that Quimseñas had imagined to be reserved for themselves.[3] Unwilling to be upstaged by such imposters, peasant women of Quimsa go to Quito prepared to prove their identity as 'authentic Quimseñas'. In order to impress potential employers, they are usually accompanied by an entourage of female relatives, women who have either worked at the Hotel Rey or at another prestigious watering hole in Quito, and who are able to vouch for their 'authenticity'. Quimseñas also carry bags stuffed with official papers verifying their origins, including birth certificates and certificates from the community's primary school. They often amass their own visual documentation of dominant settings, such as photographs of the Hacienda La Miranda, which show them engaged in some laborious task inside the manor house or posing beside a member of the Rodríguez family.

Quimseñas are aware that most élites who can afford to do so buy their sales pitch. In the élites' construction of self, most notables want to emulate the aristocratic Rodríguez family, and be equally commended for their good taste. Many élites complain that it is now difficult to find a Quimseña to work for them as merely establishing contact with the network of Quimseñas already employed in the capital does not always lead to success in procuring a native servant girl. Consequently, sophisticated Quiteños now drive to Quimsa at weekends and cruise the hillsides scouting for maids and for an occasional 'huacchiman' (i.e. a watchman or male guard hired by élite families to protect their homes or cars from theft).

Although the initial idea of Sr. Rodríguez was to promote peasant migration out of Quimsa by fomenting ethnic tourism in the nation's capital, this noble plan partially backfired as, upon retirement, several female employees from the Hotel Rey invested their savings back in Quimsa, into both the construction of homes and artisanal co-operatives. The latter enterprises provided new sources of employment for local peasants and partially curbed the flow of out-migration. Meanwhile, the weekend search for maids by cosmopolitan Quiteños is frequently combined with different forms of 'rural tourism', such as exploring the natural beauty of the area, buying embroidered goods directly from local artisans, as well as having a weekend getaway at one of the nearby 'folklorique hosterías' (cf. *Elle* 1991). Thus, despite the best intentions of Sr. Rodríguez, Quimsa, too, has the potential to rival the Hotel Rey as a tourist attraction.

CONCLUDING REMARKS

This chapter has delineated certain correspondences between contemporary practices of ethnic tourism and the experience of colonialism in highland Ecuador. Just as the last vestiges of compulsory hacienda labour were disappearing in rural Ecuador, with the arrival of the first agrarian reform in 1964, we can detect the resurgence of neo-colonial schemes of representation that sought to fix indigenous identities through the élite discourse of 'authenticity'.

My analysis of ethnic tourism demonstrates that the touristic consumption of services at the Hotel Rey was simultaneously a consumption of meanings. Hotel culture was dependent on constructs of 'differences' of gender, race and class associated with the Quimseñas, in order to establish meanings that conveyed its uniqueness *vis-à-vis* other touristic and élite establishments in the nation's capital. Such signs of difference were appropriated but, in order to be incorporated into hotel culture, these differences also had to be domesticated and made aesthetically pleasing to upper-class tastes. Thus, 'indigenous women's cultural authenticity', as staged at the hotel, was a specular image, reflecting back to the hotel management their own view of indigenous peoples.

Although they occupied subordinate positions, urban Quimseñas were not without their own agency, and they shrewdly manipulated dominant stereotypes to their advantage. Via performances which emphasized their 'cultural purity' and 'model minority status', they mimicked the dominant stereotypes regarding 'native cultural authenticity', and appropriated the Rodríguez family's name and fame as part of selfhood and group identity, in order to gain privileged access to positions in upper-class homes in Quiteño society.

ACKNOWLEDGEMENTS

Earlier versions of this chapter were delivered at the 90th American Anthropological Association meeting in Chicago in November 1991, and at the International Congress of Americanists in Uppsala, Sweden, in July 1994. The field research which forms the basis of this chapter was undertaken from 1982–4 as well as during the summer of 1992. Funding was provided by an ACLS Travel Grant, the Doherty Foundation at Princeton University, and the Institute of Latin American Studies at the University of Texas at Austin. I am indebted to these institutions for their financial support. Finally, I thank Eduardo Archetti, Jeremy Boissevain, Stephanie Kane and Kristin Koptiuch for their comments on earlier versions of this chapter.

NOTES

1 While both men and women participate in wage labour markets outside of the community of Quimsa, male participation is greater than that of women. Quimseñas' involvement in extra-local labour markets is largely restricted to service jobs, at the Hotel Rey as well as at prestigious Quiteño restaurants. They also work as domestic servants in the homes of both Quiteño and international élites, as discussed later. For more information see Crain 1989 and 1991.

2 In dominant accounts of the colonial era and subsequently, native peoples from the Otavalo culture area (of which the community of Quimsa forms a part) were always regarded to be a superior 'race' of Indians (for further information see Salomon 1973 and Walter 1981).

3 Several élites, owners of large estates in the environs of Quimsa, also confirmed that there are 'imposters', indigenous women pretending to be Quimseñas, now working in Quito.

8

CULTURAL APPROPRIATION AND RESISTANCE IN THE AMERICAN SOUTHWEST

Decommodifying 'Indianness'

David Howes

With the growing interest in things Indian in the United States and around the world, Native American culture has become a highly saleable commodity (McGowan 1993). While this commercialization of Indian culture might seem to make good business sense to the Anglo-American majority, many native people experience it as an expropriation of their heritage by the dominant society. This taking is understood to involve the alienation, popularization and corruption of native traditions and imagery through their unauthorized reproduction and commercial exploitation by non-Indians. There is widespread consensus among native spokespeople that such 'cultural appropriation' is as potentially damaging to the survival of native ways of life as the expropriation of Indian lands in the nineteenth century, or the assimilationist strategies pursued by the Indian Schools (Churchill 1992; Kahe 1993; Coombe 1993; Valaskakis 1993; Smith 1994; Burgess and Valaskakis 1995).[1]

The commercial exploitation of 'Indianness' is particularly acute in the American Southwest, an area which has a rich and vibrant heritage of native cultures, and which has long used its 'Indian' identity as a drawing card to attract tourists and sell a variety of regional goods and services. One of the most marketed cultures of the Southwest has been that of the Hopi of Arizona. Indeed, the Hopi have found that virtually every aspect of their culture has been commodified by outsiders. Some examples:

- The use of Hopi words, or the Hopi name itself, to designate commercial products or establishments, as in 'Kiva Lounge'
- The manufacture of Hopi 'fakelore' pieces, such as the Dancing Bear Kachina Doll, a figure for which there is no prototype in the Hopi pantheon
- The use of traditional Hopi motifs (copied from ancient pottery) to adorn mass-produced objects, or to decorate the interior of Southwest-style homes
- The annual spectacle of a group of Anglo businessmen, who call themselves

the Smokis, painting their bodies red, dressing in 'authentic' Hopi ceremonial costumes, and performing their version of the Snake Dance
- The teaching of the Hopi sacred art of making prayer feathers (*paho*) to the participants in a New Age workshop at the Aztec Hotel in Tucson by a self-styled expert in Native American religion
- The publication of a children's comic in which certain *kachinas* (spiritual beings) are literally turned into comic book characters and treated as the foils of the 'All-American superhero', NFL Superpro

In recent years, the Hopi have stopped simply suffering these misappropriations in silence, and started to contest them. Leigh Jenkins, the Director of the Cultural Preservation Office of the Hopi Tribe, has led some highly effective protests against the perceived misuse of Hopi culture by outsiders. One such protest involved a Hopi delegation disrupting the New Age workshop at the Aztec Hotel and, with reporters present, denouncing the (non-Indian) organizer for his commercialization of Hopi religion and spurious claim to ritual expertise. Outraged by this, the organizer declared *himself* to be the injured (or as he put it, 'persecuted') party, and vowed to fight what he perceived as Jenkins' attack on 'Freedom of Speech and investigation...the foundation stone upon which our country stands'.[2]

This incident, among others, provoked discussion and interest in finding out what 'the law' is on cultural appropriation. This chapter will accordingly explore how the resources of Anglo-American law can (and cannot) be used by the Hopi in their struggle to defend their culture and religion against vulgarization and exploitation by the outside world. We shall begin by investigating the motives behind the ceaseless production of representations of Hopi by non-Hopi, and then examine the effects of such representations on the continuity of the 'Hopi Way'. After having arrived at a preliminary understanding of the harm suffered by the Hopi, we shall examine how such harm is or can be cognized and corrected in Anglo-American law. Various recourses are considered, ranging from the common-law action for invasion of privacy to the right of publicity.

Studying these recourses with a view to determining how they may be used to protect the integrity of Native American traditions reveals a great deal about the cultural biases inherent in the Anglo-American legal system. Knowledge of these biases in turn proves useful when it comes to strategizing about how to manipulate that system from within in order to give legal effect to the 'alien' (non-commercial, non-liberal) values for which Hopi culture stands. Strategically, it emerges that the best way to keep Hopi culture *out* of the market (to whatever extent the Hopi Tribe deems this desirable) may be to invoke the same legal doctrine that North American celebrities use *to market* their personalities – the right of publicity. There are certain obvious risks associated with this strategy, and the final section of the chapter is accordingly devoted to evaluating the risks and subjecting the idea of cultural appropriation itself to critical review.

A few words are in order about the scope of this inquiry before proceeding. First, we shall not be concerned with Hopi cultural property (sacred objects, ancestral remains) because such property is, at least in principle, already covered by the regime set up under the Native American Graves Protection and Repatriation Act (NAGPRA).[3] What concerns us is Hopi intellectual property, understood as the interests of the Hopi in the reproduction of the tangible and intangible expressions of their culture, including the ideas which animate those expressions. Second, while the present study focuses on the Hopi, there are lessons and strategies to be derived from it that could equally well be used by other aboriginal groups not only in the United States, but also in other common law jurisdictions, such as Canada or Australia.

MISTAKEN IDENTITIES

The popularization of Hopi culture and religion began in 1884 with the publication of J.G. Bourke's *The Snake Dance of the Moquis of Arizona* ([1884] 1962), subtitled 'A Description of the Manners and Customs of this peculiar People, and especially the revolting religious rite, the Snake Dance'. The rite in question involved priests of the Hopi Snake Society dancing their mesmeric dance in the village plaza with live snakes clenched between their teeth. The snakes were subsequently released into the desert to carry the prayers for rain spoken over them to the appropriate deities.

The ensuing decade witnessed the publication of further sensationalist accounts of Hopi life and customs, with particular emphasis on the drama of the religious rites. Some of these accounts were commissioned by the railway companies which had begun to open up the region, and wished to promote the ceremonies as tourist attractions (Wade 1985; McLuhan 1985). Others were commissioned by magazine editors who sought to exploit the desire for tales of the Western frontier which had gripped the reading public in the industrialized East. It seems the more regimented (and dull) life became under the demands of industry, the more people sought escape through consuming this literature of adventure and discovery.

In 'The Irresistible Other', Sharyn Udall points to a further reason for the intense popular interest in the Hopi that crystallized at this time:

> The 'discovery' of the Snake Dance coincided perfectly with an accelerating American search for national identity. Hungry for a cultural past distinct from that of Europe, Americans had begun to look among the indigenous peoples of their own continent. Onto ancient American roots (surviving visibly in Native American ceremonials like the Snake Dance), Euro-Americans began to graft their aspirations for a noble past.
>
> (1992: 28)

This 'aspiration for a noble past' helps explain the noticeable transformation in the language used to describe the Snake Dance. By the early twentieth century words like 'revolting' and 'peculiar' had dropped out of public use and been replaced by a more dignified vocabulary, one which stressed the 'noble' bearing of the dancers and the profundity or 'archaic mystery' – in place of 'savagery' – of the rites. Of course, the erotic and exotic attraction of the ceremonies remained only thinly sublimated beneath this new discourse.

Representations of Hopi have continued to proliferate throughout the twentieth century, and the Hopi continue to figure as a source of national identity for Americans; but images of Hopi have also, increasingly, come to serve as identity bases for counter-cultural groups within American society. For example, in New Age books on shamanism, the Hopi are typically 'held up as icons of spiritual wisdom, exemplars in a quest toward new meaning in the malaise of modern life' (Whitely 1993: 130; cf. Mails 1994; Kaiser 1991). As a result, the Hopi Reservation has become an important stop on the path of many neo-shamans and other spiritual-seekers. To environmental groups, the Hopi symbolize the 'realization of the interdependence of living things, and the human responsibility for continual renewal [of the cosmos]' (Suagee 1982: 11). This representation is derived partly from romantic conceptions of Indian people as living 'in harmony with Nature' and partly from the Hopi's own belief that by caring for the lands at the sacred centre of the continent (i.e. the Four Corners region) in the time-honoured way, they keep the rest of the world in balance.

To peace groups, the Hopi represent the original pacifists, and Hopi society is seen as the epitome of the peaceable society. This image is based on diverse linguistic and anthropological fragments, such as that the Hopi name translates as 'People of Peace', and that Hopi rituals are dedicated to the achievement of total social harmony (cf. Thompson 1945; Waters 1963; Loftin 1991). The Hopi have even been held up as icons of *extraterrestrial* wisdom on the basis of a very particular interpretation of the 'spaceship' imagery used in certain petroglyphs and prophecies (Geertz 1992: 286 ff.). For this reason they are occasionally sought out by UFO enthusiasts wanting information.

However, of all the different representations of Hopi in circulation in American popular culture today, the most peculiar one is undoubtedly that of the Smokis. The Smokis are a virtual tribe. They were created in the Hopi image by a group of Arizona businessmen in the 1920s. In the privacy of their lodge, the Smokis probably engage in activities much like those of any other men's club. Their principal public activity, though, has until recently involved putting on their own version of the Snake Dance, complete with 'authentic' Hopi costumes and live serpents. Their motivation for staging the dance is rather convoluted, if we follow Peter Whiteley (1993: 126). It appears that the Smoki Snake Dance started out as a racist parody, but then took on additional meaning from the reactions of the wealthy Easterners who came to witness it. The 'zoo-gaze' of these high society pilgrims sensitized the frontier businessmen to the differences of geography, wealth and sensibility that divided them from their Eastern counterparts. This brought them to identify more closely with the very people they mocked, and even to feel ambivalent about their identity as whites – on account of the derision to which all aspects of their behaviour (not just the dance) were subjected by the Easterners. The Smoki Snake Dance is thus a racist joke which backfired, and then came to be taken seriously by its perpetrators.

THE BURDEN OF REPRESENTATION

We have seen how various images of Hopi have been seized upon by different groups within American society and used to construct identities. The Hopi, as both native *and* other, autochthonous *and* exotic, have been a prime source of symbols for American selves. We have also seen how the Hopi image has been adapted to stand for particular ideals in contemporary American society, such as the ideal of living in harmony with nature, or that of living in peace.

But what of the Hopi identity itself, the reputed source of all these images? Is it as timeless and unchanging as the various representations of it suggest? This question is difficult to answer because it assumes that the Hopi identity is some kind of cultural essence, whereas it is actually a way – the 'Hopi Way' – and it is understood that this way may undergo changes as new elements are incorporated into the lives of those who follow it.[4] At the same time, there is concern that the changes be directed from within, not from without. That is, to the Hopi it is important that subsequent generations continue to find the same meanings in the time-honoured images, words and practices which make up the Hopi Way as previous generations did, and not be overly influenced by the meanings which outsiders project onto them. However, this mission has grown increasingly difficult to fulfil as the representations of Hopi by outsiders have multiplied and become more invasive. The extent of this difficulty is perhaps best appreciated through a brief consideration of the Marvel Comics episode of 1992.

'The Kachinas Sing of Doom' is the title of a Marvel Comic that was published in March 1992. The story revolves around NFL Superpro, a super-hero, rescuing Laura Eagle, a Hopi maiden who has broken with tradition and become an ice figureskating champion, from the clutches of a band of *kachinas*. The latter turn out to be thugs, not spirits. They are, in fact, members of a local gambling cartel, which is trying to incite conflict between rival political factions at Hopi so as to eliminate all opposition to the cartel's bid to acquire control over the operation of the on-reserve casino. Specifically, the cartel wants to frame the Hopi traditionalist faction with Laura's abduction. NFL Super-pro's timely intervention exposes the cartel's dastardly scheme and stops the conflict between the factions from escalating.

This comic book version of their culture deeply affected many Hopi. There was anger at the impunity with which the dominant society apparently felt it could make use of Hopi sacred imagery for commercial or entertainment purposes. There was anger over how the imagery was accessed (it being suspected that the artists had secretly videotaped a Kachina Dance, and other scenes from life on the Reservation, and used this as their model). Most of all, there was worry about how the comic's representations of Hopi culture would affect Hopi youth, distorting the latter's understanding of Hopi tradition.

To pursue the last point, it is clear that the writers of 'The Kachinas Sing of Doom' conceived of the kachina costumes and masks as disguises. For the Hopi, however, they have a different meaning. According to Hopi notions, the meaning of a mask can never be grasped by looking at it, only by looking *through* it, and seeing its effect on others. Moreover, the wearer is expected to lose his personal identity and *become* that which he represents (Gill 1982: 71–2). Thus, donning a kachina mask transforms man into spirit: this act has nothing to do with disguising oneself, or concealing one's 'true' identity.

It is this belief in the transformative power of the kachina mask that makes the moment in the *Powamu* initiation ceremony, when Hopi boys and girls (*circa* age ten) are initiated into the 'secret of the kachinas' for the first time, such a poignant one. The 'secret' is that the kachinas who regularly dance in the village plaza throughout the summer months are men dressed as spiritual beings. This revelation is at once totally disenchanting and totally uplifting. The young initiates have their confidence in the reality of the spiritual beings shattered, but at the same time, they are brought to recognize the equally stunning truth that men (their own fathers and brothers!) can be as gods (Gill 1987: 32–5).

It is this moment of revelation that the Marvel Comics issue usurped. 'The Kachinas Sing of Doom' hit the newsstands at the same time as the Powamu initiation ceremonies. Instead of the revelation of one of the central mysteries of Hopi religion occurring in the controlled ritual context of the Powamu ceremony, therefore, it took place at the comic bookstand in the cornerstore. Mystery was reduced to hoax, and to add insult to injury, the men behind the kachina masks were all whites.

The Marvel Comics débâcle highlights two of the most serious threats to cultural survival posed by cultural appropriation. One is the *dilution of tradition*, or undermining of a culture's world view, which results from misconstructions entering into and becoming part of the tradition (e.g., the idea that masks are for purposes of disguise, not revelation). The other is the *dissemination of tradition*, or loss of control over the public transmission of culturally sensitive information. The Hopi are particularly concerned about the dissemination issue, because of the way it affects the very constitution of their society. As Peter Whiteley observes:

> Much ritual power and knowledge is held secret within specific sectors of Hopi society: secrecy and the attendant social care and respect accorded to esoteric knowledge guarantee both authority conferred by initiation and

instrumental efficacy when the power and knowledge are activated. Prescriptions for individual conduct in ritual, namely a purity of thought, emotion and intention, and prescriptions against the misuse of ritual knowledge, which specify supernatural retribution, are utterly central in Hopi discourse. Dissemination of ritual knowledge, either orally to unentitled parties or *ipso facto* in published accounts, violates ritual sanctity and effectiveness and may damage the spiritual health of the community.

(1993: 139)

It will be appreciated that when someone like the organizer of the New Age seminar at the Aztec Hotel, who is not a member of any Hopi clan or secret society, holds a workshop where he professes to teach Hopi religion and perform Hopi rituals, he pollutes the sanctity of the rituals and violates the constitution of Hopi society. That constitution is predicated on a strict division of ritual labour and religious knowledge among the various clans and secret societies – an arrangement which the Hopi have been able to maintain amongst themselves for centuries (Clemmer 1995: 57–61; Benedek 1993: 43–57), but which is now crumbling under the weight of the seemingly endless proliferation of representations by outsiders.[5] In the late twentieth century, maintaining a culture as a *living* tradition, and not some reified abstraction or projection of the dominant society's fantasies, has become a formidably difficult proposition (cf. Laxson 1991; Nabokov 1993).

MOBILIZING THE LAW

We have witnessed some of the harm which cultural appropriation can do to a people's sense of cultural integrity. What we want to explore now is how to characterize such damage in terms that are cognizable in Anglo-American law. To help focus the discussion, and provide us with a touchstone, I would like to introduce a hypothetical scenario. This imaginary scenario concerns the Hopi and involves the publication of a book called 'Hopi Sacred Sites and Pathways'. The book is by an enterprising writer-photographer, who got to know some members of some Hopi clans, and accompanied them on certain pilgrimages. According to the terms of the scenario, the Hopi persons involved did not object to the writer-photographer taking pictures of their ritual preparations, recording their stories (clan myths), or tracing the designs on their ritual paraphernalia, though neither were they informed these images and words would be used in a book. In addition to photographs and texts, the book is to include a detailed map and user's guide to all the sacred sites of the Hopi – including *sipapu*, the Place of Emergence (where the ancestors of the Hopi are said to have emerged into this world) in the Grand Canyon.

The publication of a book such as this hypothetical one would involve the dissemination of knowledge that, according to Hopi tradition, should remain secret, and the unauthorized use of the Hopi name and image(s) for commercial purposes. Moreover, there is a strong likelihood that the book's publication would lead to the desecration of the sacred sites by curious tourists. The publication would clearly be in violation of Hopi customary law, for interfering with the division of sacred knowledge. The question is, how can Anglo-American law be used to challenge this misappropriation and help sustain the integrity of Hopi culture?

A cursory legal analysis of this case suggests that it could be brought within the scope of the tort of invasion of privacy, and that is the first possibility we shall consider below.[6] However, as will quickly become apparent, the definitions and solutions which Anglo-American law has to offer are of very little assistance, and more often than not even *thwart* the cause of Hopi cultural sovereignty. This is because they are informed by a liberal legal philosophy which favours individual rights, free speech and free enterprise, and typically rejects arguments from cultural difference or 'tradition' in the name of Enlightenment notions of 'what is reasonable' and 'Man' – the master notions of modernity (MacIntyre 1988; Howes 1988).

In what follows, then, our search for solutions will mainly involve contemplating the pitfalls of legal liberalism. Each recourse we try out will prove flawed in some way. But this search, even though painful in certain respects, will at the same time permit us to identify the points at which the 'seamless web' of Anglo-American law can be prised open to admit the alternative construction of what it means to be human and what it means to have a culture that the Hopi, and other aboriginal peoples, have elaborated and now seek to defend. Our goal is to find some way of injecting into Anglo-American legal thought the notion of a *right to cultural integrity*, understood as a collective right (because culture is collective) that would enable aboriginal peoples to *prohibit* speech in certain circumstances and declare some things and ideas to be *extra commercium hominum* – that is, beyond the sphere of the market.

THE RIGHT TO PRIVACY

The object of the right to privacy is 'to protect the privacy of private life' because of the emotional harm and embarrassment which can result from excessive public exposure (Warren and Brandeis 1890; Howes 1993). The right is recognized to possess four distinct branches. It prohibits intrusion upon the plaintiff's physical or mental solitude, the public exposure of private facts about the plaintiff, putting the plaintiff in a false light in the public eye, and the unauthorized use of the plaintiff's name, image or likeness for the defendant's advantage (Prosser 1960).

It would appear that there are some parallels between the invasion of privacy and the appropriation of culture. For instance, there is the way both torts involve injury to feelings. There is even a case which may be seen to embody these parallels, *Nelson v. Times* (1977). This case arose out of the publication of a photograph of an Indian boy in a forest setting next to a review of the book *Glooskap's Children* in the *Maine Times*. The mother of the boy argued that the photograph of her son 'invaded the seclusion of his private life and exploited his likeness and his heritage as a member of the Penobscot Nation or Tribe of Indians', in addition to causing her mental suffering and humiliation.

The court ruled in favour of the defendant, compounding the plaintiff's humiliation. When we examine the court's decision, we are immediately struck by the many expressions of cultural bias. For example, the judge ruled that the mother had no cause of action because the right to privacy is a personal right, one which can only be invoked by the person whose *personal* privacy is invaded – namely, her son. This ruling brings out the strongly individualistic orientation of Anglo-American law. The court displayed a complete lack of comprehension of alternative (collectivist, relational) social or family and personality structures.

As for the unauthorized use of the son's photograph, the court held that this use did not constitute a recognizable cause of action because the photograph did not expose anything more about the plaintiff than would have been visible to the public eye; in other words, no details about the boy's private life were revealed. The court also dismissed the suggestion that there was exploitation involved by classifying the use of the photograph as 'incidental' or 'illustrative' rather than 'commercial'. This distinction is surely difficult to sustain, since it is evident that 'Indian features' have commercial value in North American consumer culture, and indeed have traditionally been exploited to sell everything from cigars and running shoes to automobiles (cf. Francis 1992: 171–90). The picture of the boy would certainly have functioned in this manner, even if it was not perhaps expressly set up as an advertisement for the book *Glooskap's Children*.

The court further held that in the absence of any allegation or evidence of the defendant having physically intruded on 'premises occupied privately by the plaintiff for purposes of seclusion', there was no reason to conclude that the plaintiff's solitude had been invaded. This criterion of premises having to be 'occupied privately' for there to be a cause of action is worrisome, for it raises the question of whether or not Native American sacred sites fall within this definition of premises. The answer is probably that they do not, since such sites are not normally 'occupied', nor are they treated as 'private property' by those who worship at them. This makes them fall between the cracks of Anglo-American law, and leaves them open to being trampled on by the many who remain oblivious to their spiritual significance – a situation which has sparked many calls for legal reform but has yet to issue in significant legislative action (cf. Trope 1993: 376–80, 384–90).

Eavesdropping on a person's conversations by means of hidden microphones or prying into someone's bank account are actions which are caught by the tort of invasion of privacy, because they are actively intrusive. By contrast, simple

146

presence at a scene, or the open use of a microphone to record conversations – as in our hypothetical scenario – would not be considered tortious. In addition to some degree of invasiveness, there must be an element of offensiveness in the defendant's actions for the intrusion to attract liability. That is, the private facts which the defendant makes public must be of a kind that would prove offensive and objectionable to the so-called reasonable person of ordinary sensibilities. Details of sexual relations, for example, would be caught by this, but details of religious observances probably would not, because such details are not normally considered embarrassing.

ORDINARY SENSIBILITIES

The 'ordinary sensibilities' standard has proved a major stumbling block for Native American plaintiffs bringing privacy actions. In *Bitsie v. Walston* (1973), at issue was a picture accompanying a newspaper article entitled 'Cards by Local Artists to Benefit Cerebral Palsy Fund'. The picture was of a notecard bearing a sketch of the Navajo plaintiff's daughter. The sketch was based on a photograph by the artist that was consented to when it was taken, although the publicization of it was not. The plaintiff father alleged that the publication of the picture was offensive to the 20,000 or so 'traditional Navajos' currently living in New Mexico because of the traditional Navajo belief that the publication of a photograph can have bad effects on the persons in it – particularly, as in this case, where the person in the photo is associated with a serious ailment. (The normally healthy La Verne Bitsie had, in fact, suffered many illnesses that winter.)

The court in *Bitsie* dismissed the action, holding that the plaintiff had not established that the publication would be offensive to the sensibilities of one who belonged to the 'developed society on which the interest in privacy is based' – meaning the average Anglo citizen of New Mexico. Traditional Navajo beliefs, and the sensibilities of those who hold them, were considered quaint anachronisms, relics of another age. In the words of the court:

> A traditional belief is one based on an inherited or established way of thinking; a cultural feature preserved from the past.... We cannot equate an offense to persons holding such a belief with an offense to persons of ordinary sensibilities because ... the tort relates to the customs of New Mexico at this time and does not extend to 'traditional' beliefs.
> (1973: 662)

The *Bitsie* case, with its doctrine of the intrinsic reasonableness of Anglo sensibilities and its condescending attitude toward Native American beliefs, was cited with approval in another Indian portrait case, *Benally v. Hundred Arrows Press* (1985). This makes *Bitsie* one of the leading cases on the meaning of the 'ordinary sensibilities' standard. It is astonishing that there has not been more criticism directed at this decision, yet to date there is only one law review article challenging the ethnocentrism of the *Bitsie* doctrine (Moreland 1988). What must offend Native American sensibilities the most about *Bitsie* is its 'denial of coevalness' – that is, the way it relegates the living representatives of a vital Native American culture to an outmoded past, thereby fossilizing them (Fabian 1983; Coombe 1993).

Given that the common-law standard for determining whether a publication is invasive of privacy and offensive or not denies that the beliefs and values of Native American communities can be 'reasonable', it seems pointless to try and seek protection for such beliefs and values from this branch of the law. To recur to our hypothetical scenario, one could not realistically expect a circuit court to recognize, as a legitimate concern, the fear of supernatural retribution which certain Native American plaintiffs might express as regards the unauthorized publication of photographs of them at a sacred site performing ritual actions. Highly offensive as publicization of such sacred matters might be to Native American sensibilities, the court would probably hold, as a matter of law, that 'there was no publication of private facts' and nothing to shock the conscience of a 'reasonable person' – just as it did in *Benally*.

The court in *Benally* also raised a further issue, which it did not have to decide because of its finding on the offensiveness issue, but which concerns us just the same, and that is the issue of newsworthiness. It will be appreciated that there is substantial potential for conflict between privacy claims and the claims of 'free speech' or newsworthiness. The conflict is unequal, however, because of the constitutional privilege which free speech claims enjoy. That is, there is a presumption under the US Constitution, which the US Supreme Court has consistently upheld, to the effect that all information or ideas are of legitimate public concern, and should therefore be treated as free for any member of the public to use. 'Only when faced with a contrary claim supported by an interest of the most powerful and unusual sort will the Court even consider an argument to limit that use' (Zimmerman 1992: 665), and respect for privacy is simply not such an interest (cf. Prosser 1960: 412).

To conclude, the right to privacy would not appear to be a very apt vehicle for contesting cultural appropriation because it is a personal right while the interest in cultural integrity is a collective one, because the 'ordinary sensibilities' standard discriminates against Native American beliefs and values and, above all, because the so-called public interest in information can virtually always be invoked to trump the individual interest in privacy.

COPYRIGHT

While it is true that efforts to control the use of information or ideas by others will generally be 'doomed from the outset' if the claim is classified as an attempt to interfere with freedom of speech, it is also true that 'If . . . a claimant can march the same basic dispute onto the field and successfully raise the standard of property rights, her likelihood of success will improve markedly'

(Zimmerman 1992: 669). This observation encourages us to quit the law of torts and look to that of property for other means of challenging cultural appropriation.

In what follows we shall be particularly concerned with the law of intellectual property, an area which has undergone rapid expansion in recent years (Zimmerman and Dunlop 1994). We are especially interested in the law of copyright, and how it can be used to restrict speech (cf. Buskirk 1992). A selection of cases, which illustrate what this law is capable of, is given below:

> One faction of Christian Scientists asserted copyright in an attempt to hinder another faction's spread of an unorthodox version of Mary Baker Eddy's writings . . . The holder of a copyright in a pro-choice book sued [for copyright infringement] when an anti-abortion book quoted from her volume. . . . And the Walt Disney Corporation, whose work has influenced generations of children, employed copyright to prevent those children – now adults – from using bawdy parodies of Disney images to ridicule its viewpoints.
>
> (Gordon 1993: 1535)

The last mentioned case, *Walt Disney v. Air Pirates* (1978), has shades of the Marvel Comics affair, which raises the question: If Walt Disney can use copyright law to stop the mockery of Mickey Mouse and Company then why should not the Hopi be able to use the same law to stop their deities from being turned into comic book characters, or the Smoki from performing their parody of the Snake Dance, etc.?

Salinger v. Random House (1987) is one of the leading cases in the law of copyright, and a case of particular relevance to our scenario. It concerns an unauthorized biography of the writer, J.D. Salinger, which drew extensively upon the writer's unpublished letters. The letters in question were all in the holdings of various university libraries, having been deposited there by their respective recipients. The court found that the author of the biography had infringed Salinger's copyright in the unpublished writings by virtue of the extent to which he had paraphrased the contents of the letters, and thus effectively 'taken' Salinger's particular manner of expression, even though the number of verbatim quotations from the letters was relatively small. It therefore granted an injunction barring publication of the book.

Salinger's aim was clearly to suppress the public dissemination of personal information (namely, the facts and attitudes expressed in the letters), just as our aim is to find some way to limit the circulation of certain cultural information. He succeeded by stating a property claim, whereas if he had gone the ordinary route in such cases, and tried to state a privacy claim, he would have failed, for the following reasons:

> The information at issue had been communicated freely by Salinger to his

correspondents and was legitimately available to the public by its deposit in various libraries. Additionally, the information in the [biography] was not the sort of intimate and personal disclosure the publication of which would shock the conscience [or sensibilities] of an ordinary reader. Finally, it was about a highly newsworthy subject [i.e. Salinger].

(Zimmerman 1992: 672)

The *Salinger* case points the way out of the impasse we arrived at in the last section when we sought to determine whether the right to privacy could be deployed to curtail the dissemination of certain cultural information. Reframing the issue as one of property, after Salinger, would get around the barrier thrown up by the 'ordinary sensibilities' standard. It would also, it seems, solve the problem of how to regain control over cultural information which has been communicated freely to an outsider. The question is, however, whether the specific expressions of Hopi culture with which we are concerned would be able to attract copyright protection in the first place. As will be recalled, these expressions or 'works' consist of oral renditions of clan myths and prayer formulas, and certain ritual gestures and symbols, all of which are considered sacred (i.e. not for uninitiated eyes or ears) by the Hopi.

According to Section 102 of the US Copyright Act, 'Copyright protection subsists . . . in original works of authorship fixed in any tangible medium of expression'. The authorship and original work requirements are problematic, because the elders who possess and give expression to Hopi sacred knowledge are not its authors, but rather its guardians, and the knowledge itself is not original, but rather traditional (cf. Farrer 1994; Gill 1987). In other words, none of the works the elders are authorized (by tradition) to perform are 'one man's alone', to use the standard legal expression; the Anglo-American legal idea of authorship simply does not apply. The requirement that a work be fixed in a tangible medium of expression is also problematic, given that Hopi culture is an oral culture, which means that the preponderance of its expressions are intangible by nature. Intangible expressions are outside the Copyright Act by definition because, it is presumed, only tangible expressions ('writings') are reproducible.

The latter presumption can be questioned. It reflects the chirocentrism and concomitant suspicion of unaided human memory characteristic of literate societies (Ong SJ 1982). However, various studies have shown that the power of memory in oral societies like that of the Hopi can be quite extensive, that through the use of formulaic expressions and other mnemonic techniques, the sages of oral societies can conserve texts in basically unaltered form for generations (cf. Finnegan 1988: 106–7 on 'written composition without writing' in the Pacific). Arguably, therefore, the recited word in oral societies is not intrinsically less fixed (or any less reproducible) than the written word in literate societies. The presumption underlying the US Copyright Act is thus inaccurate, as far as at least some oral traditions are concerned.

But while it would be interesting to introduce anthropological evidence on this point in court, it is doubtful that it would have much impact. The posssibility of copyright protection for the spoken word has been entertained by US courts, but it has never been established (cf. *Estate of Hemingway v. Random House*, 1968; *Falwell v. Penthouse*, 1981).[7] The Copyright Act's insistence on the work being reduced to tangible form pre-empts it. What this means with respect to the hypothetical scenario with which we are concerned is that none of the cultural expressions is susceptible to copyright protection. The only way in which any control over the reproduction of these expressions could be acquired would have been through the Hopi clan members themselves, for example, videotaping the ritual performances or tape recording the clan myths.[8] As matters stand, it is the writer-photographer who holds the copyright in these expressions, because he was the one to record them. This bizarre and perplexing scenario is indicative of how partial the Anglo-American legal system is to the norms and forms of communication peculiar to a literate or electronic society: the system virtually exposes oral cultures to appropriation by anyone with the technology and inclination to do so.

There is some question, however, as to how useful a means of cultural defence copyright represents, even if it were available. For instance, in so far as the goal of the present inquiry has been to find a way to keep certain cultural information out of the public domain *permanently*, in recognition of the inalienable and secret character of such knowledge or information, the US Copyright Act is not apposite, since it only grants protection for the life of the author plus fifty years. An even graver difficulty, of course, is that copyright protection only extends to the particular, tangible *expression* of an idea or information, not the idea or information itself. Thus, while others are not allowed to replicate the copyrighted expression, they remain free to utilize all the same information and ideas – as long as they express them differently. (For example, in the *Salinger* case, there would have been no cause of action had Salinger's biographer but varied his prose style a bit more, so that he replicated the ideas and facts but not the expression of the Salinger letters.)

To conclude, copyright would not appear to be an effective vehicle for trying to control the dissemination of culturally sensitive information. The Copyright Act does not recognize the expressions of an oral tradition as possessing the requisite degree of originality or fixity to attract protection. Furthermore, there is the difficulty of the protection which is afforded being temporal (i.e. for a term) rather than perpetual, and it being partial rather than total. In a sense, it was inevitable that we would not find copyright a very helpful instrument, because this branch of law is so deeply imbued with the values of a market economy (Buskirk 1992). The whole purpose of granting authors a limited monopoly over the reproduction of their work (which is what copyright amounts to) is to provide them with an incentive to be original and to communicate their original creations to the public. The law of copyright therefore values the commodification of knowledge over the conservation of knowledge, originality over tradition, and publicity over secrecy – all values inimical to the kind of solution being sought.

THE RIGHT OF PUBLICITY

The right of publicity, which is a creation of the judiciary (but which has now been provided for in legislation in many states), has as its object to enable persons to control and profit from the commercial use of their name and likeness, or 'image' (Howes 1993). It grew out of the appropriation branch of the right to privacy, but it differs from the latter in that it is a property right rather than a personal right; it tends to be invoked by famous persons rather than ordinary people; and it is available to groups as well as individuals. The following excerpt from *Bi-Rite Enterprises v. Button Master* (1983) explains:

> Privacy decisions limit actions to individuals, because the right of privacy is intended to protect individual personality and feelings. The right of publicity, on the other hand, seeks to protect the commercial value acquired by names and likenesses due to investments of time, energy, money, and talent . . . . It protects the persona – the public image that makes people want to identify with the object person, and thereby imbues his name or likeness with commercial value marketable to those that seek such identification . . . . A group that develops market value in its persona should be as entitled as an individual to publicity rights in its name.

> (1983: 1199)

The manner in which the right of publicity protects the persona is by prohibiting the unauthorized use of the publicly recognized attributes of a person. It bears underlining that because this right is a property right, analogous to trespass, no offence needs to be taken (or proved) by the claimant for the defendant's misappropriation to be actionable; that is, there is no 'ordinary sensibilities' standard to be met.

The range of protected attributes under the right of publicity is extensive, and continues to expand with each new case, so that now – in addition to name and likeness – protected attributes include 'a person's nickname, signature, physical pose, characterizations, singing style, vocal characteristics, body parts, frequently used phrases, car, performance style, mannerisms and gestures' (Coombe 1992: 1226), and even expressions which are merely associated with the claimant, such as 'Here's Johnny!' (*Carson v. Here's Johnny Portable Toilets*, 1983).

Most of the cases in which the right of publicity has been invoked concern the unauthorized use of the claimant's persona for advertising or promotional purposes, but the merchandising use of celebrity personas has also attracted litigation. Thus, one finds the right of publicity being invoked not only to prevent a defendant from imitating a celebrity's voice or mannerisms in a commercial, but also to prohibit 'the distribution of memorial posters, novelty souvenirs, magazine parodies, and the presentation of nostalgic musical reviews, television docudramas, and satirical theatrical performances' (Coombe 1992: 1227). An important point to note in this connection is that the right of publicity offers more comprehensive protection against misappropriation than the law of copyright, for it can be used to prohibit the copying of *intangible* as well as tangible expressions. Thus, in *Zacchini v. Scripps-Howard Broadcasting* (1977), the plaintiff blocked a television news broadcast of an unauthorized film of his human cannonball act, successfully overriding the objection made by counsel for the defence that such an order would interfere with the freedom of the Press.

Some judges and commentators have expressed concern at the expansiveness of the right of publicity. For example, the dissenting judge in the *Carson* case worried that: 'Protection under the right of publicity creates a common law monopoly that removes items, words and acts from the public domain', thus threatening democratic dialogue, not to mention free enterprise (1983: 840; cf. also Coombe 1992; Madow 1993). While the case law may certainly be interpreted as showing cause for such concern, it should be noted, in the interests of accuracy, that the right of publicity actually only penalizes those who try to avoid paying the going rate for a celebrity's endorsement or 'publicity value'. In other words, the threat of withdrawal is largely a posture adopted by the celebrity in order to enhance his or her bargaining position in the 'personality market' (cf. Howes 1993: 226; Armstrong 1991). As long as the price is right, most celebrities are only too willing to alienate aspects of their personas.

There are certain situations, however, where the right of publicity can effectively result in the removal of items from the public domain. Consider the case of *Grant v. Esquire* (1973), which involved the actor Cary Grant suing *Esquire Magazine* for using a 25-year-old photo of his face (which had been taken with his consent, and published in *Esquire* in 1946) superimposed on the torso of a model to illustrate a 1971 article/advertisement for a new line of cardigans. Grant asserted that he did 'not want anyone – himself included – to profit by the publicity value of his name and reputation'. Such language was new in publicity cases (cf. Howes 1993: 222–3), and the court was dumb-founded, but had to conclude that Grant was within his rights to take this high moral position, and have it enforced. The court arrived at this conclusion by analogy to the following principle from the law of real property: 'If the owner of Blackacre decides for reasons of his own not to use his land but to keep it in reserve he is not precluded from prosecuting trespassers' (1973: 880).

In another case, *Waits v. Frito-Lay* (1992), the singer Tom Waits sued Frito-Lay and the Tracy-Locke advertising agency for imitating his voice in a Doritos corn chips commercial. Waits had a philosophical objection against product endorsements, and had already turned down the advertising agency's offer of a substantial fee to sing on the Doritos commercial (after which it engaged the services of an impersonator to sing Waits' song). In the result, not only was the commercial pulled off the air, but the jury's award included over a million dollars in punitive damages against Frito-Lay and its agency.

The right of publicity represents one of the finest paradoxes of Anglo-American law. Its purpose is to facilitate the commodification of the celebrity persona, yet some celebrities (Grant, Waits) have used it to *de-commodify* their personalities. They have sought to reverse the process of alienation (which is so advanced among many of their peers) and, by retrieving their images from the 'economy of signs', regain a semblance of integrity – that is, of the indivisibility that used to be the defining characteristic of the individual (cf. Williams 1976: 133–6, 194–7).

The right of publicity has a number of features that commend it for purposes of containing the vulgarization and exploitation of indigenous cultures. These features include that it may be used to prohibit the unauthorized reproduction of the tangible *or* intangible expressions of a culture; that unlike the right to privacy, it is *not* a personal right, and it may therefore be invoked on behalf of a collective, be it a family, clan or tribe; and, most significantly, that it does not matter what the circumstances of the initial transfer of ideas or expressions may have been, the mere fact of unauthorized use in the present triggers liability.

What would the Hopi, or any other aboriginal people, have to show in order to benefit from the protection of the right of publicity? The court in the *Bi-Rite* case cited the following list of criteria with approval:

> An individual claiming a violation of his right to publicity must show: (1) that his name or likeness has publicity value; (2) that he himself has 'exploited' his name or likeness by acting 'in such a way as to evidence his . . . own recognition of the extrinsic commercial value of his . . . name or likeness, and manifested that recognition in some overt manner'; and (3) that defendant has appropriated this right of publicity, without consent, for advertising purposes or for the purposes of trade.
>
> (1983: 1198–9)

As for the first criterion, there is no question that the Hopi name and image has publicity value. As has been remarked:

> No ethnic group of comparable size has had as much attention trained on it as the Hopi Indians of Arizona. Ethnologists and religious specialists, linguists, art historians and collectors, hippies and 'Indian-freaks', ecologists, spiritualists and pursuers of esoterica – interest in this people oscillates among extremes. (Kunze quoted in Whiteley 1993: 137)

Legal counsel would therefore have no difficulty establishing that the Hopi possess the requisite fame. (It might not be so straightforward in the case of other Native American peoples). Nor is there any question but that the tribe, being a corporate entity, has the capacity to sue.

Regarding the second criterion, it would be possible for counsel to point to the thriving market for Hopi-made pottery and silver jewellery, basketry and *kachina* dolls, to establish that the Hopi have indeed 'exploited' the commercial value of their name and image.[9] It is important to point out in this connection that the Hopi have no objection to the commercialization of certain limited aspects of their culture. However, the point remains that such commodification must not encroach upon the sacred. Thus, for example, the Hopi have never made the creation of sandpaintings into a commercial or ethnic art the way the Navajo have done (cf. Parezo 1983); the production of such representations remains a sacred practice. *Kachina* dolls are a different matter. Originally children's toys, their function was to instruct and divert, not to propitiate, hence their easy transformation into a tourist art form. Additionally, it must be emphasized that commodification is only tolerated to the extent Hopi customary law permits. For example, pottery-making is the prerogative of specific clans in specific villages at First Mesa, just as certain other clans in other villages enjoy exclusive rights in the production of woven baskets. The enforcement of these 'monopolies' is taken very seriously.

With respect to the third criterion, counsel would have to demonstrate absence of consent on the part of the plaintiff and the commercial motives behind the defendant's appropriation of the Hopi name and image. This would not prove difficult in the case of the hypothetical scenario we have been considering. As for the remedies which a court could order in the circumstances, it is probable that a court would grant injunctive relief in the form of a publication ban, for example. Moreover, it is conceivable that a court would order punitive damages, as in the *Waits* case.[10]

CONCLUSION: AT WHAT PRICE?

Having determined that it would be possible for an aboriginal people to use the right of publicity to defend the integrity of their culture, certain questions arise, which have to do with what Roger McDonnell (1992) would call 'the politics of closure'. First, does it make any sense to attempt to protect a culture from appropriation? Second, how wise is it to invoke the law to perform the task of cultural policing? We shall consider each of these issues in turn.

One very cogent objection to the idea of trying to 'fence off' a culture from general circulation comes from the current of opinion known as post-colonial theory – a body of theory which, as we shall see presently, has a certain resonance in Hopi tradition. Thus, according to Renato Rosaldo, it is simply fallacious to regard cultures as self-contained entities with fixed boundaries:

> The view of an authentic culture as an autonomous internally coherent universe no longer seems tenable in a postcolonial world. Neither 'we' nor 'they' are as self-contained as we/they once appeared. All of us inhabit an interdependent late twentieth-century world, which is at

once marked by borrowing and lending which goes on across porous cultural boundaries . . . .

(Rosaldo quoted in Friedman 1994: 75)

A second argument, sometimes known as 'cultural internationalism', holds that cross-cultural borrowing is not only inevitable, but should be recognized as vital both to internal cultural growth and to mutual cultural tolerance and understanding. Indeed, according to John Merryman (1986), every culture should be seen as pertaining to the 'cultural heritage of all mankind', and therefore treated as public property.

A third argument holds that all cultures are marked by internal diversity, that within each culture there is to be found a plurality of equally 'authentic' (and interested) definitions of the culture. Given this irreducible multiplicity, it is impossible to settle on a single definitive account of the particular culture's essential characteristics or traits. This argument is pertinent to the Hopi situation, where the memory and legacy of the split between the Friendlies and the Hostiles at Oraibi still survive (cf. Clemmer 1995; Whiteley 1988). Some would argue, on this basis, that none of the factions of Hopi society is in a position to define authentic Hopi tradition.

The upshot of these arguments is that it is inappropriate to think of cultures either as objects that can be owned or as a determinate set of traits or properties. The only tenable position is to conceive of cultures as 'intersections' or 'processes'. However, if the intersection that is Hopi culture is constantly transforming, as post-colonial theory holds, then how can the Hopi pin down any aspects of their culture in order to assert a right to them?

As noted above, post-colonial theory on these matters has a certain resonance in Hopi tradition. The Hopi, who have interchanged cultural motives with their neighbours in the American Southwest for centuries, are well aware that their culture is neither autonomous nor bounded. Indeed, the Hopi dramatize their interdependence every time they hold a dance in which Zuni, Havasupai, or Navajo kachinas are present. Furthermore, the Hopi believe that their philosophy of life and public ceremonies should be made available to outsiders. As Peter Whiteley observes, 'it runs counter to Hopi first principles to restrict all outside representations of them: they are simply tired of the abuses' (1993: 147).

There are other indications that the Hopi themselves see their culture as a 'way' rather than an object, as a process rather than a product. For example, Hopi elders declare that 'we are not perfect yet, but through good behaviour we are trying to become Hopi' (quoted in Loftin 1991: 110). This suggests that Hopi is an ideal to be striven for, rather than an actual state (cf. Thompson 1945). Another indication is the longstanding ban on photography and all other means of visual representation at the Kachina and other dances which are otherwise open to non-Hopi visitors. The ban is designed to stop the Anglo-American spectator from making a product (or object) of the ceremony by capturing it in a photograph. The ban thus has the effect of preserving the ceremony as a live event (or process), and also, significantly, keeping it oral (cf. Ong 1969; Classen 1993). The Hopi would thus appear to hold a decidedly anti-essentialist, anti-materialistic conception of cultural identity. On this reading, there is no cultural identity in place that could be the target of appropriation.

Turning now to the question of whether the law is a fitting instrument for protecting indigenous cultures from appropriation, again there are various arguments against. The most basic argument is that to employ the law to police the boundaries of cultures would be to invest the legal system with potentially dangerous powers of social control. At a more theoretical level, it has been argued that to translate contemporary Native American aspirations for cultural sovereignty into Anglo-American legal language is to 'impose colonial juridical categories on post-colonial struggles' (Coombe 1992: 270; Pask 1993). As we have seen, to invoke the aid of the law as it now stands, the Hopi would have to come to think of their culture as property, as having a certain 'publicity value', and so on. By employing legal recourses, therefore, the Hopi would run the risk of completely redefining, secularizing and reifying their culture in the very act of trying to safeguard it.

Let us now consider some of the arguments in favour of legal intervention. First of all, it must be recognized that, while all cultures borrow from each other, this borrowing does not take place between equals. The relations between (as well as within) cultures 'are saturated by inequality, power and domination' (Rosaldo quoted in Friedman 1994: 75). As a small, marginal (Fourth World) culture encapsulated within an enormous First World power, the Hopi are in danger of being borrowed – or rather simulated – out of existence. We saw this in the case of the Marvel Comics affair, where the representation of Hopi culture by the comic book writers placed an inordinate burden on the local (indigenous) reproduction of Hopi tradition. This form of commercial exploitation and domination through representation goes far beyond what is normally meant by 'cultural borrowing', and is not something the Hopi feel they can allow to go unchallenged. The surest way to challenge it is to invoke the one language that commands respect in Anglo-American society – the language of property. Moreover, using the law is the conventional way to equalize relations between unequal parties in American culture.

As for the objection that the Hopi are in no position to bring an action for cultural appropriation, given the internal diversity (or factionalism) of their society, it bears underlining that the same objection could be levelled against almost any complex business corporation. Yet we never question the right of corporations like Disney or Nike to legally control the symbols of their identity. Why, therefore, should Indian nations (which have corporate status too) not be allowed to use the same legal controls as these corporations do to guard the 'goodwill' associated with their names and images?

The last argument to be considered has to do with the advisability of using Anglo-American law. Some would argue that to go the legal route would be against Hopi tradition, and run the risk of colonization by an alien legal system. There are two responses to this. First, the Hopi, in fact, have their own customary law of intellectual property, as suggested above. Ideally, this *lex loci* would constitute the core of any action in cultural appropriation that may be brought before the state or federal courts. Second, the Hopi have abundant experience using the official or state law to assert their rights in land and to defend their territory against encroachment (cf. Benedek 1993). Anglo-American law is not foreign law to them, therefore. Moreover, this past experience is directly relevant to the looming struggle over cultural appropriation.[11]

As to whether the Hopi risk 'de-spiritualizing' their culture through dressing it in Anglo-American legal terms, this question must remain open. It bodes well in this regard, though, that the Hopi have managed to maintain their spiritual connection to the land while using Anglo-American law to defend that connection in the course of their long-standing land dispute with the Navajo.

Finally, it is essential to recognize the gravity of the Hopi situation. The Hopi hold that the correct performance of their traditional ceremonies helps to maintain the cosmos in equilibrium. The simulation of Hopi religious practices by outsiders cannot help but disrupt and distort this process, and result in *koyaanisqatsi*, a world escalating out of balance. According to Hopi thought, therefore, the appropriation of Hopi spirituality entails not only a loss of cultural integrity but a threat to the stability of the cosmic order. Judged from this perspective, the actions taken by the Hopi to protect their cultural integrity are not only for the benefit of the Hopi themselves, but for the common good.

ACKNOWLEDGEMENTS

Part of the research on which this chapter is based was made possible by a grant from the Fonds FCAR. I wish to thank Marlene Sekaquaptewa and family for their hospitality, Leigh Jenkins for getting me thinking about the issue of cultural appropriation, and Constance Classen, Rob Wishart, Benoît Morel, Marilyn Masayesva, Ingrid Mittmannsgruber, Blaine Baker, Marlene Caplan, Nicholas Kasirer, and Chris Trott for many illuminating discussions on the subject.

APPENDIX: CASES CITED

Abernethy v. Hutchinson (1825), 47 Eng. Rep. 1313
Benally v. Hundred Arrows Press (1985), 614 F.Supp. 969
Bi-Rite Enterprises v. Button Master (1983), 555 F.Supp. 1188
Bitsie v. Walston (1973), 515 P.2d 659
Carson v. Here's Johnny Portable Toilets (1983), 689 F.2d 831

Estate of Hemingway v. Random House (1968), 244 N.E.2d 250
Falwell v. Penthouse (1981), 521 F.Supp. 1204
Grant v. Esquire (1973), 367 F.Supp. 876
Harjo v. Pro Football (1994), 30 U.S.P.Q 2D (BNA) 1828
International News Service v. Associated Press (1918), 248 US 215
Martin Luther King v. American Heritage Products (1983), 694 F.2d. 674
Nelson v. Times (1977), 373 A.2d 1221
Salinger v. Random House (1987), 811 F.2d 90
Waits v. Frito-Lay (1992), 978 F.2d 1093
Walt Disney Productions v. Air Pirates (1978), 581 F.2d 751
Zacchini v. Scripps-Howard Broadcasting (1977), 433 US 562

NOTES

1 Smith (1994) goes so far as to characterize cultural appropriation as reverse ethnocide, or extermination through symbolic assimilation.

2 From a letter of T. Mails to M. Kooyahoema, reprinted in part in 'New Ager Mails responds to Hopi critics', *Hopi Tutu-veh-ni* (15 July 1993).

3 See DuBoff (1992) and Clemmer (1995: 282–96) regarding NAGPRA and Parsley (1993) concerning the 1990 amendments to the Indian Arts and Crafts Act. Compare Clements (1991) and Blundell (1993) on the Canadian situation, and Anderson (1990) regarding Australia.

4 The situation is complicated by the fact that Hopi prophecy speaks of the inevitable dissolution of Hopi civilization (cf. A. Geertz 1992; Clemmer 1995). Then again, there is debate over the proper interpretation of the prophecies, and in any event, the prophecies do not link the end of Hopi culture to its appropriation by New Agers and other segments of American society.

5 It should be noted that there are problems of cultural appropriation 'from within' at Hopi, not only 'from without'. See Armin Geertz's *The Invention of Prophecy* for a critical discussion of the words and actions of certain self-appointed Hopi prophets.

6 The present analysis also takes into account the ways in which the Hopi conceptualize their 'rights' under Anglo-American law. Thus, some Hopi speak of their 'right to religious privacy' being violated when, for example, the Anglo spectators at a Kachina Dance crowd out the Hopi audience, or try to take photographs even when they have been instructed not to.

7 By contrast, there is an English case which involved oral statements (a course of lectures) receiving copyright protection without first having to be reduced to writing by the claimant, *Abernethy v. Hutchinson* (1825). The court in *Abernethy* also held that at common law the right to control publication of one's work includes the power to refuse publication indefinitely. This case has interesting implications for the use of copyright to challenge cultural appropriation in those jurisdictions where (unlike in the United States) the common law of copyright has not been pre-empted by statute.

8 This is the standard method of acquiring copyright in live performances and other intangible expressions. Dance choreographers, for example, commonly videotape their arrangements.

9 The second criterion may not be a necessary one, given the decision in *Martin Luther King v. American Heritage Products* (1983) as well as the decision in the only

Indian case to date where the right of publicity has been invoked, *In re Tasunke Witko* (Rosebud Sioux Tribal Court, civ. no. 93–204 [25 October 1994]).

10   There are other recourses that aboriginal peoples could employ to combat cultural appropriation, but they will have to be treated elsewhere due to limitations of space. To list some of the more promising ones: patent, passing off and the misappropriation (or unfair competition) doctrine as elaborated in *International News Service v. Associated Press* (1918). Trademark law would also seem to offer interesting, if limited, possibilities judging from *Harjo v. Pro Football* (1994).

11   As the so-called information society – or 'civilization of the image' – continues to unfold, intellectual property rights (rights in names and images) will continue to increase in value relative to land or mineral rights. Native American cultures will want to keep abreast of this shift, and in such places as Canada or Australia start to bring image claims in addition to their land claims.

9

TRANSFORMING IMAGES

Communication technologies and cultural identity in Nishnawbe-Aski

Marian Bredin

As commodities which move increasingly rapidly and freely across cultural borders, contemporary mass media are located at the intersection of the complex processes of cross-cultural consumption and those of inter-cultural communication. For the most part, the flow of electronic communication technologies and information across cultural boundaries is viewed as unidirectional, from the 'First World' to its 'others' – 'Third World' and 'Fourth World' peoples. It is now becoming apparent, however, that the cultural conditions under which electronic media and messages are received affect the uses to which technologies are put and the meanings produced. The persistence of cultural tradition is related to strategies of resistance and these often generate transformations in the dominant modes of mass communication.

In this chapter, the circulation of electronic communications media within different cultural contexts will be considered from three distinct vantage points. In the first instance, we shall examine the *contents* of media – sounds, images and ideas. Concepts of 'cultural imperialism' and 'electronic colonialism' are often applied to this type of information flow and these concepts and their critiques will be discussed. In the second instance, we shall consider communications *technologies* as objects of consumption – imported, appropriated and reconstructed in a variety of cultural conditions. Both beyond metropolitan North American and European contexts, and within them, local uses of broadcast technologies are often constrained by traditional cultural codes and values, while these traditions are themselves reinvented in the encounter with mass media. The third vantage point centres on the *practices and strategies* of communication. We shall explore how indigenous forms of media production and audience construction are shaped by dominant conventions but also refashioned according to local priorities and histories.

Each of these three aspects of the movement of media across cultural borders can be illustrated by reference to the introduction of radio and television technologies to aboriginal communities in remote areas of northern Canada, many of which have only been exposed to mass communications for a little over a decade. In the same period native communications societies have established technologically sophisticated aboriginal-language radio and television production and distribution networks, integrating technologies as simple as low-power FM community radio and as complex as transnational satellite transponders. These instances of aboriginal media use occur within specific 'conditions of possibility' at a unique socio-historical conjuncture: federal communication policies and northern 'development' agendas intersect with local needs for community-based media in Inuit and Indian languages and the struggle for self-determination in northern native communities. The emergent articulation between the northward extensions of the state and persisting aboriginal cultures, between dominant discourses of cultural policy and local priorities, shapes the ways and means by which aboriginal people have appropriated media in Canada.

The analyses and interpretations advanced in this chapter will draw upon diverse examples of native broadcasting in northern Canada and in particular from a case study conducted at Wawatay Native Communications Society, a regional aboriginal-language radio and television network based in the towns of Sioux Lookout and Moose Factory in northwestern Ontario. Wawatay has been actively engaged in the development of communication technologies for use in native communities in Nishnawbe-Aski, 'the people's land', since 1974. Nishnawbe-Aski is an area of 400,000 square kilometres which extends along the coasts of Hudson and James Bay, from Manitoba to the Québec border and south to the Canadian National Rail line between Toronto and Winnipeg. The only road or rail access to the area runs along the southern fringe, and not all the communities have year-round airstrips.

The majority of the forty-five or so villages in Nishnawbe-Aski have fewer than 500 people, and so they were not included in the extension of the national Canadian Broadcasting Corporation (CBC) radio or television service to rural areas under the Accelerated Coverage Plan initiated in 1972. Presently, Wawatay's audience consists primarily of the 20,000 Cree, OjiCree and Ojibway speaking people resident in this area who receive radio broadcasts distributed by satellite to a network of community stations, and Wawatay television programming from local TV Ontario (TVO) or Ontario Legislative Assembly Channel (OLA) transmitters. Observations originating in a case study of the Society undertaken in 1993 are presented here and juxtaposed with critical and theoretical insights into the movement of media across cultural borders.

This chapter also explores two areas of recent theoretical debate as sources of critical concepts for cross-cultural communications research. Post-modern ethnography and post-colonial theory generate concepts of culture, power, and identity, which are highly relevant to understanding the appropriation of media by indigenous people. Explanations of culture as dynamic and relational can be fruitfully applied to the analysis of the appropriation and transformation of technologies, while post-colonial perspectives on identity, agency and power are relevant to the interpretation of the indigenous use of radio and television as means of cultural self-definition and translation.

The emphasis in this chapter, then, is on the transformation of communication technologies in the cultural and political contexts of contemporary aboriginal communities. The contradictions between the commercial design and southern origin of communication systems and the forms of public and community broadcasting undertaken by northern native communications societies have to be negotiated. In considering critical concepts such as culture, power and identity I have tried to elucidate the practical and discursive conditions within which native people have appropriated and reconstructed communications technologies in resistance to dominant ideologies and the imperatives of a market economy. These strategies of resistance are embedded within aboriginal peoples' historical experience of colonialism, but are also premised upon the futurity of aboriginal communities, languages and values in Canada.

CROSS-CULTURAL MOVEMENTS OF MEDIA: CONTENT, TECHNOLOGIES AND COMMUNICATION PRACTICES

Cultural imperialism – situating experiences of imported media

The discussion of global movements of mass media is often carried out within and according to paradigms of cultural imperialism, electronic colonialism or dependency theory (cf. Schiller 1976; McPhail 1987; Mattelart *et al.* 1979). While these models make important contributions to an understanding of the political economy of media ownership and the vested interests of developed countries and metropolitan centres in promoting the 'free flow' of information, they are limited in their ability to illuminate how media messages are received in specific cultural contexts. As Tomlinson (1991:68) points out, such models encourage a spatial and synchronic perspective on cultural and national boundaries, one that fails to fully account for the historical and temporal constitution of cultural identities and the relations between cultural groups. As commodities, media are inserted into existing conditions of social interaction between groups, and circulate according to historical patterns of relationship between centre and margin – not according to some intrinsic logic of their own.

Analyses of cultural imperialism and studies of the cross-cultural impact of introduced media are premised on an assumption that imported media inevitably contribute to the cultural assimilation of minorities and promote cultural homogenization. Early studies of the introduction of television to remote Inuit communities made such assumptions, applying concepts of cultural dependency and 'electronic colonialism'. Gary Coldevin, for instance, argues that the extension of southern television programming to Inuit communities can be seen as:

designed to align native cognitions and cultural values toward main-stream Canada. Within this rubric 'cultural replacement' is ... employed as a measure of the effects of electronic colonialism or the degree of substitution of traditional Eskimo cognitive and affective orientations by Euro-Canadian structures.

(1979: 116)

From this position, the 'effects' of television can be seen as part of a broader colonial relationship which, alongside the introduction of English schools, government institutions and wage labour, contributed to the disruption of traditional Inuit cultural knowledge and social organization (cf. Graburn 1982: 12).

The presence of modern media such as television and radio in Inuit and Indian communities has undoubtedly occasioned changes in the traditional lifestyle of those communities. For example, Graburn (1982: 11) records how, in Arctic Inuit settlements, the scheduling of family hunting trips was often regulated by the desire to be at home when popular TV programmes were on. Researchers who view these effects as indications of a decline in global cultural diversity, however, often fail to account for indigenous responses to and appropriations of imported commodities or television programmes. As a model of global or national social change, notions of electronic colonialism risk a 'media-centred' distortion of complex historical and political processes and neglect to adequately situate media use within local discourses and practices.

Media content and cross-cultural 'effects'

The effects of introduced media as they cross cultural borders cannot simply be 'read off from' the visual or verbal content of television programmes or other cultural commodities. Produced in a metropolitan socio-cultural context, media texts become available for new and often conflicting interpretations when they are circulated at the margins. As Tomlinson argues;

The problem of translating the 'phenomenological' data of the viewer's experience into empirical data is common to any investigation of audiences and is central to the debate over media effects generally. The critique of media imperialism is at one level simply a version of the 'ideological effects' arguments advanced by many critical media theorists in the West. But the cross-cultural nature of the investigation in the case of media imperialism means that another layer of difficulties is added: that of *interpreting* the empirical data. The point at stake here is whether researchers can correctly interpret responses from a different cultural context in terms of their own cultural understanding.

(1991: 51)

In other words, audiences produce meanings from programmes, according to culturally specific codes and conventions, while researchers translate these initial interpretations according to their own set of codes and expectations, but there is no way to verify these translations. Furthermore, as McQuail (1983: 175) suggests, media effects studies cannot easily locate a 'cause' for given responses to media content from amongst other social and historical factors, nor predict how or when such responses might occur elsewhere.

The possibility of assessing the effects of a given medium of communication on members of a group defined in terms of cultural difference also depends upon an essentialist notion of 'culture' as a set of fixed perceptions, norms, discourses or behaviours to which an objective measure of 'change' can be applied. The connotations of 'change' in this case are often those of 'loss' – new media are associated with a degradation of the integrity and coherence of 'traditional' cultural knowledge (cf. Clifford 1988). Without minimizing the possible effects of imported television in remote aboriginal communities, especially its apparent effects on native language use, studies which rely on such essentialist models of culture must be criticized for their failure to account for the historical processes of contact and change which aboriginal groups have previously negotiated. These include 'prehistoric' intertribal contact, migration and cultural diffusion, engagement in trade with Europeans, adoption of Christianity and syllabic literacy and the transition to permanent settlements and exposure to formal education. Taking these factors into account, it is clear that media cannot be isolated as the sole or even primary cause of cognitive, affective or behavioural changes among aboriginal people, and preoccupation with the cultural impact of media alone often deflects attention away from the longer-term and more pervasive impact of colonial political institutions, territorial dispossession and economic exploitation. Ultimately, research on media effects in northern communities provides little concrete evidence that television watching brings aboriginal viewers to reject traditional values and cultural codes outright, only that these become subject to revision and negotiation.

In an early study on the introduction of television into Cree communities in northern Manitoba, Granzberg and Steinbring (1980) suggest that while the formal and technological structures of television are imported, the social functions of its use and meanings of its texts are produced according to indigenous values which are revised to include this new means of communication. There is also evidence that aboriginal youth imaginatively appropriate American prime time television characters and integrate them into existing gender and cultural models. Discussing the popularity among young male Inuit of the teenage male character known as 'the Fonz' on the sitcom *Happy Days*, Valaskakis (1988:131) suggests that this contemporary image of the 'super masculine' is located alongside the symbol of the 'real Inuk' – a skilled hunter who lives off the land and is self-sufficient – in the revision of cultural codes of masculinity. This indicates that the effects of television may be less those of cultural 'replacement' and more properly those of cultural 'transformation', involving strategies of seizing, displacing and reworking dominant codes in reference to local contexts and meanings. Clearly, the consumption of the commodified images of introduced media is not simply a unilateral process of passive assimilation but an active transformation of novel images and ideas in relation to prior cultural norms and values.

In many aboriginal communities, an unintended consequence of exposure to predominantly foreign media has been a growing demand for indigenous production. Imported television may thus have the effect of heightening awareness of cultural differences and inspiring a collective movement to appropriate communications technology as a means of promoting aboriginal languages and cultures (Roth and Valaskakis 1989: 230). It is to the study of such politically motivated reconstructions of introduced media that we turn next.

Appropriating and reconstructing communication technologies

Throughout the Canadian north, the extension of southern-based media systems has had the political effect of focusing aboriginal peoples' desire both to produce aboriginal-language programming for existing radio and television networks and to establish native-controlled community and regional communications networks. The appropriation or 'indigenization' of communication technologies in the development of native-controlled systems is, however, a complex and contradictory process. One of the earliest studies of the introduction of new media in Nishnawbe-Aski (Hudson 1974) dismissed claims that the impact of communications technologies would 'annihilate cultures and lifestyles'. As long as technologies are adequately controlled by native people, Hudson (1974: 163) argued, they become a means to an end that in fact may be the maintenance of traditional activities and communal values along with other positive changes that people want. From my own findings, I would suggest that the appropriation of technologies is not always so straightforward as Hudson indicates, that communications technologies have been designed for quite different ends to the kind that many aboriginal communities are pursuing and that there is always a dialectical tension between technology and tradition in which both are transformed.

The development of aboriginal communication networks in Nishnawbe-Aski has put a number of technologies to use, including HF radio, low power FM community radio, telephone, and satellite distribution of Cree and Ojibway radio and television programming. In each case, the appropriation of a particular medium has been constrained by prior technological design, the extent of government regulation, considerations of cost, and the degree of competition from other public and commercial broadcasters and organizations. These co-existing investments of power in communication technologies shape the way in which media are reconstructed in the political and cultural contexts of aboriginal communities. The effort to resist the one-way flow of information, challenge the centralized production of radio and television, and mediate cultural change, has transformative effects upon individual subjects, upon the public articulation of cultural identity, upon policy discourses and upon centre-margin (or north–south) relations. The meanings and lived experience of cultural tradition brought to bear upon communication technologies also have a transformative effect upon the social construction of technology itself. Whether it be the most elementary HF trail radio, packed along on hunting trips, or the volunteer operation of community radio for sending messages, telling stories and informally negotiating conflicts, or a satellite uplink used to distribute a television current affairs programme in OjiCree – these technologies are subtly and sometimes radically reconstructed in the context of their use by aboriginal peoples.

For a native person in a native community there are certain topics inappropriate to radio discussion and images unsuitable for video recording, even though such issues and images may be common in the mainstream media. At the same time, in native productions we see and hear voices, images, languages and ideas entirely absent from southern media. For example, a satellite audio subcarrier frequency is used to link high school teachers in Sioux Lookout with students in remote communities and video is used to record traditional modes of travelling and living on the land. These projects require definitions of and relations between teachers and students, radio networks and education councils, interview subjects, producers and camera operators that are created anew or strategically re-ordered.

It is necessary to explore the cultural determinants of how technologies are used to communicate, under what conditions and subject to which constraints. An example of this mode of analysis is Lisa Philips Valentine's (1990) discussion of 'telephone etiquette' in the OjiCree community of Kingfisher Lake. She suggests that, as in the case of face-to-face communication, older and middle-aged people speak most on the telephone while teenagers are considered too shy to talk to adults or even to their peers. She also notes that the caller plays a more active role in conveying a message or sharing information than does the recipient. In general, calls are brief with very truncated greetings and closings, reflecting every-day community interactions where verbal greetings and leave-takings are almost non-existent. The exchange of information through radio and television may be subject to many of the same kind of cultural constraints. Elders, for instance, are accorded substantial respect and deference in many aboriginal communities, and their role in directing the use of new media reflects this.

A further illustration of the insertion of new communication technologies into existing spheres of public discussion, negotiation and decision-making is Sackett's (1976) description of the use of Povungnituk Tusautik Radio in Northern Québec during the negotiation of the *James Bay Agreement*. The entire text of the *Agreement* was translated over the radio and residents called the station to ask for clarifications and explanations. Council members travelling to the South for negotiations would call the station in the evenings to report on their activities. The station would then host a phone-in discussion, after which the negotiators were called back and informed of people's responses. In this case, the radio station was used to engage listeners in the encounter with and negotiation of major political and social changes.

Unlike mainstream talk radio or most non-native community radio, native community radio is characterized by its strategies of horizontal communication, its inclusive, non-professional style and the integration of the station within the community – residents come and go, listen regularly, phone frequently, play radio bingo and often take part in broadcasts. In some remote communities, because community radio preceded or was established at the same time as other mass media were introduced, aboriginal people may simply regard the community station as indigenous, as something they initiated and continue to control, not compromised by its association with the foreign origin and content of other forms of public or commercial radio and television (Valentine 1990).

Communication practices and the organization of new media

Just as imported images and ideas are interpreted according to existing cultural codes, and new communications technologies are 'indigenized', so the institutional organization of media is subject to culturally specific discourses and practices. In the Wawatay case study, interviews and documentary analysis showed that production methods, organizational decisions, training formats and programme evaluation, while partially modelled on mainstream media processes, were also shaped by local priorities, communal ethics and cultural values not found in non-aboriginal media.

According to its mandate from the chiefs of Nishnawbe-Aski Nation, Wawatay is directed to test, introduce and explain new communication technologies with the provision that the technologies 'must be used for the preservation and enrichment of the languages, lifestyles and cultures of the Cree and Ojibway people' (WNCS 1989a). It is significant that in the Society's statements of principles, 'lifestyle and culture' are nowhere objectified or linked to specific traits, artefacts or beliefs. Rather 'culture' is represented in a pragmatic and dynamic manner as an open configuration of spoken and written language use, community life and the values, traditions and codes of conduct handed down by the elders; in short, culture is located in everyday practice. It is partly captured in the transaction between past and present, and between elders and youth, but grounded in meeting immediate needs in communities.

The practical nature of this definition of culture is reflected in the following suggestions from a community radio managers' conference for developing cultural policies for Wawatay Radio Network; 'WRN cultural policies include exclusive use of native language on radio, more staff time in each community, emphasis on legends and stories, translating new terminology, especially health-related, produce community profiles, establish a tape library of records of traditional activities, strengthen elders' participation and children's programming' (WNCS 1989b). The use of media technologies for the support of native culture is thus intertwined with community accountability and development. 'Culture' is not treated as a distinct category independent of its active, practical and local aspects.

Aside from a general commitment to applying technology to the promotion of Cree and Ojibway language and culture in Nishnawbe-Aski, internal structures and communicative practices at Wawatay can also be considered culturally specific. Hiring and training of staff are based on the need to bring fluent speakers of native languages and individuals committed to the principles and philosophies of the Society together with those who have some degree of technical experience. Reporting and production standards are shaped by Wawatay's close relation to the communities it serves. A degree of community control is exercised through certain traditional and ethical constraints on who may speak and under what conditions. For example, confrontational and accusatory positions are generally avoided and the right to speak on certain issues and access to some kinds of knowledge are clearly a function of age and one's position within the community. Young reporters and programme producers must understand the boundaries and limitations inherent to the traditional role of a communicator in their culture.

Since radio and television technologies require specific skills, Wawatay is also involved in training its own staff and community radio station managers from villages throughout the region that the Society serves. The technologies themselves impose demands upon trainees and Wawatay adheres to the professional standards established by public broadcasters like TVO and the CBC. But the skills being 'transferred' to Wawatay staff and community broadcasters incorporate a number of other elements as well, taken from indigenous models of community development, accountability and decision-making, on the basis of which mainstream modes of 'management' and 'journalism' are refashioned. Specific skills – the operation of a control room console, organization of community 'beats' or drawing up of an annual budget – may indeed conform closely to non-aboriginal commercial and public broadcast norms, but the social, cultural and linguistic contexts within which those skills are transferred and their public dissemination within the communities, means that those skills are ultimately transformed by the purposes to which they are put.

One final aspect of the appropriation of media that should be addressed concerns the expression of culturally specific values in indigenous media texts. In a discussion of Inuit Broadcasting Corporation (IBC) current affairs programming, Kate Madden (1990) argues that Inuit reject conventional codes of news production which construct reporter and anchorperson as expert and omniscient authorities. She proposes that the dismissal of these conventions is linked to Inuit cultural values which emphasize individual autonomy, patience and non-interference as key elements of interpersonal relationships, decentralized leadership and consensual decision-making, together with a belief in interconnectedness and co-operation which demand non-confrontational behaviour and emotional control (1990: 12). Madden locates formal and substantive expressions of each of these values in IBC programmes. Further, she suggests that IBC producers are well aware of the production values of the mainstream media and in some cases, when programmes deal primarily with non-Inuit subjects and southern news, they are shot and edited in a fashion more closely resembling mainstream television, indicating a degree of 'video bilingualism'. In her overall assessment of IBC programming, Madden (1990:9) argues that as an expression of cultural and political autonomy, Inuit-controlled media seek to promote reflexivity among Inuit audiences – 'filmic' or media reflexivity that calls attention to the conventions of television and its 'manipulation of reality', cultural reflexivity that situates Inuit cultural knowledge in relation to mainstream norms and values, and political reflexivity that uses media as a means of challenging the propagation of dominant ideologies in southern programming.

At Wawatay, the influence of cultural values and community control upon organizational strategies also shapes programme form and content. The degree of accountability to community audiences, the codes of conduct impinging upon staff members, the small-scale, non-profit character of the Society, even the structures and percepts of spoken Cree and Ojibway, each leave traces in radio and television texts. It is also apparent that regional and community radio is a unique medium for storytelling in Nishnawbe-Aski communities and that stories contain important information about local histories, narrative traditions and moral values. In each of these instances, the ways of thinking about broadcast media and the programmes produced do not derive primarily from mainstream models of how communication technologies should be used, but build upon indigenous forms of communication and extend these through new media.

The cultural politics of aboriginal media

Inquiry into the appropriation of communication technologies in aboriginal communities clearly reveals how and why native people across northern Canada have responded to introduced media and methods of communication by making them their own. By way of summary then, the phrase 'native-controlled broadcasting' must be viewed as a condensation of complex histories and discursive constructions. It marks the intersection of configurations of aboriginal identity, patterns of cultural contact, shifts within networks of power and transformations of technologies.

At Wawatay, these multiple local, regional, national and global conditions and constraints result in the overdetermination of modes of programme production, relations amongst producers, and between producers and audiences. Local practices in some ways replicate mainstream modes of media production such as might be found in other forms of community or public broadcasting but are, in important ways, culturally specific. Aboriginal communities are not engaged in a one-dimensional process in which people use existing technologies as a channel for communication 'about' their culture. In appropriating communication technologies for cultural purposes, Wawatay has participated in the transformation of the technology and how it is used, organized and situated in Nishnawbe-Aski communities. At the same time, the communities, the region and Wawatay itself are reorganized around the new communication technologies.

CULTURE, POWER AND IDENTITY: POST-COLONIAL CONDITIONS OF REPRESENTATION

Theoretical tools for reading indigenous media

The question of how to 'read' indigenous media without being complicit in colonial modes of representation and control such as those discussed by Edward Said (1993), Homi Bhabha (1994) and other post-colonial critics, is a pressing one. The following section explores theoretical tools drawn from post-modern ethnography and post-colonial theory which foreground the problems of position, authority, power and knowledge while permitting insight into strategies of resistance, emergent cultures and the possibilities of subaltern speech associated with aboriginal media. Three concepts are particularly fruitful in generating research approaches in this area: an understanding of *culture* as the conjunctural and relational organization of knowledge–discourse found in post-modern ethnography; and a model of *identity* as expressive agency along with an understanding of *power* which encompasses its strategic, productive and practical character drawn from post-colonial theory.

Emergent cultures and the politics of difference

In *The Predicament of Culture* James Clifford puts forward the notion of 'emergent' cultures and seeks to rehabilitate the culture concept for the conditions of post-modern existence. He rejects the Eurocentric assumptions upon which narratives of vanishing cultures and subsuming homogeneity are advanced. Arguing that these narratives place the cultures of the non-Western world in a context of 'present-becoming-past', Clifford (1988: 15) suggests that indigenous and post-colonial cultural politics are instead premised on the belief in the futurity of marginal cultures. Conceptions of culture as 'emergent' or as 'processual' (Rosaldo 1989) are compelling because they suggest the dynamic movement of cultural knowledge and practice within networks of power and across cultural borders. Furthermore, the notion of emergent cultures allows for the possibility that individuals and groups make strategic choices within cultures and about culture – that intending subjects are engaged in the knowledgeable occupation and appropriation of unmotivated or abstract systems of language and meaning (Spivak 1993). From these strategic choices arise articulations of subjectivity, the parameters of self-definition and the possibility of cultural identity as agency.

Homi Bhabha (1994: 31) proposes that the 'other' as cultural object becomes caught in the 'closed circle of interpretation', cited, quoted and framed but never allowed to be the active agent of signification or identification. He suggests that a renewed engagement in the 'politics of and around cultural domination' depends on a notion of cultural difference rather than cultural diversity: 'Cultural diversity is an epistemological object – culture as an object of empirical knowledge – whereas cultural difference is the process of the *enunciation* of culture as "knowledge*able*", authoritative, adequate to the construction of systems of cultural identification' (ibid.: 34). Post-modern ethnography and post-colonial thought, then, can furnish an understanding of culture as dynamic and inventive and a recognition of the conditions of cultural representation – both epistemological and enunciative – as political.

Approaches to communication and cultural politics informed by this composite model of culture can help reveal the points at which media have been integrated into contemporary aboriginal cultures. Cree and Ojibway communities in Nishnawbe-Aski are in process of transformation. Traditional values inform the use of new technologies, but traditions, cultural precepts, even languages are reconstituted in the encounter with new media. A view of culture as 'processual' illuminates the productive and strategic choices that are made by groups and individuals as they determine how social patterns, religious beliefs, linguistic structures, and technological or economic infrastructures should be maintained, transformed or relinquished.

Post-colonial discourses of agency and identity: resistance and reinscription

Post-colonial theory begins from an understanding of the productivity of colonial power in naming and locating the colonized as 'other' while effacing the possibility of subaltern subjectivity. As Spivak argues (1988: 280), the identity of the subaltern resides in its deviation from dominant Western subjectivity; it is an identity defined only in terms of its *difference*. In North America, aboriginal people have been constructed as 'other', effaced from colonial narratives, situated as outside history and discourse. The construction of indigenous cultures as distant in time and space also reflects the definition of subaltern consciousness in terms of difference and further confirms its 'unrepresentability'. A Cree television producer at Wawatay told me:

> If you look in your own books about our history you're not going to see us . . . . It's not written, you're only going to see what your father's or your mother's parents have written there for you. For you, that's all.

This is the central problem of subaltern identity and expressive subjectivity, for clearly the accounts that my ancestors have produced of 'history' are not the accounts that the Cree themselves may have produced and so in 'my' accounts, the Cree are both invisible and silent. Cree today do not find 'themselves' in these accounts, and yet as subjects are historically constituted, producing discourses in which they can locate and through which they can represent themselves.

Post-colonial writers have directed attention to the historical and spatial modes of domination and discursive occlusion, but more relevant to the question of aboriginal and indigenous appropriation of media is their concern with resistance and reinscription. It is the current fragmentation of the Western subject that may allow the possibility of an expressive subjectivity for 'others'. This potential means of self-representation by post-colonial peoples informs the cultural politics of aboriginal media use.

Central to the post-colonial rethinking of power and discourse is renewed attention to questions of subjectivity and identity, the subversion of colonial inscriptions of 'otherness' and 'difference' and the strategic reoccupation of essentialist categories of race, culture or gender. 'Difference' thus becomes 'identity', authority or agency in the rewriting of colonial narratives and the enunciation of otherness. People who do not find themselves in colonial histories may put forward competing narratives and revise historical and social definitions of self and group. Cultural identity organized within these competing narratives, as Said (1993: xxiv) suggests, is 'contrapuntal and nomadic', resistant to the monolithic constructions of 'us' and 'them' and continually undermining the 'police action' with which encompassing national identities are enforced (cf. ibid.: 15). Said also refers to the notion of recovery or reinscription in suggesting that 'resistance cultures' must work to recover forms already infiltrated by the 'culture of empire' and reoccupy the imaginative terrain common to both native and colonizer (ibid.: 121, 210). While identities may be 'negotiated' and traditions 'invented', they are not negotiated out of nowhere and invented from nothing. It is the recovery of these 'lost traces' along with claims to sovereignty, self-determination and nationhood which Spivak (1993: 63) points to as the 'agency of post-coloniality'.

In a provocative reading of post-colonial cultures and identities, Homi Bhabha (1994) suggests that post-modernism must move beyond its 'celebration of fragmentation' to a recognition of other possible histories and voices. He argues for a 'Third Space' or an 'in-between space'; not the location of singularities or 'originary narratives' but the place from which articulations of cultural difference emerge. The Third Space is that intersubjective site of negotiation and translation, contestation and collaboration where the '*inter*national' and hybrid constitution of culture becomes apparent (Bhabha 1994: 1, 38). Like Said, Bhabha seems to view the contested cultural terrain common to both colonizer and colonized as the most productive source of 'strategies of selfhood'. Above all, Bhabha argues for the 'enunciative present in the articulation of culture [as] . . . a process by which objectified others may be turned into subjects of their history and experience' (1994: 176). This enunciative present is a shifting, transformative time; neither that of pre-figurative histories nor that of traditional models but a time of cultural uncertainty and representational 'undecidability' (1994: 34).

Media and modes of identification in Nishnawbe-Aski

Post-colonial conceptions of identity help situate aboriginal peoples' appropriation of media within this enunciative present. At an early stage, for example, Wawatay's development of communications acted as a catalyst for the emergence of a regional aboriginal identity in Nishnawbe-Aski and strengthened the expression of interests common to isolated and scattered communities. Within the organization itself, cultural identity now seems to be articulated in the relation between programme producers and the community audiences they serve and in the encounter between traditional narratives and values and contemporary political and social changes. In many ways, Wawatay's communicative priorities and strategies are determined in a 'time of cultural uncertainty'. Cree and Ojibway communicators, as knowledgeable speakers within their specific linguistic and cultural contexts, must negotiate the insertion of new technologies into these discourses and use them effectively in the expression of and reflection upon past and present aboriginal experience.

In the case of television, Wawatay staff largely acquired their training and technique on site, and some had no prior experience of the medium. Many Nishnawbe-Aski communities also first encountered television at the time of Wawatay's initial broadcasts in 1987. As one Wawatay staff member suggested, a lack of extensive previous experience with the medium on the part of both producers and audiences permitted the freer use of television 'to identify ourselves', as he put it, and enabled Wawatay to engage in a mode of representation qualitatively different from that of mainstream 'propaganda organizations' like the CBC. This implicit critique of existing investments of power in communication technologies was accompanied by a suggestion that Wawatay could resist these prior constructions in the act of cultural identification. The speaker's purposeful use of the verb form in 'to identify ourselves' captures the sense of identification as an active, expressive and communicative practice.

Wawatay's media also provide information from beyond Nishnawbe-Aski. Reporting on ideas, issues and events originating outside the communities requires interpretive skills and a thorough knowledge of the internal and external contexts within which knowledge is produced and communicated.

One reporter considered his work at Wawatay as a form of translation, involving continuous shifts from internal to external definitions or locations of identity. His understanding of his own language, culture and community had to be used to situate and communicate his understanding of the larger society.

Another Wawatay staff member made a related point about the translation of language and cultural precepts in suggesting that some concepts are untranslatable. On the subject of current affairs programming the staff member put forth the example of 'famousness', in the sense of celebrity or stardom, as a concept that would not translate from English to the aboriginal languages. Instead the emphasis in a programme would, in the aboriginal linguistic and conceptual context, have to rest upon 'remembrance' of some person's activities or accomplishments and remembrance of the person themselves. A genre such as news or public affairs is subtly transformed by this necessity of translating between cultures. As an institution, Wawatay is a site where people perfect these forms of cross-cultural translation and develop a certain bicultural identity – that balance of footing that allows them to move between languages and cultural codes.

The articulation of identity through the use of media at Wawatay is most apparent at cultural boundaries. Individual and collective commitments to developing media 'for the people' and the circulation of knowledge within Nishnawbe-Aski communities are negotiated alongside economic, social and technological changes which bring these communities into more frequent contact with non-native norms and practices. In making decisions about how discursive and practical elements drawn from a native cultural and social milieu can be preserved and adapted in the appropriation and use of media, Cree and Ojibway people move between internal definitions of what it means to be Anishnawbe, to say 'who we are', and the external conditions within which such a statement can be made or understood. Identity as expression or inscription is produced in the act of identifying.

As a result of the historical isolation, geographical remoteness and linguistic and cultural vitality of these Cree and Ojibway communities, distinct cultural boundaries exist and access by outsiders is carefully regulated. But while the villages may be 'closed societies' in some respects, this does not prevent people from 'journeying out' to the larger society, finding what is useful or necessary there and adapting it for local use. Boundaries are not barriers to knowledge, as Paul Carter (1988: 163) insists, but places of communicated difference. The spatial or social location of boundaries may often be debatable, but in the articulation of cultural difference as identity they are places where meanings are produced and accumulate (Carter 1988: 137). As Bhabha (1994: 179) suggests, post-colonial subjectivities are constituted under conditions of contingency and 'liminality'. At these border crossings, cultures become 'hybrid, heterogeneous, extraordinarily differentiated and unmonolithic' (Said 1993: xxiv). Wawatay's media both facilitate and necessitate border crossings. Such crossings are not, however, one-way movements of commodities, technologies or practices from centre to margin, but involve processes of rejection, adaption, negotiation and innovation. Through these border engagements, in the movement between and within cultures, identities are articulated, inscribed and reinscribed.

CONCLUSION

This chapter has explored the movement of media across cultural borders and their appropriation and reconstruction under post-colonial conditions. Whether considered as contents, technologies or practices, dominant forms of mass communication do not cross cultural boundaries intact. In aboriginal communities in northern Canada, imported media have been incorporated into existing patterns of social interaction and communication and have been subject to culturally specific modes of interpretation and elaboration. Aboriginal media use can be seen as constrained by coexisting investments of power in communications technologies, but also as constituting a strategic and knowledgeable occupation of these technologies. Native communications societies like Wawatay are instances of the articulation between global histories and economies and local cultural priorities, and indicate the ways in which local resistance and cultural persistence transform dominant discourses and technologies of power.

Post-colonial discourses are grounded in a recognition of the occupation and reinscription of Western theories, histories and narratives by 'others'. Strategies of resistance, modes of enunciation and identification, and the implicit critique emerging from aboriginal communication practices also transform the theoretical categories described and assessed above. The use of media as a means of cultural identification in aboriginal communities embodies a tacit criticism of metropolitan constructions of communication technologies for the production and circulation of commodified images. The convergence of native-controlled media with aboriginal self-government and structures of community accountability and control represent an unstated rejection of models of 'development' as exponential economic growth. The divergence of aboriginal broadcasting from public and community broadcasting practices in Canada would suggest the need for substantial reviews of national and provincial policy in this area. In each of these instances, aboriginal communication practices have critical implications for dominant discourses and are subverting conventional categories and procedures. Research in the area of cross-cultural communication is a productive instance of practice bringing theory into crisis.

ACKNOWLEDGEMENTS

This chapter is based on research carried out for my doctoral dissertation in the Graduate Programme in Communications at McGill University in Montréal.

The dissertation benefited inestimably from the support and direction of my supervisor Ron Burnett and committee members David Crowley, Gail Valaskakis and the late Roger Keesing. I have also profited from David Howes' thorough and perceptive reading of the dissertation and editing of the material in its current form. The research and writing have been enriched throughout by the thoughtful engagement and patient response of individuals at Wawatay from whom I learned much. The opportunity to exchange ideas with individuals involved in and committed to strengthening the future of native broadcasting gave me a much greater appreciation of the importance of their work for their people and for all Canadians.

EPILOGUE

The dynamics and ethics of cross-cultural consumption

Constance Classen and David Howes

The subject of global marketing presents a prism for the researcher, glittering with a multitude of facets having to do with the production, marketing and consumption of goods and images across cultures. The chapters of this book have largely focused on the reception of imported products by various Western and non-Western societies. In the present chapter, we shall extend our focus to explore the cross-cultural interplay of the processes of the production, marketing, consumption – and reproduction – of goods. Each section of the chapter examines the phenomenon of global marketing from a different perspective: the consumption of Western goods by non-Western peoples; the global marketing of Western goods; the consumption of non-Western goods by the West; and, the global reproduction of Western-style goods. Underlying the discussion is a concern with the social and moral ramifications of the spread of consumer culture. Each section therefore ends with a number of questions which bring out the ethical dimensions of cross-cultural marketing and consumption, and the equivocal nature of the perceived effects of this marketing and consumption in different social settings.

Traditionally, cultural theorists have depicted 'the masses' as being manipulated – and even brainwashed – by consumer culture (cf. Adorno and Horkheimer 1973; Marcuse 1964). This manipulation was held to be particularly acute in the case of the Third World consumer, who was deemed to be at the mercy of the 'dream machine' of Western marketing. As a result of the relentless promotional drive of transnational corporations, Third World consumers were said to be coerced to buy goods – jeans, watches, perfumes, televisions – which had no real meaning for them and played no authentic role in their culture (Wilk 1994; Tomlinson 1991).

The more recent approach in the study of consumer culture, put forward by authors such as Miller (1987), Hannerz (1992) and Willis (1990), among others, has been to stress the agency of consumers to select and adapt products according to their own desires, knowledge and interests.[1] This is the approach taken by most of the contributors to this book. According to this model, although Third World people may *seem* to be manipulated into buying consumer goods which are alien to, and destructive of, their cultures, in fact, they are actively employing consumer goods to express and forge their own unique cultural identities. The term 'creolization' was proposed to refer to this 'indigenization' of consumer goods.

The present chapter recognizes the transformations which global goods and images undergo in local marketplaces, but it is attentive to the conflicts of values which occur when consumer goods are marketed across cultures as well. In other words, the fact that consumers can creatively construct their own identities through the products they consume should not be taken to mean that the diffusion of consumer culture presents no dilemmas for the world's peoples.

CONSUMING THE WEST

The ethical concern most commonly raised with respect to the transcultural marketing of consumer goods is that the spread of a single regime of products and values around the world will work to destroy cultural diversity and end up creating a globally standardized culture. According to this view, we will one day live in a world in which everyone has access to and consumes the same things. No matter where you go in the world, there will be a McDonald's restaurant, Hollywood movies, Adidas running shoes, and an American Express office. This vision of a global consumer culture is particularly disturbing for diverse Third World peoples, some of whom have only recently emerged from colonial regimes, and now find themselves being apparently 'Coca-colonized' by an influx of consumer goods from the West. In India, for example, fear that an influx of Western products would herald a return to colonial domination recently led Hindu fundamentalists to organize a boycott of Coca-Cola and Pepsi as 'the most visible symbols of the multinational invasion of this country' (Bose 1994).

Even in the First World country of Japan, there has been widespread concern over the proliferation of Western goods and images and a call for a rejection of the process of Westernization together with a return to a 'traditional' Japanese way of life.

> To some Japanese nativists, their people's best hope of liberating themselves from Western cultural domination and rediscovering their Japanese souls lies in the process of *jikkan* – 'retrospection through actual sensation.' Thus the smell of incense at a shrine or the tactile and kinesthetic sensations of sitting on tatami (*suwaru*) rather than sitting on a chair (*koshikakeru*) can produce a reconnection with the eternal, authentic Japanese culture and soul.
>
> (Tobin 1992: 34)

The global marketing of Western products is criticized not only for spreading Western values (while enriching Western coffers), but also for spreading what many people perceive as materialist, decadent values. Junk food, Barbie dolls, designer jeans, Playboy magazines. Happiness in a dish-washer, social status in an automobile, beauty in a bottle of hair colour. These are the goods and values the West is ostensibly offering the rest of the world. These are the goods and values which, in the minds of many critics of the consumer society, have already brought the West to a state of moral and social decay.

Criticism of the shallow, self-serving way of life ostensibly promoted by Western consumer goods has been world-wide. In Chile, intellectuals claimed that Donald Duck and other American comic book characters were spreading the materialist and imperialist ideology of the United States under the guise of harmless entertainment for children (Dorfman and Mattelart 1975). In Iran, the government considered banning the import of satellite dishes in order to preserve Iranian culture from infiltration by 'immoral' Western television shows. 'These programs, prepared by international imperialism, are part of an extensive plot to wipe out our religious and sacred values' declared an official of the Iranian Ministry of Culture and Islamic Guidance (Barber 1995: 207; cf. also Arnould 1989: 251–2).

Yet, unless they result in the institution of outright bans, such protests are rarely sufficient to deter the consumption of Western commodities in the non-West. For example, the fact that Western-style public displays of affection are considered improper in India has not prevented Indians from watching such displays in American movies and television shows broadcast on the cable network Star TV. The expectation on the part of the global marketers is that this watching will soon turn to imitating, and, in turn, create a need for a whole new range of consumer products. A transnational business executive explains: 'When you want to be physically closer to people a lot, then you tend to want to look better, smell better. So the market [in India] will grow for cosmetics, perfumes, after-shaves, mouthwashes and so on' (Dyer 1994). This illustrates how closely allied Western consumer goods are with Western lifestyles, and the difficulty of receiving the former while ignoring or rejecting the latter (Sinha 1991).

Even official bans on Western consumer goods are often not sufficient to keep such goods from entering the country. In Iran a ban on American movies led to underground video clubs springing up all over the country. A widespread prohibition on imports in India (in order to boost the Indian economy as well as to appease Indian nationalists) similarly resulted in a thriving black market in foreign goods (Barnet and Cavanagh 1994: 140–1). Such strong popular interest in consumer goods reinforces the fears of those who worry that their cultural and religious identity will be swept away by a flood of Michael Jackson videos and McDonald's hamburgers if their country's borders are opened to the global marketers.

One concern, common to many people both within and without the West, is that consumer goods and values will be presented and perceived as so eminently desirable that they will not only alter or displace traditional cultural and religious values, but become an object of worship in themselves. In this regard Roland Barthes has written of the automobile: 'Cars today are almost the exact equivalent of the great Gothic cathedrals . . . consumed in image if not in usage by a whole population which appropriates them as . . . purely magical object[s]' (quoted in Durning 1992: 81).

Such investment of Western commodities with religious or magical properties has occurred in many non-Western countries. In Malaysia, for example, the Temiar people believe that they encounter spirits in their dreams, who endow them with sacred power and knowledge in the form of songs. Whereas these spirits customarily came from natural objects, such as flowers and mountains, they now increasingly come from consumer goods such as watches and motorcycles (Roseman 1993). In Mexico, the Tzotzil people have constituted Pepsi-Cola as a means of communicating with the divine and a symbol of religious belief. On the third Thursday of every month Tzotzil elders meet to ceremonially drink Pepsi and *Poch* – an alcoholic beverage – and thereby enter into communion with God (Robberson 1994).

Perhaps the most famous example of the sacralization of commodities is found in the cargo cults of Melanesia. These cults were based on the belief that following certain ritual practices would ensure the arrival of an enormous ship or plane-load of Western goods – iron axes, tinned food, firearms, automobiles – for the cultists. The ritual practices ranged from wearing Westernized dress in anticipation of the arrival of the Western goods to performing traditional dances, and from creating mock stores with stones and leaves for goods to making mock aircraft and airstrips (Worsley 1970; Burridge 1960).

To some observers such practices may seem to indicate a disturbing devotion to things Western – a colonization of the soul by consumer goods. However, the reality is more complex. The incorporation of certain Western products into local cults is often an attempt to acquire some of the perceived power of the West in order to turn it to the advantage of one's own community. In Melanesia, the objective of many cargo cults was not only to attain consumer goods, but also to enable the local people to gain ascendency over the white colonists. In the Madang district of Papua New Guinea, for example, imported products were said by cargo cult leaders to have been made, in fact, by the ancestors of the native inhabitants and then stolen by whites. According to this belief, imported goods were more native than foreign and consequently more the property of indigenous people than whites. Ultimately, it was believed, the ancestors would arrive in a ship bringing the goods directly, and the corrupt Westerners would be driven away (Worsley 1970: 115–16).

The example above, like many of the examples presented in the various chapters of this book, demonstrates that, while Western consumer goods are indeed spreading across the globe, there is none the less a significant amount of variation in the ways in which these goods are received by different peoples. When non-Western peoples consume Western goods, therefore, they do not necessarily 'swallow them whole', symbolic values and all, but rather 'season' them according to their own tastes and customs. Yet might it not be the case, as some nationalists and nativists fear, that instances of syncretism between local cultures and global goods are just steps on the route to homogenization? Can modern consumer goods ultimately belong anywhere but in a consumer society?

SELLING TO THE 'OTHER'

We have seen that a major critique of global marketing is that, by selling the same goods in essentially the same way all over the world, transnational corporations ignore and eradicate cultural difference. What, however, are the attitudes of the people directing this global marketing of goods? Are they insistent on blanketing the world with Western goods and advertising images – with complete disregard for cultural difference? This would certainly appear to be the case from many of the statements made by transnational executives (cf. Magrath 1992: 130–58; Filman 1992a, 1992b). The director of an international advertising agency (one of whose clients happens to be the Bayer pharmaceutical company) puts it this way:

> 'A lie has been perpetuated for years and years... The lie is that people are different. Yes there are differences among cultures, but a headache is a headache.' And aspirin is aspirin.
>
> (Barnet and Cavanagh 1994: 169)

The rationale expressed here is that people are basically the same (or have the same headaches) everywhere, and that products designed to satisfy North American 'needs' will also satisfy the 'needs' of people in Bolivia or China.[2] To take this rationale further, there is nothing *inherently* American about McDonald's restaurants or Hollywood movies, they are just good responses to what are fundamentally universal desires for food and entertainment.

A more subtle attitude, even though it produces similar effects, holds that, yes, cultural differences exist, but the power (symbolic, technological, aesthetic, etc.) of Western products is so great that it can overcome any local differences. As a Harvard business professor states: 'the products and methods of the industrialized world play a single tune for all the world and all the world eagerly dances to it' (Levitt 1983: 92). Thus, to take a random example, even if sunglasses are of little use to rain forest dwellers in Malaysia, the prestigious connotations of the product, enhanced by advertising, would make them desirable possessions.

A third view is that, as foreign products, imported goods should not be expected to conform to local values, and may even violate them with impunity. For example, in an African society, such as that of the Ndembu of Zambia, the colours red and white might be strongly associated with blood and milk (cf. Turner 1967). These colours would therefore seem inappropriate for marketing a soft drink. Yet a red and white Coca-Cola can might be deemed by members of the culture to stand so far outside tribal experience, that the colours are not interpreted according to the local system of classification, and instead assume a transcendent signification.

These three points of view have all been partially borne out in practice. Certain First World goods, such as televisions and cars, would seem to be so attractive in themselves as to have an almost universal appeal, cutting across cultural difference.[3] Other goods, such as Western clothing, may not be immediately alluring, but are so invested with symbolic authority and attraction that they appeal to many Third World people in spite of cultural difference. Finally, due to their foreign nature, many imported goods are not expected by local peoples to conform to local lifestyles. In Japan, for example, Western products often have better sales when advertised with Western models in Western settings than with Japanese models in Japanese settings, where they may seem out of place and inappropriate (O'Barr 1994: 174–87).

Given these scenarios, there would seem to be no pressing need for Western marketers to take into account the cultural values of the non-Western peoples to whom they sell their products. In fact, there would even seem to be compelling reasons why marketers should *not* attempt to respond to these values for, in many cases, the commercial appeal of Western products has been shown to be predicated on their associations with a Western lifestyle.

Yet, if imported products can sometimes impose their own cultural logic on the markets they enter, there are none the less plenty of instances where imported products are not able to override local sensibilities. For example, a camellia-scented perfume popular in the United States failed to attract buyers in Latin America because camellias are associated with funerals in Latin America (Ricks 1993: 46).

Such clashes of cultural values often occur not just with the product, but with the advertising used to promote it. One American advertising campaign which attempted to evoke a sense of masculinity by using an image of a deer became an object of ridicule in Brazil where the deer is a symbol of homosexuality. A soap company which tried to promote its products in the Middle East with an ad depicting soiled clothes to the left of the detergent and clean clothes to the right achieved the opposite from the intended effect due to the fact that Arabic peoples read from right to left (Ricks 1993: 52–3).

Transnational corporations cannot simply ignore local sensibilities and customs, therefore, and, in fact, such corporations have increasingly abandoned or modified the three views described above in favour of a fourth approach: tailoring global products and advertisements to local markets (cf. Piirto 1991: 142–53; J. James 1993: 54–8). For example, while Unilever's Impulse fragrance was promoted with a 'boy meets girl' theme in most countries, in the Middle East, where Islamic law forbids a strange man to approach a woman, the theme was dropped and the fragrance was positioned as a perfumed deodorant (Hogan 1989: 29–30). Even the world-famous name of Coca-Cola was changed for the Chinese market when it was found that the Chinese characters literally mean 'Bite the Wax Tadpole' (Berkowitz 1994).

Transnational companies which *do* try to present themselves as 'cultural insiders' to their global clients, however, have to make sure they 'get things right'. United Airlines advertised flights to Asia by boasting 'We Know the Orient', but then mismatched pictures of Eastern currencies and the names of Eastern countries (Berkowitz 1994). An advertisement by a shoe company depicted Japanese women performing footbinding, a practice which was exclusive to China (Solomon 1994: 485).

An area where global marketers frequently come to cross-cultural grief is that of slogans, idiomatic expressions which often translate poorly from English to other languages. For example, a Taiwanese translation of the Pepsi-Cola slogan 'Come Alive with the Pepsi Generation' turned out to mean 'Pepsi will bring your ancestors back from the dead'. Similarly, the Coors slogan 'Get Loose With Coors' came out in Spanish as 'Get the runs with Coors' (Solomon 1994: 480). Such errors point to the problems which can arise when marketers are not sufficiently knowledgeable about and in tune with their target markets. It is not therefore simply a case of the West 'playing a single tune for all the world to dance to'.

Cultural differences, of course, also occur *within* the West, and can influence the marketing and reception of products in different regions. For instance, a citronella-scented laundry detergent which sold well in Europe had poor sales in North America where the scent of citronella is associated with mosquito repellent (Classen, Howes, and Synnott, 1994: 194–5). Even within one country, there may be a variety of ethnic groups and social classes with different cultural and consumer profiles (Peñaloza 1994; García Canclini 1995). For this reason, American marketing texts, for example, now contain sections on how to successfully market goods to the African-American, Asian-American and Hispanic-American populations (Rossman 1994; Solomon 1994).

Even when marketers appear to be sensitive to cultural difference, however, the issue of 'Coca-colonization' remains. Does it really make a difference to the globalization of consumer culture if marketers emphasize the family in advertisements directed towards family-oriented Latin Americans or if Coca-Cola is sold under a different name in China? Could it just be an *illusion* of cultural difference that is preserved (or created)?

CONSUMING THE 'OTHER'

The West not only sells goods to the rest of the world, it also consumes goods – Japanese cars, Mexican food – from the rest of the world. Global marketing would seem to entail, therefore, not only a 'Westernization' of the world, but also a certain 'Japanization' or 'Mexicanization' of the West. This state of affairs is a matter of some concern to Westerners, who fear a loss of cultural integrity (and hegemony) and worry about importing more goods than they export. The trade imbalance between Japan and the United States (which currently favours the former), for example, has been a source of significant political and social anxiety in the United States. In response to this tense situation, as well as to the rising costs of labour in Asia, hundreds of Japanese companies have located their factories in Mexico close to the American border. When the goods these factories produce enter the United States they count as Mexican, rather than Japanese, thus apparently lessening the number of Japanese exports sold in America. This state of affairs has led American Members of Congress to call the Mexican/US border a 'Japanese Trojan horse', spilling out an army of Japanese goods to conquer the American economy (Barnet and Cavanagh 1994: 64).

Non-Western marketers who sell to the West usually try to take Western sensitivities and values into consideration. When imported goods are not immediately identifiable as foreign, as is the case with cars or tape recorders, for instance, their manufacturers will sometimes try to disguise or downplay their foreign origins. Brand names, for example, will often be Westernized, such as the Japanese-based Panasonic or the Korean-based Gold Star. The Japanese electronics giant Sony so successfully disguised its Japanese origins with its choice of company name that 'a high percentage of [American] retailers who carried Sony products claimed that they had never sold anything made in Japan and never would' (Barnet and Cavanagh 1994: 59–60). One Sony creation, the Walkman, is an interesting case of a Japanized English neologism becoming naturalized in the rest of the world.

Advertising will usually be employed to make the foreign product appear reassuringly Western. Therefore, while Western cars may be advertised in Japan with Western actors, Japanese cars are not advertised in the West with Japanese actors, but in 'typical' Western settings. This situation may have to do both with a distrust of foreignness in the West and the lack of a 'prestige-value' associated with non-Western peoples (O'Barr 1994).

Non-Western marketers also try to take into account the lifestyles and aesthetic preferences of Westerners in their product design and advertising. When the Walkman was first invented, its Japanese creators thought of providing it with two sets of headphones because, from a traditional Japanese perspective, it seemed 'rude' for individuals to retreat into a private world (Barnet and Cavanagh 1994: 49). Yet in the individualized culture promoted by the modern West, consumers are less interested in sharing than in pleasing themselves, and thus the Walkman ended up being sold with only one headphone set (cf. Chambers 1994: 49–53; Barber 1995: 77).

As an example of the difficulty that non-Westerners sometimes have in fathoming Western likes and dislikes, a recent issue of *China Trade News* advised Chinese marketers that: 'Elephants are taboo to the British. When exporting goods to Britain make sure you do not put any pictures of elephants on the good's trademarks or its packaging.' Marketers were similarly told to avoid the number thirteen, deemed unlucky in the West (Anon. 1995).

In general, the only time when the foreign nature of an imported product is emphasized in the West by its marketers (whether these be Western or non-Western) is when part of its appeal to Westerners lies in its exotic nature. Examples of this are Colombian coffee, Middle-Eastern carpets, or African folk art. In such cases stereotypical imagery of otherness is usually employed to promote the products, such as an illustration of a Colombian coffee picker in traditional clothing leading a donkey, or of a Middle-Eastern man with billowing pants and turned-up shoes flying a magic carpet. The broad smiles on the faces of these product mascots indicate that 'the natives are friendly' to Westerners – in other words, that the product's foreignness is appealing rather than threatening. As Carol Hendrickson points out in her chapter on the marketing of Guatemalan handicrafts in the United States, the traditionalist settings and descriptions employed in the ads for such products – 'handmade in a tiny town high above the Guatemalan rainforests' – play both on a Western appetite for exotica, and on a Western nostalgia for a pre-industrial way of life, widely perceived by Westerners as still existing in most of the Third World. At the same time, the evident Western desire to perceive Third World peoples as 'primitive' indicates an interest on the part of the West in locating Third World peoples in a subordinate position (cf. Bhabha 1983).

The Western consumption of 'cultural difference' occurs not only within the West itself (Figure 10), but also within non-Western countries through the tourist trade. Westerners who travel to Mexico, to Bali or to Kenya, want to see the traditional imagery they have come to associate with these countries. In

Figure 10 POINT ZERO fashion billboard in Montreal
Source: photograph by Mediacom

186

other words, not just skyscrapers and shopping malls, but native villages, dances, and handicrafts. In order to keep the tourist dollars coming in, such nativist spectacles and products must be produced for travellers, regardless of whether they form part of the contemporary local scene (MacCannell 1989; Little 1991).

This Western consumption of otherness, whether inside or outside the West, does not take place without affecting the 'others' whose products and supposed lifestyles are being consumed. The simplistic and traditionalistic imagery of 'otherness' used in product promotions and travel advertisements hinders the inhabitants of the countries concerned in asserting an identity as modern, industrially developed or developing peoples with complex lifestyles. Furthermore, perceiving their exoticized image in the mirror of the West, non-Westerners sometimes exoticize themselves, in turn. This can have two contrasting effects. The first is to try and de-exoticize oneself by becoming more Western – wearing Western clothing, living in Western-style houses, and so on. The second is to internalize the West's exotic image of oneself. For example, it has been suggested in Japan that the 'samurai bravado' admired by the Japanese 'not only does not represent an authentic Japanese sensibility but is an occidentally inspired burlesque of what it means to be Japanese' (Tobin 1992: 31).

While Western consumers often manifest a desire for 'authenticity' when consuming the products and images of other cultures, it is authenticity from a Western, and not an indigenous, perspective. As will be recalled from Mary Crain's chapter on native identity in Ecuador, native women working in an international hotel in Quito are required by the management to wear a pastiche of traditional clothing calculated to appeal to tourists as 'authentic native costume'. Another example concerns the production of wood sculptures for the tourist trade. As tourists to Africa and New Guinea are often only interested in buying carvings that are black in colour (in keeping with their association of Africa and New Guinea with 'blackness') local wood carvers find themselves having to rub black shoe polish into their light-coloured carvings in order to make them saleable (Graburn 1976; cf. also Jules-Rosette 1994). A further example is that of the recreation of 'authentic' African or Melanesian tribal villages complete with natives in grass skirts solely for the purpose of satisfying foreign sightseers (Gewertz and Errington 1991).

What kinds of social and psychological disjunctions might occur when imagery and products, which supposedly convey the 'essence' of a culture, are created not in response to local traditions and values, but to the wishes of Western consumers? Will it not be the case, as seems to have occurred with the cult of the samurai in Japan, that local peoples will come to think of the Westernized version of their culture as authentic? How does the West reconcile its desire for exotic, pre-industrial 'otherness' with its marketing drive to globalize consumer culture? Finally, when Japanese exports to the United

States exceed American exports to Japan, is not the spectre of Western consumer imperialism an outdated myth?

RECREATING THE WEST

If stereotypical representations of otherness abound in the West, stereotypical representations of the West are even more abundant, both inside and outside of the West. Many of these representations originate in the West and are disseminated by, among other things, advertising, movies, and television shows. The United States, for example, uses the popular image of the American cowboy to push products, while Great Britain promotes itself to tourists with pictures of quaint thatched cottages. One can argue that these kinds of representations are not as potentially misleading as the images of foreignness found in the West, for most of the world knows that the United States is not *just* a land of cowboys and that Britain is not *just* a land of thatched cottages. Furthermore, representations of the West – while hardly true portraits of Western life with all its complexities – show a variety of lifestyles, urban life as well as life on the range, apartment buildings as well as cottages.

In the late twentieth century, people in non-Western countries are increasingly producing their own representations of the West for purposes of product promotion. Entrepreneurs around the world have learned that 'Westernness' or 'Americanness' is a highly valuable selling feature, and have been quick to capitalize on this in their production and packaging of commodities. Classen has noted how in Argentina domestic products will sometimes be given English or pseudo-English names in order to give them an 'American' prestige-value. The same occurs with even greater frequency in Japan, where one finds products such as 'American Cola', 'Class' cigarettes, and 'Creap' powdered milk (Tobin 1992: 1–38).[4] These are the products of peoples who have consumed the imagery of the West, and are now regurgitating, or recreating, it in their own way. From a Western, English-speaking perspective, such representations may appear unauthentic – 'Class' is too broad a term for a brand name, 'Creap' is not a real English word (and not a very enticing made-up English word, either). Yet from a local perspective, all that matters is that these names and products convey the intended image to their intended market. Western views on the matter are as irrelevant to local marketers as the views of Asians or Latin Americans on their stereotypical representation in Western media are to Western marketers.[5]

The production of 'Western' imagery, therefore, is no longer exclusively in the hands of the West. It is true that in many cases the factories producing Western products in Indonesia or Mexico belong to, or are contracted on behalf of, Western companies. For example, the American sports shoe company Nike contracts out virtually all of its actual production to Asian factories (Clifford 1992).[6] However, while Western consumer culture is still on the march around the world, it is not being driven solely by Western interests. The very success of the West in promoting its consumer products and consumer culture has spawned a world of local variations.

In the broadest sense, such products as Japanese cars and watches might be regarded as foreign imitations of originally Western products. What has been 'copied', and developed, however, is the technology and general concept, rather than any particular Western model. Many 'imitation goods' produced outside the West, none the less, *do* closely copy actual Western products. In Middle-Eastern markets, for example, one can find 'Tibe' and 'Tipe' boxes of detergent on the shelf, alongside their Western prototype, 'Tide'. In Japan, 'Chamel' and 'Canal' imitation perfumes compete with Chanel (Fenby 1983: 58, 111–12).

While imitation products sometimes only approximate the brand name of the models they copy, they often simply duplicate it. Fake Levi's, Citizen watches, Johnnie Walker Scotch and Raleigh bicycles, among many other products, can be found all over the world, but particularly in Asia, Africa and Latin America. Classen makes reference in her chapter, for example, to the prevalence of imitation goods in the marketplaces of Bolivia. The Third World, indeed, displays a post-modern proliferation of consumer 'simulacra', which can blur the border between real and fake.

In the 1960s, a merchant in Mexico City named Fernando Pelletier, opened a shop called 'Cartier' and started selling precise imitations of goods – watches, leather goods, pens – produced by the French company of the same name, at discount prices. When it discovered that its goods were being counterfeited, the original Cartier company decided to open up its own shop in Mexico. The Mexican Cartier, in response, sent a letter to the President of Mexico denouncing the French Cartier's lack of respect for Mexican industry and government, and suggesting that the *French* products were fakes. This letter was printed in major Mexican newspapers and soon became the subject of angry editorials against the French invaders. The French Cartier also ran into problems when it tried to register its trademark designs in Mexico, for it found that Pelletier had already registered them and thus had prior rights in them.

Eventually, in 1981, Pelletier – by then a millionaire – made the mistake of travelling to France where he was arrested for counterfeiting. In exchange for his release and the right to become one of Cartier's authorized agents in Mexico, Pelletier agreed to stop using the Cartier name for his own products. However, the end of this one counterfeiting operation has not prevented fake Cartier products from continuing to be produced in millions around the world (Fenby 1983: 60–9).

The example of Cartier illustrates how difficult it can be for companies to stop their goods from being counterfeited. As Jonathan Fenby notes in *Piracy and the Public*, the inhabitants of the Third World countries where many counterfeit products are made 'do not necessarily see things in the same way as Western holders of copyrights and trademarks' (1983: 5). Counterfeiting goods can be an important source of revenue and employment in developing nations. Furthermore, counterfeiting may seem like the only option when Third World countries find that their own local products cannot compete in consumer appeal with prestigious Western goods. Fenby writes:

> If people want jeans that look like Levis and local workshops can turn out a reasonable imitation, why spend much-needed hard currency on importing the real thing? The only sufferer is a distant firm with a famous name which can easily be dismissed as a rich multinational that does not need the money and is probably exploiting Third World markets in any case.
>
> (1983: 5)

Western individuals may also sympathize with this point of view, until they are told that their own livelihoods and even lives can be jeopardized by counterfeiting.

While the imitation goods made by counterfeiters are sometimes of high quality – for example, certain Korean copies of Apple and IBM computers – more often they have the look of the original without the quality. Product counterfeiters know that it is the image that attracts buyers in consumer culture – the classic shape of the Chanel No. 5 perfume bottle or the alligator in the Lacoste trademark – and it is the image that they therefore concentrate on replicating. This has led to a number of potentially hazardous products entering the marketplace, from poor-quality imitations of car parts to fake medicines. Such products have the 'look' of the real thing, but their lack of substance makes them harmful to First World and Third World consumers alike.

Although in the West 'cheap imitations' are usually thought of as coming from the East, products are counterfeited on a large scale within the West itself, and sometimes end up being sold to the Third World. Singapore, for example, was sold fake aircraft parts by a British firm, with fatal consequences. Kenya was sold a fake brand-name fungicide by a European company, resulting in a significant loss of the country's coffee crop (Fenby 1983: 4).[7] Moreover, many brand-name products from the East, such as Seiko watches or Nissan car parts, are also the target of counterfeiters. What matters is not the origin of the product, but what will sell.

It is none the less true that most of the originals of the products counterfeited or imitated come from the West, and that a vast amount of this counterfeiting goes on outside the West. The 'West' is therefore not only being marketed around the world, but is continually being recreated around the world, from local perspectives. Given this situation, are Third World countries which replicate Western products and imagery *ad infinitum* taking over the colonial role of the West and colonizing themselves? Should First World trademark holders be able to monopolize the global market with their products just because they have the money and resources to design and promote them?[8] Can a line be drawn between 'harmless' imitations and 'dangerous' fakes? Why should the production of fake Cartier watches or fake Levi's jeans be more of an issue than the production of fake Hopi *kachina* dolls or fake Mayan textile designs?

DYING OF CONSUMPTION

Situations where imported products are successfully incorporated into local lifestyles often seem to provide a 'happy solution' to the problem of maintaining cultural diversity in the face of global marketing. Rather than let consumer goods colonize them, local peoples instead 'colonize' consumer goods, imposing their own systems of values and practices on them and maintaining their cultural integrity. We saw examples of this in the chapter by Philibert and Jourdan on the indigenous classification of consumer goods in Melanesia, and in Marian Bredin's chapter on northern native appropriations of communications technology.[9] Yet the merging of consumer products and values with local traditions does not always have happy results for the communities concerned.

In India, for example, expensive consumer goods such as televisions and motorcycles are increasingly demanded as part of a bride's dowry by grooms avid to acquire the enticing products of Western culture. There have been many hundreds of cases of women being killed – often by being set on fire – by their husbands or in-laws when their families failed to produce the desired goods. The presumption is that the men can then remarry and receive another dowry elsewhere. Feeling themselves unable to cope with the growing economic burden of providing dowries for their daughters, some parents practise female infanticide (Bordewich 1986; Kronholz 1986). In India, consequently, the materialist values of consumer culture have had deadly results when combined with the traditional practice of the dowry.

In the Colombian Amazon, the Barasana Indians believe that consumer goods are infused with *ewa*, 'an irresistibly attractive and potent force which leads [the Barasana] to act in an uncontrolled manner and do things against their better judgement' (Hugh-Jones 1992: 46). One thing which the Barasana do against their better judgement in order to obtain such goods is to grow coca for the cocaine industry. A Barasana man comments:

> To begin with the old people all said 'don't work coca, working coca is bad'. But those guns and all those other things, they have such *ewa* that everybody – the shamans, the elders, even my old uncle Christo – they're all working coca now. There's no way to avoid it. These White people are really bad but we want their goods so much that we have to act as if we liked them.
>
> (Hugh-Jones 1992: 47)

The manufactured goods which the Barasana desire – guns, fishing hooks, cooking pots – are often those which they find eminently useful in their forest environment. Yet as a result of their self-professed irresistible desire for consumer goods, many Barasana end up in a situation of perpetual debt to their 'white' bosses, obliged to provide them with a constant flow of coca leaves, rubber, wood, gold, and other valuable forest products (Hugh-Jones 1992: 49).

The compulsion to obtain consumer goods whatever the cost, manifest in the dowry deaths of India or in the debt peonage of the Barasana, is certainly not unknown in the West where children have been killed in schoolyards for their brand-name running shoes. Such incidents often trigger a backlash against the self-centred materialist values of the consumer society. Yet in *Culture and Consumption*, Grant McCracken asserts that '[the] goods that are so often identified as the unhappy, destructive preoccupation of a materialist society are in fact one of the chief instruments of its survival, one of the ways in which its order is created and maintained' (1988: ix). It is undoubtedly the case that consumer goods are integral to the order of modern First World society, but this point should not be allowed to negate the serious difficulties that many people have both with consumerism and with the social structure it supports (cf. Gell 1988; Appleby 1994). If the West, the home of the consumer society, is not by any means comfortable with consumerism and its social effects, why should it be thought that non-Western peoples, for whom consumerism is a more recent phenomenon, should be any more comfortable with it (cf. Sherry 1987)?

Even when imported goods *do* appear to be harmoniously integrated into non-Western societies, they can be producing a number of troubling effects within those societies. Jean Comaroff, in her chapter, described how Africans were able to take elements of Western dress and give them their own meanings and uses in colonial Africa. Yet the widespread availability of imported clothing in Africa has hindered the development of local textile industries, which find their products cannot compete with the imports. This is especially the case when second-hand clothing from the West is bought in bulk by Western entrepreneurs (often from charity organizations, such as Goodwill) and shipped to Africa where it is sold at bargain prices (Todd 1993).

The availability of consumer goods may also have disastrous consequences for local and global environments by dramatically increasing levels of garbage production and pollution. Alan Durning writes in his study of the impact of consumerism on the environment:

> The consumer society's exploitation of resources threatens to exhaust, poison, or unalterably disfigure forests, soils, water, and air. We, its members, are responsible for a disproportionate share of all the global environmental challenges facing humanity.
>
> (1992: 23)

The environment simply cannot support a whole world of people with the consumer habits of the First World. Yet who should be excluded from the consumer society?

Certain consumer products put public health directly at risk. An obvious culprit here is the cigarette, aggressively marketed by multinationals around the globe. Another widely criticized product is baby formula (Van Esterik 1989). Baby formula is usually marketed as a healthy and modern (First World) alternative to breast milk. As used in the Third World, however, such formula is often neither healthy nor convenient. Lacking information and resources, Third World women sometimes mix the formula with contaminated water or fail to refrigerate it, resulting in the growth of potentially deadly bacteria. Another problem arises when nursing mothers start using baby formula, sometimes after having received free samples, and then discover that they cannot afford to continue using the product but are likewise unable to return to nursing as their own flow of milk has stopped. The misuse of baby formula in developing countries has resulted in the deaths of untold numbers of infants.

The situations described above are deeply disturbing. While it is evident that the exportation of Western consumer goods and values has been instrumental in bringing about these situations, it is not clear what, if anything, the West should now do to prevent them. To stem the spread of consumer goods from the First World to the Third would be to deny the agency of Third World peoples and to deprive them of the goods most people in the First World would on no account like to do without themselves. For instance, in response to the number of infant deaths caused by the improper use of milk formula, the World Health Organization recommended a ban on the advertising and marketing of breastmilk substitutes in the Third World. This recommended ban has been attacked, however, as an example of First World paternalism towards, and deprivation of, the Third World (Finkle 1994).

Different economic, political and cultural pressures, both from within and without, in turn, work to hinder Third World peoples from controlling the spread of consumerism in their countries themselves – if they are so inclined. So closely are the products and values of the consumer society tied to First World status, in fact, that any country which tries to avoid becoming 'consumerized', risks being completely marginalized from the global centres of power, as was the case in Indonesia for a time (Anderson 1984: 153–88).

Just as the marketing of consumer goods is now global in scope, so are the problems such marketing may create. Is the World Health Organization justified in calling for a ban on milk formula in the Third World when cigarettes – with their well-documented carcinogenic effects – are not banned in the First World? Can the Third World be expected to control the environmental damage caused by consumer goods in its countries, when the First World has been ravaging the environment for decades with its own cars, refrigerators, and throwaway products? Is there a 'dark side' to consumerism which will inevitably surface regardless of the particular cultural context? Have consumer goods become simply too attractive for anyone in the world to resist?

NOTES

1 Mica Nava discusses this shift in the theoretical models used to analyse consumer culture in *Changing Cultures* (1992: 162–99). See further, Tomlinson (1990).

2 On the classification of headaches among the Ainu of Japan, whose complex system of classification gives the lie to the claim 'a headache is a headache', see Ohnuki-Tierney (1977).

3 Aside from their inherent attractiveness, of course, televisions and cars often have a potent symbolic appeal. In Sri Lanka, for example, prosperous fishermen in remote villages buy televisions although they have no electricity, and add garages to their houses although they have no roads. It is as signs of status and modernity that these possessions are valued by the fishermen, rather than for their practical use (Gell 1986: 114).

4 A study of the use of English in Japan can be found in Stanlaw (1992).

5 In this regard it is informative to read Homi Bhabha (1984) on the unease occasioned in 'imperialist' nations when colonial peoples 'mimic' the discourse of their colonizers. See also Herzfeld (1987).

6 Interestingly, the fact that many 'American' products, such as those bearing the name Nike or Levi's, are manufactured *in* Mexico does not seem to affect attributions of their country of origin: they remain American products in the minds of Mexicans (Peñaloza 1994: 45). On product-country images generally see Popadopoulos and Heslop (1993).

7 The batches of expired Western medicines which sometimes end up in Third World markets also constitute fakes of a kind.

8 For a probing discussion of the copyright issue as it relates to world music see *Music Grooves* (Keil and Feld 1994).

9 As a further example, Homa Hoodfar (in press) reports that in low-income neighbourhoods of Cairo, people invest in household goods as a means of 'saving money', for in this way they are able to insulate their earnings from the potential demands of kin. Moreover, the selection and acquisition of Western appliances is often motivated by their potential to augment opportunities for social exchange. Thus, kerosene burners are preferred to gas stoves, because the former are portable and therefore enable women to do their cooking out of doors where they can converse with their friends.

BIBLIOGRAPHY

Adam, M. (1980) 'La contre culture coca-cola: le mirage des objets et la dépendance du consommateur dans le tiers-monde', *L'homme et la société* 56–8: 149–60.

Adorno, T. and Horkheimer, M. (1973) *Dialectics of Enlightenment*, London: Allen Lane.

Agnew, J.-C. (1994) 'Coming up for air: consumer culture in historical perspective', in J. Brewer and R. Porter (eds) *Consumption and the World of Goods*, London: Routledge.

Anderson, M. H. (1984) *Madison Avenue in Asia: Politics and Transnational Advertising*, Toronto: Associated University Press.

Anderson, P. (1990) 'Aboriginal imagery: influence, appropriation, or theft?', *Eyeline* 12: 8–11.

Anon. (1995) 'Chinese newspaper warns elephants unnerve the British', *The Gazette*, 1 April 1995.

Appadurai, A. (1986) 'Introduction: commodities and the politics of value', in A. Appadurai (ed.) *The Social Life of Things: Commodities in Cultural Perspective*, Cambridge: Cambridge University Press.

—— (1990) 'Disjuncture and difference in the global cultural economy', *Theory, Culture and Society* 7 (2–3): 295–311.

—— (1993) 'Consumption, duration, and history', *Stanford Literary Review* 10(1–2): 11–33.

Appleby, J. (1994) 'Consumption in early modern social thought', in J. Brewer and R. Porter (eds) *Consumption and the World of Goods*, London: Routledge.

Armstrong, G. M. (1991) 'The reification of celebrity: persona as property', *Louisiana Law Review* 51: 445–68.

Arnould, E. (1989) 'Toward a broadened theory of preference formation and the diffusion of innovations: cases from Zinder Province, Niger Republic', *Journal of Consumer Research* 16: 239–66.

Arnould, E. and Wilk, R. (1984) 'Why do the natives wear Adidas?', *Advances in Consumer Research* 11: 748–52.

Austen, R. (1968) *Northwest Tanzania Under German and British Rule: Colonial Policy and Tribal Politics, 1889–1939*, New Haven, CT: Yale University Press.

Austen, R. and Smith, W. (1990) 'Private tooth decay as public economic virtue: the slave–sugar triangle, consumerism and European industrialization', *Social Science History* 14(1): 95–115.

Barber, B. R. (1995) *Jihad vs. McWorld*, New York: Random House.

Barley, N. (1986) *The Innocent Anthropologist*, Harmondsworth: Penguin.

Barnet, R. J. and Cavanagh, J. (1994) *Global Dreams: Imperial Corporations and the New World Order*, New York: Touchstone.

Baudrillard. J. (1968) *Le système des objets*, Paris: Denoel-Gonthier.

—— (1970) *La société de consommation*, Paris: Gallimard.

—— (1975) *The Mirror of Production*, trans. M. Poster, St. Louis, MO: Telos Press.

—— (1981) *For a Critique of the Political Economy of the Sign*, trans. C. Levin, St Louis, MO: Telos Press.

—— (1988) *America*, trans. C. Turner, London: Verso.

Beattie, J. (1958) 'The blood pact in Bunyoro', *African Studies* 17: 198–203.

Bell, Q. (1949) *On Human Finery*, New York: A. A. Wyn.

Benedek, E. (1993) *The Wind Won't Know Me: A History of the Navajo-Hopi Land Dispute*, New York: Vintage.

Benjamin, W. (1969) 'The work of art in the age of mechanical reproduction', in *Illuminations*, trans. H. Zohn, New York: Schocken Books.

—— (1989) *Paris, Capitale du XIXe Siècle. Le livre des passages*, trans. J. Lacoste, Paris: Editions du CERF.

Berger, J. (1983) *Ways of Seeing*, London: British Broadcasting Corporation.

Berkowitz, H. (1994) 'Top firms' slogan translations a disaster', *The Gazette*, 21 June 1994.

Bhabha, H. K. (1983) 'Difference, discrimination, and the discourse of colonialism', in F. Barker *et al.* (eds.) *The Politics of Theory: Proceedings of the Essex Conference on the Sociology of Literature*, Colchester: University of Essex Press.

—— (1984) 'Of mimicry and man: the ambivalence of colonial discourse', *October* 28: 125–33.

—— (1994) *The Location of Culture*, London: Routledge.

Blundell, V. (1993) 'Aboriginal empowerment and souvenir trade in Canada', *Annals of Tourism Research* 20: 64–84.

Bocock, R. (1993) *Consumption*, London: Routledge.

Bordewich, F. M. (1986) 'Dowry murders', *The Atlantic* July 1986: 21–7.

Bose, A. (1994) 'Cola influx gets cold reception', *The Gazette* 9 July 1994.

Bourdieu, P. (1979) *Algeria 1960*, Cambridge: Cambridge University Press.

—— (1984) *Distinction: A Social Critique of the Judgement of Taste*, trans. R. Nice, Cambridge, MA: Harvard University Press.

Bourke, J. G. [1884] (1962) *The Snake Dance of the Moquis of Arizona*, Glorieta, NM: Rio Grande Press.

Bowlby, R. (1985) 'Modes of shopping: Mallarmé at the Bon Marché', in N. Armstrong and L. Tennenhouse (eds) *The Ideology of Conduct: Essays in Literature and the History of Sexuality*, New York: Methuen.

Brewer, J. and Porter, R. (eds) (1994) *Consumption and the World of Goods*, London: Routledge.

Brookfield, H.C. (1972) *Colonialism, Development and Independence*, Cambridge: Cambridge University Press.

Bruner, E. M. (1994) 'Abraham Lincoln as authentic reproduction: a critique of postmodernism', *American Anthropologist* 96(2): 397–415.

Buck-Morss, S. (1989) *The Dialectics of Seeing: Walter Benjamin and the Arcades Project*, Cambridge, MA: The MIT Press.

Buell, F. (1994) *National Culture and the New Global System*, Baltimore, MD: The Johns Hopkins University Press.

Bulmer, R. (1967) 'Why the cassowary is not a bird? A problem of zoological taxonomy among the Karam of the New Guinea Highlands', *Man* (n.s.) 2(1): 5–25.

Burchell, W. J. (1822–4) *Travels in the Interior of Southern Africa*, (2 vols), London: Longman, Hurst, Rees, Orme, Brown & Green.

Burgess, M. and Valaskakis, G. (1995) *Indian Princesses and Cowgirls*, Montreal: Oboro.

Burke, T. (1990) '"Nyamarira that I love": commoditization, consumption, and the social history of soap in Zimbabwe', paper read at the Africa Studies Seminar, Northwestern University.

Burridge, K. (1960) *Mambu: A Study of Melanesian Cargo Movements and Their Social and Ideological Background*, New York: Harper Torchbooks.

Buskirk, M. (1992) 'Commodification as censor: copyrights and fair use', *October* 26: 83–109.

Carr, C. (1993) *On Edge: Performance at the End of the Twentieth Century*, Middletown, CT: Wesleyan University Press.

Carrier, J. (1990) 'The symbolism of possession in commodity advertising', *Man* (n.s.) 25(4): 693–705.

—— (1992) 'Occidentalism: the world turned upside-down', *American Ethnologist* 19:195–212.

Carrington, L. (1989) *The Seventh Horse and Other Stories*, London: Virago.

Carter, P. (1988) *The Road to Botany Bay*, London: Faber and Faber.

Chambers, I. (1986) *Popular Culture: The Metropolitan Experience*, London: Methuen.

—— (1990) *Border Dialogues: Journeys in Postmodernity*, London: Routledge.

—— (1994) *Migrancy, Culture, Identity*, London: Routledge.

Charles, N. and Kerr, M. (1988) *Women, Food and Families*, Manchester: Manchester University Press.

Chase, H. (1992) 'The *meyhane* or McDonald's – change in eating habits and the evolution of fast food in Istanbul', in S. Zubaida (ed.) *Culinary Cultures of the Middle East*, London: Centre of Near and Middle Eastern Studies.

Churchill, W. (1992) *Struggle for the Land: Indigenous Resistance to Genocide, Ecocide and Expropriation in Contemporary North America*, Toronto: Between the Lines.

Classen, C. (1993) *Worlds of Sense: Exploring the Senses in History and Across Cultures*, London: Routledge.

Classen, C., Howes, D. and Synnott, A. (1994) *Aroma: The Cultural History of Smell*, London: Routledge.

Clements, R. (1991) 'Misconceptions of culture: Native peoples and cultural property under Canadian Law', *University of Toronto Faculty of Law Review* 49: 1–26.

Clemmer, R. O. (1995) *Roads in the Sky: The Hopi Indians in a Century of Change*, Boulder, CO: Westview Press.

Clifford, J. (1988) *The Predicament of Culture: Twentieth-Century Ethnography, Literature, and Art*, Cambridge, MA: Harvard University Press.

Clifford, M. (1992) 'Spring in their step', *Far Eastern Economic Review*, 5 November 1992. Reprinted in *Consumerism* (vol. 4), Boca Raton, FL: Social Issues Resources Series Inc.

Coldevin, G. (1979) 'Satellite television and cultural replacement among Canadian Eskimos', *Communication Research* 6(2): 115–33.

Comaroff, J. (1985) *Body of Power, Spirit of Resistance: The Culture and History of a South African People*, Chicago: University of Chicago Press.

Comaroff, J. and Comaroff, J. L. (1991) *Of Revelation and Revolution: Christianity, Colonialism, and Consciousness in South Africa* (vol. 1), Chicago: University of Chicago Press.

—— *Of Revelation and Revolution* (vol. 2) (in preparation).

Comaroff, J. L. and Comaroff, J. (1992) *Ethnography and the Historical Imagination*, Boulder, CO: Westview Press.

Coombe, R. J. (1992) 'Publicity rights and political aspiration: mass culture, gender identity, and democracy', *New England Law Review* 26: 1221–80.

—— (1993) 'The properties of culture and the politics of possessing identity: Native claims in the cultural appropriation controversy', *The Canadian Journal of Law and Jurisprudence* 6(2): 249–85.

Crain, M. (1989) *Ritual, memoria popular y proceso político en la Sierra Ecuatoriana*, Quito, Ecuador: Abya Yala Press and Corporación Editora Nacional.

—— (1990) 'The social construction of national identity in Highland Ecuador', *Anthropological Quarterly* 63(1): 43–59.

—— (1991) 'Poetics and politics in the Ecuadorean Andes: women's narratives of death and devil possession', *American Ethnologist* 18(1): 67–89.

—— (1994a) 'Opening Pandora's box: a plea for discursive heteroglossia', *American Ethnologist* 21(1): 219–24.

—— (1994b) 'Unruly mothers: gender identities, political discourses and struggles for social space in the Ecuadorean Andes', *PoLAR (Political and Legal Anthropology Review)* 15(2): 98–110.

Crick, M. (1989) 'Representations of international tourism in the social sciences: sun, sex, sights, savings and servility', *Annual Review of Anthropology* 18: 307–44.

Curtis, K. (1989) 'Capitalism fettered: state, merchant and peasant in Northwestern Tanzania, 1917–1960', unpublished PhD thesis, University of Wisconsin.

Davenport, W. H. (1986) 'Two kinds of value in the Eastern Solomon Islands', in A. Appadurai (ed.) *The Social Life of Things: Commodities in Cultural Perspective*, Cambridge: Cambridge University Press.

Davidoff, L. and Hall, C. (1987) *Family Fortunes: Men and Women of the English Middle Class, 1780–1850*, Chicago: University of Chicago Press.

Davidson, A. (1988) *A Kipper with My Tea*, London: Macmillan.

de Certeau, M. (1984) *The Practice of Everyday Life*, trans. S. Rendall, Berkeley: University of California Press.

di Leonardo, M. (1990) 'Otherness is in the details', *The Nation* 5 November 1990: 530–6.

Dorfman, A. (1983) *The Empire's Old Clothes: What the Lone Ranger, Babar, and Other Innocent Heroes Do to our Minds*, New York: Pantheon Books.

Dorfman, A. and Mattelart, A. (1975) *How to Read Donald Duck: Imperialist Ideology in the Disney Comic*, New York: International General Editions.

Douglas, M. (1966) *Purity and Danger: An Analysis of the Concepts of Pollution and Taboo*, London: Routledge and Kegan Paul.

—— (1975) *Implicit Meanings*, London: Routledge and Kegan Paul.

Douglas, M. and Isherwood, B. (1979) *The World of Goods: Towards an Anthropology of Consumption*, New York: W.W. Norton & Co.

DuBoff, L. (1992) '500 years after Columbus: protecting Native American culture', *Cardozo Arts and Entertainment Law Journal* 11: 43–58.

Durning, A. T. (1992) *How Much is Enough? The Consumer Society and the Future of the Earth*, New York: W. W. Norton.

Dyer, G. (1994) 'How Star TV can sell aftershave and curb totalitarianism at the same time', *The Gazette*, 21 May 1994.

Enloe, C. (1990) *Bananas, Beaches and Bases: Making Feminist Sense of International Politics*, Berkeley: University of California Press.

Etherington, N. (1978) *Preachers, Peasants, and Politics in Southeast Africa, 1835–1880: African Christian Communities in Natal, Pondoland, and Zululand*, London: Royal Historical Society.

Ewen, S. (1988) *All-Consuming Images: The Politics of Style in Contemporary Culture*, New York: Basic Books.

Fabian, J. (1983) *Time and the Other; How Anthropology Makes Its Object*, New York: Columbia University Press.

Farrer, C. (1994) 'Who owns the words? An anthropological perspective on public law 101–601', *The Journal of Arts Management, Law and Society* 23(4): 317–26.

Faurschou, G. (1990) 'Obsolescence and desire: fashion and the commodity', in H. Silverman (ed.) *Postmodernism in Philosophy and Art*, London: Routledge.

Featherstone, M. (1990a) *Consumer Culture and Postmodernism*, London: Sage.

—— (1990b) 'Global culture: an introduction', *Theory, Culture and Society* 7(2–3): 1–15.

Feld, S. (1982) *Sound and Sentiment: Birds, Weeping, Poetics and Song in Kaluli Expression*, Philadelphia: University of Pennsylvania Press.

Fenby, J. (1983) *Piracy and the Public: Forgery, Theft and Exploitation*, London: Frederick Muller.

Ferguson, J. (1988) 'Cultural exchange: new developments in the anthropology of commodities', *Cultural Anthropology* 3: 489–513.

Filman, H. (1992a) 'A brand new world', *Marketing*, 6 April 1992.

—— (1992b) 'Marketers and ad agencies grapple with globalization', *Marketing*, 21 December 1992.

Fine, B. and Leopold, E. (1993) *The World of Consumption*, London: Routledge.

Finkelstein, J. (1989) *Dining Out*, Cambridge: Polity Press.

Finkle, C. L. (1994) 'Nestlé, infant formula, and excuses: the regulation of commercial advertising in developing nations', *Northwestern Journal of International Law and Business* 14: 602–19.

Finnegan, R. (1988) *Literacy and Orality: Studies in the Technology of Communication*, Oxford: Basil Blackwell.

Firat, F. (1995) 'Consumer culture or culture consumed?', in J. A. Costa and G. J. Bamossy (eds) *Marketing in a Multicultural World: Ethnicity, Nationalism and Cultural Identity*, London: Sage.

Fiske, J. (1989) *Understanding Popular Culture*, Boston: Unwin Hyman.

Foster, R. (1991) 'Making national cultures in the global ecumene', *Annual Review of Anthropology* 20: 235–60.

Foucault, M. (1978) *The History of Sexuality*, trans. R. Hurley, New York: Pantheon Books.

—— (1980) *Power–Knowledge: Selected Interviews and Other Writings*, trans. C. Gordon, New York: Pantheon Books.

Francis, D. (1992) *The Imaginary Indian*, Vancouver: Arsenal Pulp Press.

Friedman, J. (1990) 'Being in the world: globalization and localization', *Theory, Culture and Society* 7(2–3): 311–29.

—— (1994) *Cultural Identity and Global Process*, London: Sage.

Gaitskell, D. (1988) 'Devout domesticity? Continuity and change in a century of African women's Christianity in South Africa', paper read at Meeting of African Studies Association, Chicago.

García Canclini, N. (1992) *Culturas Híbridas: Estrategias para entrar y salir de la modernidad*, Buenos Aires: Editorial Sudamericana.

—— (1995) *Consumidores y Ciudadanos: Conflictos multiculturales de la globalización*, Mexico: Editorial Grijalbo.

Geertz, A. (1992) *The Invention of Prophecy*, Knebel, Denmark: Brunbakke.

Gell, A. (1986) 'Newcomers to the world of goods: consumption among the Muria Gonds', in A. Appadurai (ed.) *The Social Life of Things: Commodities in Cultural Perspective*, Cambridge: Cambridge University Press.

—— (1988) 'Anthropology, material culture and consumerism', *Journal of the Anthropological Society of Oxford*, 19(1): 43–7.

Gewertz, D. B. and Errington, F. K. (1991) *Twisted Histories, Altered Contexts: Representing the Chambri in a World System*, Cambridge: Cambridge University Press.

Gill, S. (1982) *Native American Religions: An Introduction*, Belmont, CA: Wadsworth.

—— (1987) *Native American Religious Action: A Performative Approach to Religion*, Columbia, SC: University of South Carolina Press.

Giroux, H. A. (1994) 'Consuming social change: the "United Colors of Benetton"', *Cultural Critique* 26:5–32.

Goldman, R. (1992) *Reading Ads Socially*, London: Routledge.

Goody, J. (1982) *Cooking, Cuisine and Class*, Cambridge: Cambridge University Press.

Gordon, W. (1993) 'A property right in self-expression: equality and individualism in the natural law of intellectual property', *Yale Law Journal* 102: 1533–607.

Graburn, N. (1976) 'Introduction: arts of the Fourth World' in N. Graburn (ed.) *Ethnic and Tourist Arts of the Fourth World*, Berkeley: University of California Press.

—— (1982) 'Television and the Canadian Inuit', *Etudes Inuit Studies* 6(1): 7–19.

Granzberg, G. and Steinbring, J. (eds) (1980) *Television and the Canadian Indian: Impact and Meaning Among Algonkians of Central Canada*, Winnipeg, Man.: University of Winnipeg.

Greenblatt, S. J. (1980) *Renaissance Self-Fashioning: From More to Shakespeare*, Chicago: University of Chicago Press.

Gregory, C. (1982) *Gifts and Commodities*, London: Academic Press.

Grossberg, L. (1992) *We gotta get out of this place: Popular Conservatism and Postmodern Culture,* New York: Routledge.

Hall, S. and Jefferson, T. (eds) (1976) *Resistance Through Rituals*, London: Hutchinson.

Handler, R. (1986) 'Authenticity', *Anthropology Today* 2(1): 2–4.

Hannerz, U. (1987) 'The world in creolisation', *Africa* 57(4): 546–59.

—— (1990) 'Cosmopolitans and locals in world culture', *Theory, Culture and Society* 7(2–3): 237–51.

—— (1992) *Cultural Complexity: Studies in the Social Organization of Meaning*, New York: Columbia University Press.

Hartwig, G. (1976) *The Art of Survival in East Africa: The Kerebe and Long-Distance Trade, 1800–1895*, New York: Africana.

Haug, W. (1986) *Critique of Commodity Aesthetics: Appearance, Sexuality and Advertising in Capitalist Society*, trans. R. Bock, Minneapolis: University of Minnesota Press.

Hebdige, D. (1979) *Subculture: The Meaning of Style*, London: Methuen.

Hendrickson, C. (1986) 'Handmade and thought-woven: the construction of dress and social identity in Tecpn Guatemala', unpublished PhD thesis, University of Chicago.

Hertzfeld, M. (1987) *Anthropology Through the Looking Glass: Critical Ethnography in the Margins of Europe*, Cambridge: Cambridge University Press.

Hill, J. H. (1993) 'Hasta La Vista, Baby: Anglo Spanish in the American Southwest' *Critique of Anthropology* 13(2): 145–76.

Hogan, K. (1989) 'Impulse selling', *Marketing*, 7 December 1989.

Holub, E. (1881) *Seven Years in South Africa: Travels, Researches, and Hunting Adventures, between the Diamond-Fields and the Zambesi (1872–79)* (2 vols), trans. E. E. Frewer, Boston: Houghton Mifflin.

Hom, K. (1984) *Chinese Cookery*, London: British Broadcasting Corporation.

Hoodfar, H. *Between Marriage and the Market: Intimate Politics and Survival in Cairo*, Berkeley: University of California Press (in press).

Hornik, J. (1992) 'Tactile stimulation and consumer response', *Journal of Consumer Research* 19: 449–58.

Howes, D. (1988) 'Dialogical jurisprudence', in W. Pue and B. Wright (eds) *Canadian Perspectives on Law and Society*, Ottawa: Carleton University Press.

—— (1990a) '*We Are the World* and its counterparts: popular song as constitutional discourse', *International Journal of Politics, Culture and Society* 3(3): 315–39.

—— (1990b) 'Les techniques des sens', *Anthropologie et Sociétés* 14(2): 99–116.

—— (1993) 'Inverted precedents: legal reasoning as "mytho-logic"', *Journal of Legal Pluralism* 33: 213–29.

Howes, D. and Classen, C. (1991) 'Conclusion: sounding sensory profiles', in D.

Howes (ed.) *The Varieties of Sensory Experience: A Sourcebook in the Anthropology of the Senses*, Toronto: University of Toronto Press.

Hudson, H. (1974) 'Community communication and development: a Canadian case study', unpublished PhD thesis, Stanford University.

Hughes, I. (1841) 'Missionary labours among the Batlapi', *Evangelical Magazine and Missionary Chronicle* 19: 522–3.

Hugh-Jones, S. (1992) 'Yesterday's luxuries, tomorrow's necessities: business and barter in Northwest Amazonia', in C. Humphrey and S. Hugh-Jones (eds) *Barter, Exchange and Value: An Anthropological Approach*, Cambridge: Cambridge University Press.

Hunt, N. R. (1990) '"Single ladies on the Congo"': protestant missionary tensions and voices', *Women's Studies International Forum* 13: 395–403.

Hyden, G. (1968) *Political Development in Rural Tanzania: Tanu Yajenga Nchi*, Nairobi: East African Publishing House.

Jaffrey, M. (1989) *Far Eastern Cookery*, London: British Broadcasting Corporation.

James, A. (1990) 'The good, the bad and the delicious: the role of confectionery in British society', *The Sociological Review* 38(4): 666–88.

—— (1993) 'Change or continuity in English food preferences', paper presented at ICAF Conference, Oxford.

James, J. (1993) *Consumption and Development*, New York: St. Martin's Press.

Jourdan, C. (1994a) 'Créolisation, urbanisation et identité aux îles Salomon', *Journal de la Société des Océanistes* 99(2): 177–86.

—— (1994b) 'Objets du désir et désir des objets aux îles Salomon', *Anthropologie et Sociétés* 18(3): 125–32.

Joy, A. and Venkatesh, A. (1994) 'Postmodernism, feminism, and the body: the visible and the invisible in consumer research', *International Journal of Research in Marketing* 11: 333–57.

Jules-Rosette, B. (1994) 'Simulations of postmodernity: images of technology in African tourist and popular art', in L. Taylor (ed.) *Visualizing Theory*, London: Routledge.

Kahe, M. (1993) [Untitled], *Hopi Tutu-veh-ni* 2(92): 8.

Kaiser, R. (1991) *The Voice of the Great Spirit: Prophecies of the Hopi Indians*, trans. W. Wünsche, Boston: Shambhala.

Kay, S. (1834) *Travels and Researches in Caffraria* (2 vols), New York: Harper & Brothers.

Keesing, R. M. (1982) *Kwaio Religion: The Living and the Dead in a Solomon Island Society*, New York: Columbia University Press.

—— (1994) 'Foraging in the urban jungle: notes from the Kwaio underground', *Journal de la Société des Océanistes* 99(2): 167–76.

Keil, C. and Feld. S. (1994) *Music Grooves: Essays and Dialogues*, Chicago: University of Chicago Press.

King, A. D. (1991) 'Introduction: spaces of culture, spaces of knowledge', in A. D. King (ed.) *Culture, Globalization and the World-System*, London: Macmillan.

Kondo, D. K. (1990) *Crafting Selves: Power, Gender, and Discourses of Identity in a Japanese Workplace*, Chicago: University of Chicago Press.

Kopytoff, I. (1986) 'The cultural biography of things: commoditization as process', in A. Appadurai (ed.) *The Social Life of Things: Commodities in Cultural Perspective*, Cambridge: Cambridge University Press.

Kronholz, J. (1986) 'Dowry-linked burnings in India', *The Gazette*, 25 August 1986.

Laermans, R. (1993) 'Bringing the consumer back in', *Theory, Culture and Society* 10: 153–61.

Laxson, J. D. (1991) 'How "we" see "them": tourism and Native Americans', *Annals of Tourism Research* 18: 365–91.

Leach, E. (1964) 'Anthropological aspects of language: animal categories and verbal abuse', in E. H. Lennenberg (ed.) *New Directions in the Study of Language*, Cambridge, MA: The MIT Press.

Lederman, R. (1986) 'Changing times in Mendi: notes towards writing highland New Guinea history', *Ethnohistory* 33(1): 1–30.

Lee, M. (1993) *Consumer Culture Reborn: The Cultural Politics of Consumption*, London: Routledge.

Leiss, W., Kline, S. and Jhaly, S. (1988) *Social Communication in Advertising: Persons, Products and Images of Well-Being*, Toronto: Nelson.

Levenstein, H. A. (1988) *Revolution at the Table: The Transformation of the American Diet*, New York: Oxford University Press.

Lévi-Strauss, C. (1962) *Totemism*, trans. R. Needham, Harmondsworth: Penguin.

—— (1974) *Tristes Tropiques*, trans. J. and D. Weightman, New York: Atheneum.

Levitt, T. (1983) 'The globalization of markets', *Harvard Business Review*, 83(3): 92–102.

Levy, P. (1986) *Out to Lunch*, Harmondsworth: Penguin.

Little, K. (1991) 'On safari: the visual politics of a tourist representation', in D. Howes (ed.) *The Varieties of Sensory Experience*, Toronto: University of Toronto Press.

Loftin, J. (1991) *Religion and Hopi Life in the Twentieth Century*, Bloomington: Indiana University Press.

London Missionary Society (1824) 'Kurreechane', *Missionary Sketches*, No. XXV, April, London: London Missionary Society. [South African Public Library: South African Bound Pamphlets, No. 54.]

—— (1828) 'Sketch of the Bechuana Mission', *Missionary Sketches*, No. XLIII, October, London: London Missionary Society. [South African Library: South African Bound Pamphlets, No. 54.]

Lowenthal, D. (1990), *The Past Is a Foreign Country*, Cambridge: Cambridge University Press.

Lutz, C. A. and Collins, J. L. (1993) *Reading National Geographic*, Chicago: University of Chicago Press.

MacCannell, D. (1989) *The Tourist: A New Theory of the Leisure Class*, London: Macmillan.

—— (1992) *Empty Meeting Grounds: The Tourist Papers*, London: Routledge.

McCracken, G. (1988) *Culture and Consumption: New Approaches to the Symbolic Character of Consumer Goods and Activities*, Bloomington: Indiana University Press.

McDonnell, R. (1992) 'Contextualizing the investigation of customary law in contemporary native communities', *Canadian Journal of Criminology* 34: 299–316.

McGowan, J. C. (1993) 'Going Indian', *Whole Earth Review* 81: 106–9.

MacIntyre, A. (1988) *Whose Justice? Which Rationality?*, Notre Dame, IN: University of Notre Dame Press.

Mackenzie, J. (1871) *Ten Years North of the Orange River: A Story of Everyday Life and Work among the South African Tribes*, Edinburgh: Edmonston and Douglas.

—— (1883) *Day Dawn in Dark Places: A Story of Wanderings and Work in Bechwanaland*, London: Cassell. Reprinted 1969, New York: Negro Universities Press.

McLuhan, T. C. (1985) *Dream Tracks: The Railroad and the American Indian, 1890–1930*, New York: Harry N. Abrams.

McPhail, T. (1987) *Electronic Colonialism*, Beverly Hills, CA: Sage.

McQuail, D. (1983) *Mass Communication Theory*, London: Sage.

Madden, K. (1990) 'Inuit Broadcasting Corporation', paper presented at International Communication Association Meeting, Dublin.

Madow, M. (1993) 'Private ownership and public image: popular culture and publicity rights', *California Law Review* 81: 125–240.

Magrath, A. (1992) *The 6 Imperatives of Marketing: Lessons from the World's Best Companies*, New York: Amacom.

Mails, T. E. (1994) *Secret Native American Pathways: A Guide to Inner Peace*, Tulsa, OK.: Council Oaks Books.

Marcuse, H. (1964) *One-Dimensional Man*. London: Routledge and Kegan Paul.

Marx, K. (1967) *Capital: A Critique of Political Economy* (3 vols), F. Engels (ed.), New York: International Publishers.

Mattelart, A. (1994) *Mapping World Communication: War, Progress, Culture*, trans. S. Emanuel and J.A. Cohen, Minneapolis: University of Minnesota Press.

Mattelart, A. *et al.* (1979) *Communication and Class Struggle* (vol. 1), New York: International General.

Mayer, P. (1961) *Townsmen or Tribesmen: Conservatism and the Process of Urbanization in a South African City*, Cape Town: Oxford University Press.

Mayle, P. (1990) *A Year in Provence*, London: Pan.

—— (1991) *Toujours Provence*, New York: Knopf.

Mears, W.G.A. (1934) 'The educated native in Bantu communal life', in I. Schapera (ed.) *Western Civilization and the Natives of South Africa*, London: George Routledge & Sons.

Mennell, S. (1985) *All Manners of Food*, Oxford: Basil Blackwell.

Merryman, J. H. (1986) 'Two way of thinking about cultural property', *American Journal of International Law* 80: 831–57.

Miller, D. (1987) *Material Culture and Mass Consumption*, Oxford: Blackwell.

—— (ed.) (1993) *Unwrapping Christmas*, Oxford: Clarendon Press.

—— (1994) *Modernity: An Ethnographic Approach*, Oxford: Berg.

Miller, I. (1994) 'Creolizing for survival in the city', *Cultural Critique* 27: 153–88.

Mintel International (1992) *Eating Out*, London: Mintel.

Mintz, S. (1985) *Sweetness and Power: The Place of Sugar in Modern History*, New York: Viking.

Mitchell, T. (1991) *Colonising Egypt*, Berkeley: University of California Press.

Moffat, M. (1967) 'Letter to a well-wisher', *Quarterly Bulletin of the South African Library* 22: 16–19.

Moffat, R. (1825) 'Extracts from the journal of Mr Robert Moffat', *Transactions of the Missionary Society*, 33: 27–9.

—— (1842) *Missionary Labours and Scenes in Southern Africa*, London: Snow.

Moreland, J. W. (1988) 'American Indians and the right to privacy: a psycholegal investigation of the unauthorized publication of portraits of American Indians', *American Indian Law Review* 15(2): 237–77.

Muldoon, J. (1975) 'The Indian as Irishman', *Essex Institute Historical Collections* 3: 267–89.

Nabokov, P. (1993) 'Unto these mountains: toward the study of sacred geography', *New Scholar* 10: 479–89.

Nag, D. (1991) 'Fashion, gender, and the Bengali middle class', *Public Culture* 3: 93–112.

Nava, M. (1992) *Feminism, Youth and Consumerism*, London: Sage.

Neave, P. (1992) 'The High Life in the Andes', *Elle* September 1992: 210–24.

Northcott, W. C. (1961) *Robert Moffat: Pioneer in Africa, 1817–1870*, London: Lutterworth Press.

O'Barr, W. M. (1994) *Culture and the Ad: Exploring Otherness in the World of Advertising*, Boulder, CO: Westview Press.

Ohnuki-Tierney, E. (1977) 'An octopus headache? A lamprey boil?' *Journal of Anthropological Research* 33(3): 245–57.

Ong, A. (1987) *Spirits of Resistance and Capitalist Discipline: Factory Work in Malaysia*, Albany, NY: State University of New York Press.

Ong SJ, W. J. (1969) 'World as view and world as event', *American Anthropologist* 71: 634–47.

—— (1982) *Orality and Literacy: The Technologizing of the Word*, London: Methuen.

Ortner, S. (1978) *Sherpas Through Their Rituals*, Cambridge: Cambridge University Press.

Packard, R. M. (1989) 'The "healthy reserve" and the "dressed native": discourses on black health and the language of legitimation in South Africa', *American Ethnologist* 16: 686–703.

Parezo, N. (1983) *Navajo Sandpainting: From Religious Art to Commercial Art*, Tucson, AZ: University of Arizona Press.

Parsley, J. K. (1993) 'Regulation of counterfeit Indian arts and crafts: an analysis of the Indian Arts and Crafts Act of 1990', *American Indian Law Review* 18(2): 487–514.

Pask, A. (1993) 'Cultural appropriation and the law: an analysis of legal regimes concerning culture', *Intellectual Property Journal* 8: 57–86.

Peñaloza, L. (1994) '*Atrevesando fronteras*/border crossings: a critical ethnographic exploration of the consumer acculturation of Mexican immigrants', *Journal of Consumer Research* 21: 32–54.

Pendergrast, M. (1993) *For God, Country and Coca-Cola: The Unauthorized History of the Great American Soft Drink and the Company that Makes It*, Toronto: Maxwell Macmillan.

Philibert, J.-M. (1982) 'Vers une symbolique de la modernisation au Vanuatu', *Anthropologie et Sociétés* 6(1): 69–98.

—— (1984) 'Adaptation à la récession économique dans un village péri-urbain du Vanuatu', *Journal de la Société des Océanistes* 40(79):139–50.

—— (1986) 'The politics of tradition: toward a generic culture in Vanuatu', *Mankind* 16(1):1–12.

—— (1988) 'Women's work: a case study of proletarianization of peri-urban villagers in Vanuatu', *Oceania* 58(3): 161–75.

—— (1989) 'Consuming culture: a study of simple commodity consumption', in H. Rutz and B. Orlove (eds) *The Social Economy of Consumption*, Lanham, MD: University Press of America.

—— (1992) 'Social change in Vanuatu', in A. B. Robillard (ed.) *Social Change in the Pacific Islands*, London: Kegan Paul.

—— (1994a) 'Nouvelles-hybrides', *Journal de la Société des Océanistes* 99(2): 197–205.

—— (1994b) 'Erakor ou la lente consommation d'un capital collectif imaginaire', *Anthropologie et Sociétés* 18(3): 75–89.

Philip, J. (1828) *Researches in South Africa; Illustrating the Civil, Moral, and Religious Condition of the Native Tribes* (2 vols), London: James Duncan.

Piirto, R. (1991) *Beyond Mind Games: The Marketing Power of Psychographics*, Ithaca: American Demographic Books.

Polanyi, K. (1944) *The Great Transformation*, New York: Farrar & Rinehart.

Popadopoulos, N. and Heslop, L. (eds) (1993) *Product-Country Images: Impact and Role in International Marketing*, New York: International Business Press.

Pouillon, J. (1975) *Fétiches sans fétichisme*, Paris: François Maspéro.

Powdermaker, H. (1967) *Stranger and Friend*, London: Secker and Warburg.

Price, S. (1991) *Primitive Art in Civilized Places*, Chicago: University of Chicago Press.

Prosser, W. L. (1960) 'Privacy', *California Law Review* 48(3): 383–423.

Rald, J. and Rald, K. (1975) *Rural Organization in Bukoba District, Tanzania*, Uppsala: Scandinavian Institute of African Studies.

Read, J. (1850) 'Report on the Bechuana Mission', *Evangelical Magazine and Missionary Chronicle* 28: 445–7.

Religious Tract Society, The (n.d.) *Rivers of Water in a Dry Place: An Account of the Introduction of Christianity into South Africa, and of Mr. Moffat's Missionary Labours, Designed for the Young*, London: The Religious Tract Society.

Richards, A. I. [1956] (1982) *Chisungu: A Girl's Initiation Ceremony among the Bemba of Northern Rhodesia'*, London: Faber & Faber.

Ricks, D. (1993) *Blunders in International Business*, Oxford: Blackwell.

Riggins, S. H. (ed.) (1994) *The Socialness of Things: Essays on the Socio-Semiotics of Objects*, New York: Mouton de Gruyter.

Robberson, T. (1994) 'Pepsi and poch', *The Gazette*, 6 February 1994.

Robertson, R. (1992) *Globalization: Social Theory and Global Culture*, London: Sage.

Roden, C. (n.d.) *A Book of Middle Eastern Food*, Harmondsworth: Penguin.

Rodó, J. E. (1988) *Ariel*, trans. M. Sayers Peden, Austin: University of Texas Press.

Rojek, C. (1985) *Capitalism and Leisure Theory*, London: Tavistock.

—— (1995) *Decentring Leisure: Rethinking Leisure Theory*, Thousand Oaks, CA,: Sage.

Rosaldo, R. (1989) *Culture and Truth: The Remaking of Social Analysis*, Boston: Beacon Press.

Roseberry, W. (1991) *Anthropologies and Histories: Essays in Culture, History and Political Economy*, New Brunswick, NJ: Rutgers University Press.

Roseman, M. (1993) 'The spiritualization of the commodity among the Temiar of Malaysia', public lecture at Concordia University, Montreal, 23 November 1993.

Rossman, M.L. (1994) *Multicultural Marketing: Selling to a Diverse America*, New York: Amacom.

Roth, L. and Valaskakis, G. (1989) 'Aboriginal broadcasting in Canada: a case study in democratization', in M. Raboy and P. Bruck (eds) *Communication For and Against Democracy*, Montreal: Black Rose Books.

Rutherford, P. (1994) *The New Icons? The Art of Television Advertising*, Toronto: University of Toronto Press.

Rutz, H. and Orlove B. (eds) (1989) *The Social Economy of Consumption*, Lanham, MD: University Press of America.

Rybczynski, W. (1986) *Home: A Short History of an Idea*, New York: Viking.

Sackett, B. (1976) 'There are no impersonal call letters here . . .', *Broadcaster* March 1976: 31–2.

Sahlins, M. D. (1976) *Culture and Practical Reason*, Chicago: University of Chicago Press.

—— (1988) 'Cosmologies of capitalism: the trans-Pacific sector of "the world system"', *Proceedings of the British Academy* LXXVI: 1–51.

Said, E. W. (1978) *Orientalism*, New York: Random House.

—— (1993) *Culture and Imperialism*, New York: Knopf.

Salomon, F. (1973) 'Weavers of Otavalo', in D.R. Gross (ed.) *Peoples and Cultures in Native South America*, New York: Doubleday.

Sarlo, B. (1994) *Escenas de la vida posmoderna*, Buenos Aires: Ariel.

Savigliano, M. E. (1955) *Tango and the Political Economy of Passion*, Boulder, CO: Westview Press.

Scaravelli, P. and Cohen, J. (1987) *A Mediterranean Harvest*, Wellingborough: Thorsons.

Schama, S. (1988) *The Embarrassment of Riches: An Interpretation of Dutch Culture in the Golden Age*, New York: Knopf.

Schapera, I. (1947) *Migrant Labour and Tribal Life: A Study of Conditions in the Bechuanaland Protectorate*, London: Oxford University Press.

—— (1953) *The Tswana*, London: International African Institute. Revised edition, I. Schapera and J. L. Comaroff (1991), London: Kegan Paul International.

Schiller, H. (1976) *Communication and Cultural Domination*, New York: M. E. Sharpe.

Schivelbusch, W. (1992) *Tastes of Paradise: A Social History of Spices, Stimulants, and Intoxicants*, New York: Pantheon Books.

Scott, J. C. (1990) *Domination and the Arts of Resistance: Hidden Transcripts*, New Haven, CT: Yale University Press.

Sherry, J.F. (1987) 'Cultural propriety in a global marketplace', in A.F. Firat, N. Dholakia and R. Bagozzi (eds) *Philosophical and Radical Thought in Marketing*, Toronto: Lexington Books.

Shields, R. (ed.) (1992) *Lifestyle Shopping: The Subject of Consumption*, London: Routledge.

Simmel, G. (1904) 'Fashion', *International Quarterly* 10: 130–55.

Sinha, P.K. (1991) 'Marketing research', in S.C. Sahoo and P.K. Sinha (eds) *Emerging Trends in Indian Marketing in the '90s*, Delhi: Academic Foundation.

Smith, A. (1939) *The Diary of Dr. Andrew Smith, 1834–1836* (2 vols), P. R. Kirby (ed.), Cape Town: The Van Riebeeck Society.

Smith, A. (1994) 'For all those who were Indian in a former life', *Cultural Survival Quarterly* 17(4): 70–1.

Smith, C. and Stevens, P. (1988) 'Farming and income-generation in the female-headed smallholder household: the case of a Haya village in Tanzania', *Canadian Journal of African Studies* 22: 552–66.

Solomon, M.R. (1994) *Consumer Behavior* (2nd edn), Needham Heights, MA: Allyn and Bacon.

Solway, J. and Lee, R. (1990) 'Foragers, genuine or spurious: situating the Kalahari San in history', *Current Anthropology* 31: 109–46.

Spivak, G. C. (1988) 'Can the subaltern speak?', in C. Nelson and L. Grossberg (eds) *Marxism and the Interpretation of Culture*, Urbana, IL: University of Illinois Press.

—— (1993) *Outside in the Teaching Machine*, New York: Routledge.

Stallybrass, P. and White, A. (1986) *The Politics and Poetics of Transgression*, Ithaca, NY: Cornell University Press.

Stanlaw, J. (1992) '"For beautiful human life": the use of English in Japan', in J. J. Tobin (ed.) *Re-Made in Japan: Everyday Life and Consumer Taste in a Changing Society*, New Haven, CT: Yale University Press.

Suagee, D. B. (1982) 'American Indian religious freedom and cultural resources management: protecting Mother Earth's caretakers', *American Indian Law Review* 10: 1–59.

Tambiah, S. J. (1969) 'Animals are good to think and good to prohibit', *Ethnology* 8(4): 424–59.

Tannahill, R. (1973) *Food in History*, Harmondsworth: Penguin.

Taussig, M. (1993) *Mimesis and Alterity: A Particular History of the Senses*, London: Routledge.

Taylor, C. (1991) *Milk, Honey and Money*, Washington, DC: Smithsonian Institution Press.

Taylor, D. (1994) 'Opening remarks', in D. Taylor and J. Villegas (eds) *Negotiating Performance: Gender, Sexuality, and Theatricality in Latin America*, Durham, NC: Duke University Press.

Tester, K. (ed.) (1994) *The Flâneur*, London: Routledge.

Thomas, N. (1991) *Entangled Objects: Exchange, Material Culture and Colonialism in the South Pacific*, Cambridge, MA: Harvard University Press.

Thompson, L. (1945) 'Logico-aesthetic integration in Hopi culture', *American Anthropologist* 47: 540–53.

Tobin, J. J. (1992) 'Introduction: domesticating the West', in J. J. Tobin (ed.) *Re-made in Japan: Everyday Life and Consumer Taste in a Changing Society*, New Haven, CT: Yale University Press.

Todd, D. (1993) 'From rags to riches', *The Gazette*, 13 November 1993.

Tomlinson, A. (1990) 'Introduction: consumer culture and the aura of the commodity', in A. Tomlinson (ed.) *Consumption, Identity and Style: Marketing, Meaning and the Packaging of Pleasure*, London: Routledge.

Tomlinson, J. (1991) *Cultural Imperialism*, Baltimore, MD: Johns Hopkins University Press.

Torgovnick, M. (1991) *Gone Primitive: Savage Intellects, Modern Lives*, Chicago: University of Chicago Press.

Trope, J. (1993) 'Protecting Native American religious freedom: the legal, historical, and constitutional basis for the proposed Native American Free Exercise of Religion Act', *Review of Law and Social Change* 20: 373–405.

Turner, T. S. (n.d.) 'The social skin', unpublished manuscript. Published in abridged form in J. Cherfas and R. Lewin (eds) (1980) *Not Work Alone*, Beverly Hills, CA: Sage.

Turner, V. W. (1967) *The Forest of Symbols: Aspects of Ndembu Ritual*, Ithaca: Cornell University Press.

Udall, S. (1992) 'The irresistible other: Hopi ritual drama and Euro-American audiences', *The Drama Review* 36(2): 23–43.

Urry, J. (1990) *The Tourist Gaze: Leisure and Travel in Contemporary Societies*, London: Sage.

Valaskakis, G. (1988) 'Television and cultural integration: implications for native communities in the Canadian North', in R. Lorimer and D. C. Wison (eds) *Communication Canada: Issues in Broadcasting and New Technologies*, Toronto: Kagan & Woo Ltd.

—— (1993) 'Postcards of my past: the Indian as artefact', in V. Blundell, J. Shepherd and I. Taylor (eds) *Relocating Cultural Studies: Developments in Theory and Research*, London: Routledge.

Valentine, L. P. (1990) '"Work to create the future you want": Contemporary discourse in Severn Ojibwe', unpublished PhD thesis, University of Texas.

Van Esterik, P. (1989) *Beyond the Breast-Bottle Controversy*, New Brunswick, NJ: Rutgers University Press

Veblen, T. (1912) *The Theory of the Leisure Class*, New York: Macmillan.

Volkman, T. A. (1988) 'Out of South Africa: *The Gods Must Be Crazy*', in L. Gross, J. S. Katz and J. Ruby (eds) *Image Ethics: The Moral Rights of Subjects in Photographs, Film and Television*, New York: Oxford University Press.

Wade, E. (1985) 'The ethnic art market in the American Southwest, 1880–1980', in G. W. Stocking Jr (ed.) *Objects and Others: Essays on Museums and Material Culture*, Madison: University of Wisconsin Press.

Waldman, S. (1992) 'Freedom's just another word for much too much to choose', *Globe and Mail*, 25 January 1992. Reprinted in *Consumerism* (vol. 4), Boca Raton, FL: Social Issues Resources Series Inc.

Wallerstein, I. (1974) *The Modern World System*, New York: Academic Press.

—— (1984) *The Politics of the World Economy*, New York: Cambridge University Press.

—— (1991) *Geopolitics and Geoculture: Essays on the Changing World System*, Cambridge: Cambridge University Press.

Walter, L. (1981) 'Otavaleño development, ethnicity, and national integration', *America Indígena* 41(2): 319–37.

Warren, S. and Brandeis, L. (1890) 'The right to privacy', *Harvard Law Review* 4: 193–220.

Waters, F. (1963) *Book of the Hopi*, Harmondsworth: Penguin.

Wawatay Native Communications Society (1989a) *Wawatay General Meeting, Peawanuck Ontario*, Sioux Lookout, Ont.: Wawatay Native Communications Society.

—— (1989b) *Editorial Policy for Journalists of Wawatay Native Communications Society*, Sioux Lookout, Ont.: Wawatay Native Communications Society.

Weismantel, M. J. (1989) 'The children cry for bread: hegemony and the transformation of consumption' in H. Rutz and B. Orlove (eds) *The Social Economy of Consumption*, Lanham, MD: University Press of America.

Weiss, B. (1992) 'Plastic teeth extraction: the iconography of Haya gastro-sexual affliction', *American Ethnologist* 19(3): 538–52.

—— (1996) *The Making and Unmaking of the Haya Lived World: Consumption, Commoditization and Everyday Practice in Northwest Tanzania*, Durham, NC: Duke University Press.

White, L. (1988) 'Domestic labour in a colonial city: prostitution in Nairobi, 1900–1952', in S. Stichter and J. Parpart (eds) *Patriarchy and Class: African Women in the Home and the Workforce*, Boulder, CO: Westview Press.

Whiteley, P. (1988) *Deliberate Acts: Changing Hopi Culture through the Oraibi Split*, Tucson: University of Arizona Press.

—— (1993) 'The end of anthropology (at Hopi)?', *Journal of the Southwest* 35(2): 125–57.

Wicke, J. (1988) *Advertising Fictions: Literature, Advertisement and Social Reading*, New York: Columbia University Press.

Wilk, R. (1994) 'Consumer goods as dialogue about development: colonial time and television time in Belize', in J. Friedman (ed.) *Consumption and Identity*, Chur, Switzerland: Harwood Academic Publishers.

Williams, R. (1976) *Keywords: A Vocabulary of Culture and Society*, Glasgow: Collins.

Williamson, J. (1992) 'I-less and gaga in the West Edmonton mall: towards a pedestrian feminist reading', in D. H. Currie and V. Raoul (eds) *The Anatomy of Gender: Women's Struggle for the Body*, Ottawa: Carleton University Press.

Willis, P. (1990) *Common Culture: Symbolic Work at Play in the Everyday Cultures of the Young*, Milton Keynes: Open University Press.

Willoughby, W. C. (n.d. [*c.* 1899]) *Native Life on the Transvaal Border*, London: Simpkin, Marshall, Hamilton, Kent.

Worsley, P. (1970) *The Trumpet Shall Sound: A Study of 'Cargo' Cults in Melanesia*, London: Paladin.

Young, I. M. (1994) 'Women recovering our clothes', in S. Benstock and S. Ferriss (eds) *On Fashion*, New Brunswick, NJ: Rutgers University Press.

Zelizer, V. A. (1989) 'The social meaning of money: "special monies"', *American Journal of Sociology* 95(2): 342–77.

Zimmerman, C. S. and Dunlop, L. J. (1994) 'Overview: intellectual property – the new global currency', in M. Simensky and L. G. Bryer (eds) *The New Role of Intellectual Property in Commercial Transactions*, Toronto: John Wiley and Sons.

Zimmerman, D. (1992) 'Information as speech, information as goods: some thoughts on marketplaces and the Bill of Rights', *William and Mary Law Review* 33: 665–740.

INDEX